Ready-to-Use

Citizenship Activities

For Grades 5-12

Prentice
Hall

**THE CENTER FOR APPLIED
RESEARCH IN EDUCATION**
West Nyack, New York 10994

Fay R. Hansen

Library of Congress Cataloging-in-Publication Data

Hansen, Fay R.
   Ready-to-use citizenship activities for grades 5-12 : 200
skillsheets for real-world democratic participation / Fay R. Hansen.
     p.   cm.
  ISBN 0-87628-357-1
  1. Civics—Problems, exercises, etc. 2. Civics—Study and
teaching—United States. I. Title.
H62.3.H35 1998
320.473—DC21

98-41361
CIP

© 1999 by The Center for Applied Research in Education

Every effort has been made to ensure that no copyrighted material has been used without permission. The author regrets any oversights that may have occurred and would be happy to rectify them on future printings of this book.

Printed in the United States of America

10 9 8 7 6 5 4 3

ISBN 0-87628-357-1

ATTENTION: CORPORATIONS AND SCHOOLS

The Center for Applied Research in Education books are available at quantity discounts with bulk purchase for educational, business, or sales promotional use. For information, please write to: Prentice Hall Direct Special Sales, 240 Frisch Court, Paramus, New Jersey 07652. Please supply: title of book, ISBN number, quantity, how the book will be used, date needed.

 **THE CENTER FOR APPLIED RESEARCH
IN EDUCATION**
West Nyack, NY 10994

On the World Wide Web at http://www.phdirect.com

About the Author

Fay Hansen received a B.A. in political science from New College, a M.A. in American History from Florida State University, and a M.A. in European History from Cornell University. After years of teaching at the University of South Florida and at Cornell University, she is now a writer and editor specializing in books, articles, and research reports on political and economic trends. Ms. Hansen also works as a research analyst for state legislative reforms and prepares white paper reports for national organizations and federal agencies.

Her forthcoming *American History Teacher's Book of Lists* will be published by The Center for Applied Research in Education in 1999.

About This Resource

How do you register to vote? Run a political campaign? Protect your constitutional rights? Track a bill? Follow election results? Impeach a president?

Where does tax money come from and where does it go? Why is the federal debt so large? What makes the economy run? What is a recession? How does the stock market work? How do you measure unemployment or define a labor market?

How do you write a letter to the editor? Report for jury duty? Get a pothole fixed? Speak at a town meeting?

With the readiness activities in *Ready-to-Use Citizenship Activities for Grades 5-12*, your students can step into the real world of politics and economics. These 200 reproducible skillsheets help you prepare students for their lives as citizens in a democratic society. You can use this book to teach your students how government works *and* where they fit in.

Each activity is a one-page reproducible worksheet geared to grades 5-12. Photocopy each worksheet as many times as needed for student use. A complete answer key appears at the back of the book.

Most of the activities can be completed in 10-15 minutes. You can use the worksheets as:

- stand-alone class assignments
- individual or team assignments
- launching points for group discussions

At the bottom of some activity sheets, a short "Step Ahead!" exercise is provided for students who complete the main assignment quickly or who need more advanced work. You can also assign the "Step Ahead!" exercise for bonus points.

This book will help you teach students the skills they need to participate as full citizens in political and economic life. The activities focus on the most important rights and responsibilities of citizenship:

- **political participation** – voting, running for office, and following legislation at all levels of government
- **legal participation** – exercising constitutional rights and protecting the rights of others

- **economic participation** – working, paying taxes, saving, investing, and approving public budgets

You can use these activities to teach the structure of government at the national, state, and local levels. Students learn to enter the democratic process by voting, campaigning, lobbying, letter-writing, or even running for office. They also become familiar with the main vehicles for participating in the economic life of the nation and the relationship between political and economic decisions.

The activities in this book help you prepare students for political life by reinforcing the following readiness skills:

- critical thinking
- making decisions
- gathering data
- organizing ideas
- solving problems
- mediating conflicts
- creating new systems

You can also help your students become familiar with the following aspects of citizenship:

- Concepts of democracy and citizenship
- Forms of participation at the local, state, and national levels
- Rights and responsibilities under the Constitution
- Structure of the federal government
- Duties of the president, the cabinet, and the executive agencies
- The legislative and judicial processes
- Economic policy and major economic institutions
- State and local services

Ready-to-Use Citizenship Activities for Grades 5-12 helps teachers take an integrated approach to political issues. The activities weave math and reading skill development into the process of learning about the government and the economy. Some of the activities call on students to build their math skills by calculating, charting, or graphing data. Some focus on reading skills by asking students to read for bias, read for the main point, or write summaries. Others combine geography and spelling skills.

Citizenship is a life-long activity. This resource can help students prepare for their first steps.

Fay Hansen

Contents

PART III. ECONOMIC PARTICIPATION

PART IV. STATE AND LOCAL GOVERNMENTS

I. EMPOWERMENT AND PARTICIPATION

- Democracy and Citizenship
- Participating in Democracy
- The Constitution
- Voting

Section 1

Democracy and Citizenship

1.1 Citizenship

"Citizen" means an inhabitant of a city or a town who possesses certain rights and privileges. As we use the term today, it means membership in a political community. The term is rooted in the classical Greek and Roman idea of humans as political beings, with the capacity to govern and to be governed. Citizenship is tightly linked to the idea of equality before the law and active political participation, and its emergence is tied to the birth of democracy. However, citizenship in the Greek democratic city–states was restricted to free and native-born men, and citizens only represented a minority of the population, even in Athens. Their participation in public life was only possible because of the existence of slaves, who were responsible for performing the main economic functions.

In ancient Rome, citizenship was still defined in terms of office holding, but it was extended first to plebeians and then to conquered peoples. This produced a much more heterogeneous body of citizens, and the term began to refer more to protection under the law than to active participation in its execution. Instead of indicating membership and active participation in a political community, citizenship became a legal status. By edict of the emperor Caracalla, citizenship was granted to the great majority of imperial subjects; only the very lower classes and women were excluded.

The ideal of citizenship culminated in the French Revolution and the Declaration of the Rights of Man and Citizen. The French political philosopher Jean-Jacques Rousseau, in *The Social Contract* (1762), established the modern figure of the citizen by connecting it to the idea of consent. The citizen for Rousseau is a free and independent individual who is entitled to take part in making decisions that all are required to obey. Rousseau's concept of citizenship attempts to link the republican conception of political community with the premises of individualism.

With the development of liberalism during the nineteenth century, the republican conception of the active citizen was displaced by a view of citizenship expressed in the language of natural rights. The ideas of civic activity, public spiritedness, and political participation in a community of equals were discarded by most liberal writers. Citizenship was reduced to a legal status, indicating the possession of rights that the individual holds against the state. This idea of citizenship as a set of rights became important in shaping modern societies. In the United States, for example, this conception of citizenship was gradually expanded to include blacks and women as citizens in the political world.

Debates continue about the meaning of citizenship. Is citizenship more than just the legal rights of individuals? Should everyone be a citizen of the country in which he or she lives? On the back of this sheet write a paragraph that answers these two questions.

1.2 Forms of Government

You'll find the words to complete this puzzle in the box.

DOWN
1. system in which a highly centralized government is controlled exclusively by one party and maintained by political suppression
2. autocratic rule; the ruler maintains absolute power
3. government in which the powers of the monarch are limited by and defined by a constitution
4. sovereign control of a government by a hereditary ruler
5. one-party system of government with individuals subjected to the control of the state
6. government in which a ruler possesses absolute power

ACROSS
2. government in which political power is retained by all the people
5. union of several states under a central government
7. government in which the clergy rules
8. rule of the government by a few persons
9. rule by one person who has total control over all others; dictatorship
10. a representative democracy, where elected officials exercise power vested in them by sovereign citizens
11. government ruled by the wealthy or upper class

| Aristocracy |
| Autocracy |
| Constitutional monarchy |
| Democracy |
| Despotism |
| Dictatorship |
| Fascism |
| Federalism |
| Monarchy |
| Oligarchy |
| Republic |
| Theocracy |
| Totalitarianism |

Name _____ Date _____ Class _____

1.3 "We hold these truths..."

Drafted by Thomas Jefferson at the Second Continental Congress in 1776, the Declaration of Independence declared the thirteen colonies independent from Great Britain and established the United States as its own nation. As Americans, we sometimes wonder about the famous phrase contained in Jefferson's writing: "all Men are created equal...." We question how our founding fathers could have included this statement and yet have allowed slavery to continue to flourish in this new land. In fact, many of the delegates to the Second Continental Congress argued in favor of abolishing slavery. Benjamin Franklin and John Adams, among others, believed the practice would harm the young nation and Jefferson himself originally included in the document this passage condemning the slave trade:

> *He (King George III) has waged cruel war against human nature itself, violating its most sacred rights of life & liberty in the persons of a distant people, who never offended him, captivating & carrying them into slavery in another hemisphere, or to incur miserable death in their transportation thither.*

The delegates from the southern colonies of Georgia and South Carolina forced the deletion of Jefferson's words. They argued that unless this anti-slavery clause was removed from the document, they would not sign it. After considerable debate, the remaining delegates ultimately agreed to the deletion. It was better, they reasoned, to deal with the slavery issue later than to risk not ratifying the Declaration now and thus jeopardize the very existence of the new country.

Do you agree with the decision the patriots made? Was it wrong for them to go forward in building a democratic nation while still remaining slaveholders? Or were they correct in recognizing the need to establish separation first, and to take up the cause of abolition later when the country was more secure? Were, indeed, "all men created equal"? On the back of this sheet, write down your thoughts and reactions to the Declaration of Independence and to the words that this great document does—and does not—contain.

1.4 Reading the Declaration of Independence

Read this passage from the Declaration of Independence, then answer the questions. Use a dictionary if you need to check the meanings of words.

> *When in the course of human events it becomes necessary for one people to dissolve the political bands which have connected them with another, and to assume among the powers of the earth, the separate and equal station to which the Laws of Nature and of Nature's God entitle them, a decent respect to the opinions of mankind requires that they should declare the causes which impel them to the separation.*
>
> *We hold these truths to be self-evident, that all men are created equal, that they are endowed by their Creator with certain unalienable rights, that among these are life, liberty and the pursuit of happiness. That to secure these rights, governments are instituted among men deriving their just powers from the consent of the governed. That whenever any form of government becomes destructive of these ends, it is the right of the people to alter or to abolish it, and to institute new government, laying its foundation on such principles and organizing its powers in such form, as to them shall seem most likely to effect their safety and happiness. . . .*

1. What does "unalienable" mean? _____

_____

_____

2. What are the "unalienable rights" spelled out in the Declaration? _____

_____

_____

3. According to the Declaration, what is the purpose of government? _____

_____

_____

4. What course of action does the Declaration advocate when a government "becomes destructive" of its proper purpose? _____

_____

_____

Name _____ Date _____ Class _____

1.5 Jefferson's Inaugural—Key Concepts

The first paragraph of Thomas Jefferson's first inaugural address, delivered in 1801, contains many of the most important concepts of the American political system. Read the paragraph carefully. Select three of the concepts expressed here, underline them in the paragraph, and then describe them in your own words on the lines provided below.

During the contest of opinion through which we have passed the animation of discussions and of exertions has sometimes worn an aspect which might impose on strangers unused to think freely and to speak and to write what they think; but this being now decided by the voice of the nation, announced according to the rules of the Constitution, all will of course arrange themselves under the will of the law, and unite in common efforts for the common good. All, too, will bear in mind this sacred principle, that though the will of the majority is in all cases to prevail, that will to be rightful must be reasonable; that the minority possesses their equal rights, which equal law must protect, and to violate would be oppression. Let us, then, fellow citizens, unite with one heart and one mind. Let us restore to social intercourse that harmony and affection without which liberty and even life itself are but dreary things.

1. _____
_____
_____

2. _____
_____
_____

3. _____
_____
_____

1.6 Allegiance—Taking the Oath

When immigrants become citizens of the United States, they are required to take the oath of allegiance printed below. Look up the underlined words in a dictionary if you are unsure of their meanings. Then rewrite the oath in your own words in the space provided.

Oath of Allegiance

I hereby declare, on <u>oath</u>, that I absolutely and entirely <u>renounce</u> and <u>abjure</u> all <u>allegiance</u> and fidelity to any foreign prince, potentate, state or <u>sovereignty</u> of whom or which I have heretofore been a subject or citizen; that I will support and defend the Constitution and the laws of the United State of America against all enemies, foreign and domestic; that I will bear true <u>faith</u> and allegiance to the same; that I will bear arms on behalf of the United States when required by law; that I will perform <u>noncombatant</u> service in the Armed Forces of the United States when required by the law; or that I will perform work of national importance under civilian direction when required by the law; and that I take this obligation freely without any mental reservation or purpose of <u>evasion</u>: SO HELP ME GOD....

_____

_____

_____

_____

_____

_____

_____

Step Ahead!

Why does the Oath of Allegiance require immigrants to renounce any loyalty to a foreign government? Can you think of some historical events that might have made this seem particularly important? _____

_____

_____

_____

1.7 Spelling Democracy

Discussions of the different forms of government require a new vocabulary and new spelling skills. Study the words below. Then team up with a classmate and test each other. Take turns calling out the words for a written quiz, then check each other's work.

1. democracy
2. pluralism
3. majority
4. minority
5. representation
6. ballot
7. congress
8. president
9. polling
10. citizenship

Step Ahead!

1. parliamentarian
2. endorsement
3. filibuster
4. federalism
5. participation

1.8 Patriotic Songs

Do you mumble when the band strikes up "The Star-Spangled Banner"? Do you fake your way through the second verse of "America"? Test yourself. Some of the words are missing from the lyrics given below. For each blank, write the missing word near the line where it should appear, then draw a line to the space where the word should go. The first word is done for you.

THE STAR-SPANGLED BANNER
Oh, say can you see by the dawn's _____ light,   early
    What so proudly we hailed at the _____ last gleaming?
Whose broad stripes and bright stars through the perilous fight,
    O'er the _____ we watched were so gallantly streaming?
And the rocket's red glare, the _____ bursting in air,
    Gave proof through the night that our flag was still there.
Oh, say does that star-spangled banner yet wave
    O'er the land of the free and the _____ of the brave?

AMERICA
    My country, 'tis of thee,
_____ land of liberty, of thee I sing.
Land where my fathers _____!
Land of the Pilgrims' _____!
From ev'ry _____, Let freedom ring.
    Our fathers' God, to Thee,
_____ of liberty,
To Thee we sing.
Long may our _____ be bright
With freedom's _____ light;
Protect us by Thy might,
_____ God, our King!

AMERICA, THE BEAUTIFUL
    O beautiful for spacious skies, For _____ waves of _____,
For purple mountain _____ above the _____ plain:
America! America! God shed His grace on thee,
And _____ thy good with brotherhood
From sea to shining sea.
    O beautiful for _____ dream that sees beyond the years,
Thine _____ cities gleam, Undimmed by human _____.
America! America! God shed His grace on thee,
And crown thy good with brotherhood
From sea to shining sea.

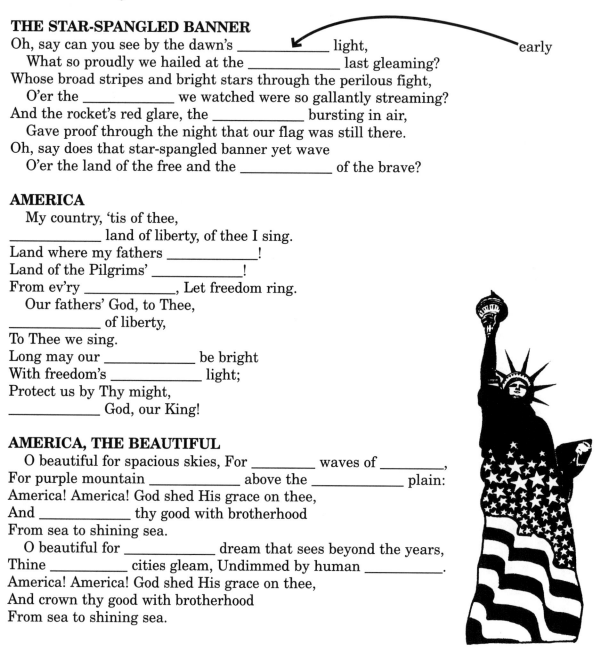

©1999 by The Center for Applied Research in Education

1.9 Powerful Political Writing

The Gettysburg Address, delivered by President Abraham Lincoln at Gettysburg, Pennsylvania on November 19, 1863, is considered one of the finest pieces of political writing in American history. Read the passage below, then answer the questions.

> *Four score and seven years ago our fathers brought forth on this continent a new nation, conceived in liberty and dedicated to the proposition that all men are created equal.*
>
> *Now we are engaged in a great civil war, testing whether that nation, or any nation so conceived and so dedicated, can long endure. We are met on a great battlefield of that war. We have come to dedicate a portion of that field, as a final resting-place for those who here gave their lives that that nation might live. It is altogether fitting and proper that we should do this.*
>
> *But, in a larger sense, we cannot dedicate—we cannot consecrate—we cannot hallow—this ground.... It is rather for us to be here dedicated to the great task remaining before us—that from these honored dead we take increased devotion to that cause for which they gave the last full measure of devotion—that we here highly resolve that these dead shall not have died in vain—that this nation, under God, shall have a new birth of freedom—and that government of the people, by the people, for the people, shall not perish from the earth.*

1. If you had to pick *one* word to describe the thoughts and feelings expressed in this speech, what would that one word be? _____

2. Using your own words, write *one* sentence that expresses the main idea of the speech.

_____

_____

_____

_____

Section 2

Participating in Democracy

2.1 An "Exceptional" Government

The French writer Alexis de Tocqueville described the early United States as "exceptional," qualitatively different from other nations. The government of the United States is still exceptional in many ways. The United States is the oldest continuing democracy in the world, and its Constitution is the oldest in the world. More people hold a political office here than in any other country in the world. The U.S. has the largest number of elected positions, with more than 500,000 offices filled through elections. But fewer people vote here than in most other democracies—only about 50 percent in presidential-year elections and even less in many local elections.

The U.S. system of government is also unique in many ways. The American Constitution established a divided form of government, the presidency and two houses of Congress, which differs from those of Europe and reflects a deliberate decision by the country's founders to create a weak and internally conflicted political system. The leaders of the Revolution, with their opposition to a powerful monarchy, strongly distrusted the state. The first constitution, the Articles of Confederation, provided for a Congress to pass laws, but not for an executive.

The second constitution—the one we still follow today—divided the government into different units, with each serving different terms or periods of office. The president is elected every four years by an electoral college. Senators, two from each state, are chosen by the state legislators for six-year terms, with one-third of the seats open every two years. The popularly elected House of Representatives is filled every two years, with the number from each state roughly proportionate to its share of the national population. Supreme Court justices are appointed by the president for life, but their nomination, like those of other federal justices, cabinet members, and high ranking office-holders, must be ratified by the Senate.

The president may veto legislation passed by Congress, but the veto can be overridden by two-thirds of each house. Changes to the Constitution require a two-thirds vote in both houses of Congress and ratification by three-quarters of the states.

Answer the following questions.

1. What makes the United States government different from most other democracies? _____

_____

_____

2. How did the framers of the Constitution ensure that no one part of government would gain too much control?

_____

_____

_____

3. Is it possible to change the Constitution? How? _____

_____

_____

2.2 Voter Registration and Turnout

Use the table below and the definitions given to answer the questions.

STATE	1996 VAP	1996 REG	% REG of VAP	TURNOUT	% T/O of VAP
California	22,826,000	15,662,075	68.62%	10,019,484	43.90%
Florida	11,043,000	8,077,877	73.15%	5,300,927	48.00%
Illinois	8,754,000	6,663,301	76.12%	4,311,391	49.25%
Maryland	3,820,000	2,587,978	67.75%	1,780,870	46.62%
Massachusetts	4,649,000	3,459,193	74.41%	2,556,459	54.99%
Michigan	7,072,000	6,677,079	94.42%	3,848,844	54.42%
New Jersey	6,034,000	4,320,866	71.61%	3,075,860	50.98%
New York	13,564,000	10,162,156	74.92%	6,439,129	47.47%
North Carolina	5,519,000	4,318,008	78.24%	2,515,807	45.58%
Ohio	8,347,000	6,879,687	82.42%	4,534,434	54.32%
Pennsylvania	9,197,000	6,805,612	74.00%	4,506,118	49.00%
Texas	13,597,000	10,540,678	77.52%	5,611,644	41.27%
Virginia	5,083,000	3,322,135	65.36%	2,416,642	47.54%
Washington	4,115,000	3,078,128	74.80%	2,253,837	54.77%
UNITED STATES	196,511,000	146,211,960	74.40%	96,456,345	49.08%

DEFINITIONS:
   1996 VAP refers to the total Voting Age Population of the State as reported by the Bureau of Census. The VAP includes all persons over the age of 18. **1996 REG** refers to the total number of registered voters as reported by the States. **TURNOUT** refers to the total vote cast for the highest office 1996 President.

   Source: Congressional Research Service.

1. Which state has the largest voting age population? _____
2. In which state is the largest proportion of voting age population registered to vote? _____
3. Which state had the highest turnout in 1996? _____
4. Which state had the lowest? _____
5. How many people in the U.S. voted in the 1996 election?_____
6. What percentage of the voting age population voted? _____

2.3 Civil Disobedience

Civil disobedience is the open, deliberate, nonviolent breaking of a law. When citizens resort to civil disobedience, it is usually because they believe a law is not valid because it was not created in a democratic way. People may resort to civil disobedience if they believe a law contradicts a higher moral principle or a religious belief. Civil disobedience may be practiced by individuals, small groups, or masses of people.

Civil disobedience may be practiced solely to avoid participating in activities believed to be wrong. It may be practiced as part of an organized campaign planned to achieve a specific objective, such as the repeal of a law. Civil disobedience has been widely practiced in the United States and in other countries. In our own time, civil disobedience has been used in the United States in the civil rights movement, the anti-Vietnam War movement, and the controversy over abortion rights.

Answer the following questions.

1. Name some other situations where civil disobedience might be used.

_____

_____

2. We live in a democracy that offers a number of opportunities to block or repeal offensive laws. Is civil disobedience still justified in some circumstances? Why?

_____

_____

3. Should all citizens obey laws regardless of their content or purpose?

_____

_____

4. Does the willful breaking of laws lead to social chaos?

_____

_____

5. Would you participate in an act of civil disobedience? If so, under what circumstances? Would you be willing to go to jail for your beliefs?

_____

_____

2.4 Lincoln's Second Inaugural

This is a passage from President Abraham Lincoln's second inaugural address, delivered in 1865 when the outcome of the Civil War was certain but the war still dominated national life. Fourteen months earlier, Lincoln had delivered the Gettysburg Address, which many considered his finest speech. But the final sentences of the second inaugural represent some of Lincoln's best writing. Read the passage carefully, then answer the questions below.

Fondly do we hope, fervently do we pray, that this mighty scourge of war may speedily pass away. Yet, if God wills that it continue until all the wealth piled by the bondsman's two hundred and fifty years of unrequited toil shall be sunk, and until every drop of blood drawn with the lash shall be paid by another drawn with the sword, as was said three thousand years ago, so still it must be said the judgments of the Lord are true and righteous altogether.

With malice toward none, with charity for all, with firmness in the right as God gives us to see the right, let us strive on to finish the work we are in, to bind up the nation's wounds, to care for him who shall have borne the battle and for his widow and his orphan—to do all which may achieve and cherish a just and lasting peace among ourselves and with all nations .

1. In the second sentence, what is Lincoln saying about the length of the war? How long might the war continue?

   _____

   _____

   _____

2. What is Lincoln's point in the final sentence?

   _____

   _____

   _____

3. Under what circumstances would you participate in a civil war? Would you be able to wish for "malice toward none" at the end of the war?

   _____

   _____

   _____

2.5 Kennedy's Inaugural

This is a passage from President John F. Kennedy's inaugural address, delivered on January 20, 1961, as Kennedy assumed office as the youngest president in U.S. history. His speech was widely hailed as one of the finest ever delivered by an American president. Read the passage carefully, then answer the questions below.

In the long history of the world, only a few generations have been granted the role of defending freedom in its hour of maximum danger. I do not shrink from this responsibility—I welcome it. I do not believe that any of us would exchange places with any other people or any other generation. The energy, the faith, the devotion which we bring to this endeavor will light our country and all who serve it—and the glow from that fire can truly light the world.

And so, my fellow Americans, ask not what your country can do for you: Ask what you can do for your country.

My fellow citizens of the world: Ask not what America will do for you, but what together we can do for the freedom of man.

Finally, whether you are citizens of America or citizens of the world, ask of us the same high standards of strength and sacrifice which we ask of you. With a good conscience our only sure reward, with history that final judge of our deeds, let us go forth to lead the land we love, asking His blessing and His help, but knowing that here on earth God's work must truly be our own.

1. What is Kennedy's challenge to the American people in this speech?

   _____

   _____

   _____

2. What challenge does he give to all citizens of the world?

   _____

   _____

   _____

3. Rewrite the final sentence in your own words.

   _____

   _____

   _____

2.6 Your Country

A government is the system by which a country, state, city, or other group of people is ruled. There are many types of governments, and the people who rule a country, state, or city must decide which to use. Imagine that you are starting a new country and have to set up a government. Answer the questions below to determine how your country will be ruled. Continue on another sheet of paper if you need more space.

1. What is the name of your country? _____

2. Who will be in charge of your country? How much power will they have?

_____

_____

3. How will those who rule be chosen?

_____

4. How will the government raise money?

_____

5. How will the government decide on which laws will be made?

_____

6. How will the government enforce the laws?

_____

7. What laws will be made and why?

_____

_____

_____

_____

_____

2.7 The Selective Service System

The Selective Service System is an independent agency within the Executive Branch of the Federal Government. The Director of Selective Service is appointed by the President and confirmed by the Senate.

The Federal law under which the agency operates is the Military Selective Service Act. Under this law, the mission of the Selective Service System is to provide the numbers of men needed by the Armed Forces, within the time required, should Congress and the President decide to return to a draft, in the event of a national emergency.

Registration is the process of providing the Selective Service with personal information, such as name, address, date of birth, Social Security number, and other related information about one's self. Even though no one is currently being drafted, men are required to register with Selective Service as soon as they reach age 18.

Registration provides the U.S. with a means to develop and maintain an accurate list of names and addresses of men who might be called upon if a return to the draft is authorized.

Failure to register or otherwise comply with the Military Selective Service Act is, upon conviction, punishable by a fine of up to $250,000, imprisonment for up to five years, or both.

Answer the following questions.

1. Do you believe men should be forced to register with the Selective Service at age 18? Why?

_____

_____

_____

2. Should women be forced to register at age 18? Why?

_____

_____

_____

3. Thousands of young men refused to register with the Selective Service during the Vietnam War. Some fled to Canada; some went to jail. Others registered and were drafted. More than 50,000 died in Vietnam. What might you have done?

_____

_____

_____

_____

2.8 International Citizenship—the UN

The United Nations (UN) was founded on October 24, 1945. It is the most important international organization in the world. The UN emerged from world war when the twenty-six Allied countries pledged to fight against Germany, Italy, and Japan. World War II not only showed the need for an effective international organization to replace the unsuccessful League of Nations, but also demonstrated the possibilities of international cooperation as a basis for resisting threats to the peace.

At the center of the UN is the UN Charter. The charter was adopted by the representatives of fifty states meeting at San Francisco in 1945. Membership is limited to states. In accord with article 7 of the charter, there are six principal organs of the UN: the General Assembly, the Security Council, the Economic and Social Council, the Trusteeship Council, the International Court of Justice, and the Secretariat.

The General Assembly controls much of the UN's work. Meeting in regular session for the last quarter of every year, it approves the budget, adopts priorities, calls international conferences, oversees the work of many smaller groups or committees, and adopts resolutions on a wide range of issues.

The Security Council has primary responsibility for the maintenance of international peace and security. It has the "big five" permanent members (China, France, the United Kingdom, the United States, and Russia) plus 10 others to be elected for two-year terms by the General Assembly. Each of the "big five" has a power of veto. The Security Council meets frequently throughout the year, and is empowered to make decisions binding on all UN members.

There are sixteen specialized agencies associated with the UN, each with its own constitution, membership, and budget. Apart from the main financial agencies (the International Monetary Fund and the World Bank), the "big four" are the International Labor Organization (ILO) in Geneva, the Food and Agriculture Organization (FAO) in Rome, the UN Educational, Scientific and Cultural organization (UNESCO) in Paris, and the World Health Organization (WHO) in Geneva.

Answer the following questions.

1. When and why was the UN founded?

_____

_____

2. Describe the structure of the UN.

_____

_____

3. Which countries are members of the Security Council and what are the functions of the Council?

_____

_____

©1999 by The Center for Applied Research in Education

2.9 The UN—Part II

The actual role and influence of the UN have differed significantly from what was foreseen in 1945. In particular, peacekeeping and observer forces, not mentioned in the charter, have been an important aspect of UN action in numerous conflicts and crises. Other issues not addressed in the charter, such as environmental management, have become more central to the work of the organization. Also, the secretary-general's functions have grown, especially the use of the position's influence to mediate between members.

The Middle East crisis of 1956 gave rise to a major innovation in UN practice: peacekeeping, or the use of multinational forces under UN command to help control and resolve conflict between hostile states or between hostile communities within a state.

In the decades after 1956, many other peacekeeping forces were created under UN auspices. They were deployed in Lebanon, West Iran, Yemen, Cyprus, Sinai, Golan Heights, and the Congo. In 1992, the UN sent peacekeeping forces into Cambodia and Yugoslavia to bring internal wars to an end.

One method of pressure provided for in the UN Charter is mandatory economic sanctions, but these have been used only rarely. The Security Council has applied them against Rhodesia and South Africa, and in August 1990 sanctions were imposed on Iraq following its invasion of Kuwait.

The UN has become the first genuinely global international organization, bringing almost all sovereign states together under one set of principles—those of the UN Charter. It remains central to the survival and advancement of the idea that states exist as part of a universal international society.

Answer the following questions.

1. How has the work of the UN changed since 1945?

_____

_____

2. What is the peacekeeping function of the UN and where has it been used?

_____

_____

3. When has the UN imposed economic sanctions?

_____

_____

4. What is the purpose of the UN?

_____

_____

5. Would you be willing to serve in a UN peacekeeping force? Why?

_____

_____

Section 3

The Constitution

3.1 Constitutions

The word "constitution" refers both to the principles that define a system of government and to the written document that establishes such a system. Every government has a constitution in the first sense of the word and, since World War II, virtually every state—Britain, New Zealand, and Israel are among the exceptions—has a written constitution as well.

The first written constitutions were made during the American and French revolutions. These constitutions restructured government institutions, set out political principles and, in the case of the United States, proclaimed independence from colonial rule. In both France and the United States, written constitutions attempted to establish governments based on popular consent and respect for individual rights.

These eighteenth-century French and American constitutions became models for constitutions around the world. Now, a written constitution has become almost a prerequisite to international recognition for new nations.

A constitution creates a nation or state in a number of ways. First, a constitution marks the existence of a group that claims its own sphere of authority. This authority may be defined in terms of a particular region or a group of people. Second, a constitution not only asserts that there is a nation or state, it also describes how that nation or state will be governed. Finally, a constitution provides a set of terms that will be used to discuss government. For example, the U.S. Constitution established terms such as "due process" and "equal protection" that became the basis for enforcing certain rights.

Interpreting the constitution and its application is usually the job of a nation's courts. In the U.S., the Supreme Court is charged with interpreting and upholding the Constitution.

Answer the following questions.

1. What does "constitution" mean? _____

_____

_____

2. When were the first constitutions written, and what was their purpose?

_____

_____

3. What issues are covered in most constitutions? _____

_____

_____

_____

_____

3.2 We the people . . .

The United States Constitution is the oldest written constitution in the world and the basis of our political system. Yet this remarkable document, which defines the purpose and function of our government, remains a mystery to many Americans. Are you among them? Take the following quiz to test your own knowledge. Circle the letter of the correct answer for each question.

1. In the summer of 1787, 55 delegates from 12 states met to revise the Articles of Confederation and to frame a new American government. This gathering was called the:
   a. Continental Congress
   b. Constitutional Convention
   c. Jamestown Colony
2. Of the thirteen original states, the one that refused to send a delegate to the Convention was:
   a. New Jersey
   b. Rhode Island
   c. Ohio
3. The delegates met in:
   a. Trenton
   b. Williamsburg
   c. Philadelphia
4. The former military hero who was chosen presiding officer of the Convention was:
   a. George Washington
   b. John Paul Jones
   c. John Adams
5. The delegate (and future President) known as the chief framer of the Constitution was:
   a. James Madison
   b. Thomas Jefferson
   c. John Adams
6. The delegate who put all the Convention's resolutions and decisions into final written form was:
   a. Myles Standish
   b. Patrick Henry
   c. Gouverneur Morris
7. The two factions supporting and opposing ratification of the Constitution were known as:
   a. Federalists and Anti-Federalists
   b. Republicans and Democrats
   c. Loyalists and Tories
8. The Constitution divides the powers of the national government into this number of branches:
   a. Three
   b. Five
   c. Seven
9. The system written into the Constitution ensuring that these branches of government share responsibilities and power is known as:
   a. Advice and Consent
   b. Checks and Balances
   c. Separate but Equal

©1999 by The Center for Applied Research in Education

3.3 Unscramble the Preamble!

Put the following parts of the Preamble of the Constitution in the correct order. Rewrite the Preamble on the lines below.

1. Posterity, do ordain and
2. United States, in order
3. provide for the common defense,
4. establish this Constitution
5. We the People of the
6. Liberty to ourselves and our
7. promote the general Welfare,
8. to form a more perfect
9. for the United States of America
10. Union, establish Justice,
11. insure domestic Tranquility,
12. and secure the blessings of

_____

_____

_____

_____

_____

_____

_____

_____

_____

_____

_____

_____

_____

3.4 Article I

The first seven sections of Article I of the U.S. Constitution sketch the structure of Congress and its operations. The main clauses of these first seven sections are given below. Read them carefully, then rewrite the seven sections in your own words.

Article I

   Section 1. All legislative powers herein granted shall be vested in a Congress of the United States, which shall consist of a Senate and House of Representatives.

   Section 2. The House of Representatives shall be composed of members chosen every second year by the people of the several States, and the electors in each State shall have the qualifications requisite for electors of the most numerous branch of the State legislature.

   Section 3. The Senate of the United States shall be composed of two senators from each State, *(chosen by the legislature thereof*)*, for six years; and each senator shall have one vote.

   Section 4. The times, places and manner of holding Elections for senators and representatives, shall be prescribed in each State by the Legislature thereof, but the Congress may at any time by law make or alter such regulations. . . .

   Section 5. Each House shall be the judge of the elections, returns and qualifications of its own members, and a majority of each shall constitute a quorum to do business; but a smaller number may adjourn from day to day, and may be authorized to compel the attendance of absent members, in such manner, and under such penalties as each House may provide. Each House may determine the rules of its proceedings, punish its members for disorderly behavior, and, with the Concurrence of two thirds, expel a member.

   Section 6. The senators and representatives shall receive a compensation for their services, to be ascertained by law, ...

   Section 7. All bills for raising revenue shall originate in the House of Representatives; but the Senate may propose or concur with amendments as on other bills.

*Amended for popular election in 1913.

1. _____
   _____

2. _____
   _____

3. _____
   _____

4. _____
   _____

5. _____
   _____

6. _____
   _____

7. _____
   _____

3.5 Judicial Powers

Article III of the Constitution grants certain powers to the federal courts and defines the cases that the federal courts may decide. Read the passage carefully, then list in your own words ten types of cases that the federal courts may hear.

Article III
   Section 1. The judicial power of the United States, shall be vested in one Supreme Court, and in such inferior courts as the Congress may from time to time ordain and establish.
   Section 2. The judicial power shall extend to all cases, in law and equity, arising under this Constitution, the laws of the United States, and treaties made, or which shall be made, under their authority;—to all cases affecting ambassadors, other public ministers and consuls;—to all cases of admiralty and maritime jurisdiction;—to controversies to which the United States shall be a party;—to controversies between two or more States;—between a State and citizens of another State;—between citizens of different States;—between citizens of the same State claiming lands under grants of different States, and between a State, or the citizens thereof, and foreign States, citizens or subjects.
   In all cases affecting ambassadors, other public ministers and consuls, and those in which a State shall be party, the Supreme Court shall have original jurisdiction. In all the other cases before mentioned, the Supreme Court shall have appellate jurisdiction, both as to law and fact, with such exceptions, and under such regulations as the Congress shall make.

1. _____
2. _____
3. _____
4. _____
5. _____
6. _____
7. _____
8. _____
9. _____
10. _____

3.6 The Bill of Rights

The Bill of Rights, another name for the first ten amendments to the United States Constitution, lists the fundamental rights and freedoms of the citizens of the United States. Authored by Virginians James Mason and James Madison, and ratified in 1791, the Bill of Rights guarantees certain basic individual liberties to all people and limits the powers of the federal government. Use this summary of the first ten amendments to study the protections they provide. Then team up with a partner and test each other on your knowledge of each amendment.

First Amendment: Forbids the Congress from interfering with freedom of religion, speech or press, or with the right to assemble peaceably, or to petition the government.

Second Amendment: Guarantees the right to bear arms.

Third Amendment: Assures that soldiers cannot be arbitrarily lodged in private homes without the consent of the owner.

Fourth Amendment: Forbids unreasonable search or seizure of persons, homes, and effects without a warrant.

Fifth Amendment: Guarantees specific rights when on trial; stipulates that no one may be forced to testify against him- or herself.

Sixth Amendment: Assures the accused the right to speedy and public trial, the right to be represented by an attorney, and the right to be faced by accusing witnesses.

Seventh Amendment: Guarantees the right to trial by jury.

Eighth Amendment: Forbids excessive fines and cruel or unusual punishments.

Ninth Amendment: States that people may be entitled to rights not mentioned in the Constitution.

Tenth Amendment: Powers not delegated to the federal government are reserved for the states.

3.7 The Right Stuff . . .

Below are some real-life situations made possible for Americans under the protection offered by the Bill of Rights. Match these situations to the rights that follow, and place the correct letter in each blank.

_____ 1. Newspapers release evidence incriminating the President

_____ 2. Judge removes herself from hearing trial in which defendant is her brother

_____ 3. Nazi group is given permission to hold orderly parade on Main Street

_____ 4. Shop owner of small store in high crime area keeps licensed pistol in locked drawer

_____ 5. Court rules that pepper spray may not be used against nonviolent prisoners

_____ 6. On trial for tax fraud, defendant chooses not to take the stand

_____ 7. Maple Avenue is home to six churches, four synagogues, two mosques, and one Hindu temple

_____ 8. Anti-war activists stage series of protest speeches outside White House gates

_____ 9. Although Mr. Smith looked somewhat like the notorious Pickpocket Peterman, Detective Miller merely questioned him and did not insist on examining the contents of Smith's briefcase

A. Freedom of the press
B. The right to keep and bear arms
C. Freedom of religion
D. Freedom of speech
E. The right to assemble peacefully
F. The right to be protected against cruel and unusual punishment

G. The right not to testify against oneself in court
H. The right to protect one's home and belongings from unreasonable search without warrant
I. The right to a speedy, fair, and impartial trial

3.8 The "Other" Amendments

The first ten amendments to the Constitution are known as the Bill of Rights. Although these amendments receive a great deal of attention, there are 16 additional amendments to the Constitution, some of which have had tremendous impact on citizens of the United States. Read the amendments listed below. Pick the three amendments you think are the most important, list them in the space provided, and explain why you think they are important.

Amendment XI (1795) prohibited citizens of one state from suing the government of another state

Amendment XII (1804) established separate ballots for president and vice president in electoral college

Amendment XIII (1865) abolished slavery

Amendment XIV (1868) made slaves citizens and forbade states from denying civil rights

Amendment XV (1870) prohibited states from denying a person the right to vote on account of race

Amendment XVI (1913) gave Congress the right to levy an income tax

Amendment XVII (1913) provided for direct election of Senators

Amendment XVIII (1919) permitted Congress to ban the sale of liquor

Amendment XIX (1920) gave women the right to vote

Amendment XX (1933) changed the date of the presidential inauguration and set congressional sessions to begin in January

Amendment XXI (1933) repealed Amendment XVIII

Amendment XXII (1951) limited president to two elected terms

Amendment XXIII (1961) granted people of the District of Columbia the right to vote for residential electors

Amendment XXIV (1964) prohibited use of the poll tax to deny people voting privileges

Amendment XXV (1967) provided a procedure to fill the vice presidency in the event of a vacancy

Amendment XXVI (1971) lowered the voting age nationally to 18

Amendment XXVII (1992) Prohibited varying congressional compensation until election of Representatives has intervened

I think the three most important amendments are:

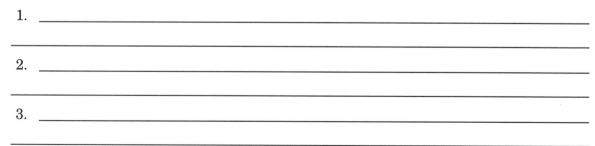

1. _____

   _____

2. _____

   _____

3. _____

   _____

Section 4

Voting

4.1 Voting Rights

The U.S. Constitution does not specify any uniform voting age. Until recently, all states had established 21 years as the minimum age for voting. The twenty-sixth amendment to the Constitution, passed in 1971, lowered the voting age from 21 to 18. In most states, voters must be citizens of the U.S., they must be at least 18 years old, and they must have lived in the county and voting precinct for a certain number of days. States also prohibit certain classes of citizens from voting, usually mental incompetents and convicted felons.

In colonial America, voting was not considered an inherent right but a privilege to be granted only to certain members of the community—those who could be trusted to make the proper decisions in sharing power with the colonial authorities. Voting was limited largely to white men who owned property and worshipped in the established churches. When the Constitution left it up to the states to determine voting laws, most extended the vote to all white men but continued to exclude Native Americans, blacks, many immigrant groups, and women.

After the Civil War, the fifteenth amendment to the Constitution guaranteed blacks the right to vote. Terrorist groups such as the Ku Klux Klan organized to keep blacks from voting. Southern states passed laws designed to stop blacks from voting by requiring voters to pay poll taxes and pass literacy tests. Voting rights were largely denied to black voters until the Voting Rights Act of 1965 finally banned literacy tests and ensured the rights of blacks and other minorities.

Women did not gain the right to vote until a constitutional amendment was finally passed in 1920. Until then, women who tried to vote were turned away from the ballot box, arrested, fined and ridiculed.

Answer the following questions.

1. Which groups of people were denied the right to vote through much of U.S. history?

_____

_____

2. Which groups of people are not allowed to vote today?

_____

_____

3. Do you agree with the law that sets the minimum voting age at 18 years? Why?

_____

_____

_____

_____

4.2 Register to Vote!

When you reach voting age, you can register to vote through the local election officials in your county, or through registration outreach programs sponsored by groups such as the League of Women Voters. You can also register to vote at state drivers' licensing offices, state offices providing public assistance, and at armed forces recruitment offices. In addition to these locations, many states offer registration opportunities at public libraries, post offices, unemployment offices, public high schools, and universities. Registering to vote is as easy as filling out the form below. Go ahead! Practice for the real day by completing the form.

Qualifications of an Eligible Applicant

You must be a citizen of the United States and, by the date of the next election, at least 18 years old and a resident of New Jersey and your county for at least 30 days.

The Commissioner of Registration will notify you upon receipt of this form.

The Registration deadline to vote at the next election is 29 days prior to election day.

Check if you wish to be a board worker/poll clerk in future elections. ❏

Check if you are permanently disabled, unable to go to the polls to vote, and wish to receive information on an Absentee Ballot. ❏

Sign or Mark ➡

If applicant is unable to complete this form, print name and address of individual who completed this form.

Voter Registration Application

1 Check one:
❏ New Registration   ❏ Address Change   ❏ Name Change

2 Last Name | First Name | Middle Initial | Jr. Sr. II III

3 Street Address Where You Live | Apt. #

4 City or Town | County | Zip Code

5 Address Where You Get Your Mail (if different from above)

6 Date of Birth- Month, Day, Year   **7** Telephone Number (optional)

8 Name And Address Of Your Last Voter Registration

County

9 Declaration - I swear or affirm that:

• I am a U.S. citizen
• I live at the above address
• I will be at least 18 years old on or before the next election
• I am not on parole, probation or serving sentence due to a conviction for an indictable offense under any federal or state laws.
• I understand that any false or fraudulent registration may subject me to a fine up to $1,000, imprisonment up to 5 years or both pursuant to R.S. 19:34-1.

Signature or Mark | Date

For Office Use Only

Clerk

Registration No.

Office Time Stamp

10 Name

Address

4.3 Voting—Interpret the Data

The numbers below represent the actual total voting age population, voter registration, and national voter turnout in federal elections from 1980–1996. As you can see, there are significant differences among the number of people of voting age, the number of people who are registered to vote, and the number of people who actually go to the polls and cast ballots. In the space provided, write a paragraph describing some of the trends revealed in the data.

Year	Voting Age Population	Registration	Turnout	% T/O of VAP
1996	196,511,000	146,211,960	96,456,345	49.08%
1994	193,650,000	130,292,822	75,105,860	38.78%
1992	189,529,000	133,821,178	104,405,155	55.09%
1990	185,812,000	121,105,630	67,859,189	36.52%
1988	182,778,000	126,379,628	91,594,693	50.11%
1986	178,566,000	118,399,984	64,991,128	36.40%
1984	174,466,000	124,150,614	92,652,680	53.11%
1982	169,938,000	110,671,225	67,615,576	39.79%
1980	164,597,000	113,043,734	86,515,221	52.56%

% T/O of VAP = Percent Turnout of Voting Age Population

Source: Congressional Research Service reports, Election Data Services Inc., and State Election Offices.

_____

_____

_____

_____

_____

_____

_____

_____

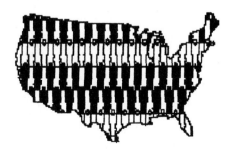

4.4 Voter Turnout—Graph It!

The numbers below represent national voter turnout in federal elections from 1976-1996.
Using some or all of the data, draw a graph to represent the information provided.

Year	Voting Age Population	Registration	Turnout	% T/O of VAP
1996	196,511,000	146,211,960	96,456,345	49.08%
1994	193,650,000	130,292,822	75,105,860	38.78%
1992	189,529,000	133,821,178	104,405,155	55.09%
1990	185,812,000	121,105,630	67,859,189	36.52%
1988	182,778,000	126,379,628	91,594,693	50.11%
1986	178,566,000	118,399,984	64,991,128	36.40%
1984	174,466,000	124,150,614	92,652,680	53.11%
1982	169,938,000	110,671,225	67,615,576	39.79%
1980	164,597,000	113,043,734	86,515,221	52.56%
1978	158,373,000	103,291,265	58,917,938	37.21%
1976	152,309,190	105,037,986	81,555,789	53.55%

% T/O of VAP = Percent Turnout of Voting Age Population

Source: Congressional Research Service reports, Election Data Services Inc., and State Election Offices.

4.5 Vote for Your Choice! ✔

Gubernatorial elections are only days away. You've been out of town for several weeks and have missed much of the campaign coverage by the media. Tonight's televised debate is your last chance to evaluate the three candidates who are vying to be your state's governor. Review their statements and use the questions below to analyze their positions and your reactions to them.

Candidate Allison Andrews: In my concerns about moral issues and the future of young people today, I have led the fight to eliminate the distribution of condoms in schools. I also support the death penalty. In my push to get government out of your pocketbook, I favor an across-the-board tax cut. And, if you elect me, I will work to eliminate fraud in our welfare system.

Candidate Bernie Billings: My campaign is the working class alternative to the candidates who promote big business. I am in favor of "jobs for all." We must shorten the work week and spread available work around. I identify with struggles of the oppressed; we must march for immigrant rights!

Candidate Carmen Carruthers: I support the Brady bill on gun control and am in favor of legalizing marijuana for medical purposes. My office will ensure there is money in the budget to increase pollution reduction efforts statewide and to provide healthcare for all our citizens. Elect me for a better tomorrow!

1. Which candidate do you think is *least* likely to win support from corporations? Why?

   _____

   _____

2. Which candidate do you think is *most* likely to favor school prayer? Why?

   _____

   _____

3. Which candidate would be *most* likely to advocate an active government? Why?

   _____

   _____

4. Which candidate would you vote for? Why?

   _____

   _____

   _____

   _____

4.6 Picture Perfect

In analyzing political trends, data are sometimes more easily understood when presented in pictorial or graph format. Line graphs, bar graphs, and pie charts can help show patterns of voter behavior or shifts in voter demographics. Below are two fictional scenarios. Read the information contained in each and follow the directions for constructing a corresponding graph.

1. In a recent campaign, the two candidates for school board election—and their supporters—differed sharply over how to allocate the newly passed school budget. Twelve percent of the citizens who voted for Jane Phippson believed that the school should sponsor work–study programs in the local quarry, a belief shared by three times that number of Wilma Morton's supporters. Moreover, while each group agreed with the need to bolster the student lunch program, 91% of Phippson's people believed that meant installing individual microwave ovens in each student's locker, compared with only two percent of Morton's voters supporting that expenditure. Using bar graphs, compare how Phippson's and Morton's supporters differ on these main voter issues.

2. Since 1965, the percentage of citizens of Wrightstown who favor mandatory schooling until age 30 has been climbing almost steadily, to a near 100% approval rating today. Starting from a near zero base when first proposed in 1965, support for the measure has shown solid increase over each five-year period (aside from a ten-year interval between 1970 and 1980 when enthusiasm leveled off). In the space below, use a line graph to depict this trend.

4.7 Picture Perfect—Part II

In analyzing political trends, data are sometimes more easily understood when presented in pictorial or graph format. Line graphs, bar graphs, and pie charts can help show patterns of voter behavior or shifts in voter demographics. Read the information in the fictional scenario below and follow the directions for constructing a graph.

Between 1985 and 1995, the work patterns of female voters living in Stanford County have changed greatly. In 1985, just 10% of the women voters held full-time jobs outside the home; half of all the women polled said they were full-time homemakers and the remainder were employed part-time. By 1995, however, the percentage of full-time workers had tripled while those employed part-time had fallen by half (leaving homemakers to make up the rest of the picture). Using two pie charts, present these changing demographics of the women of Stanford County.

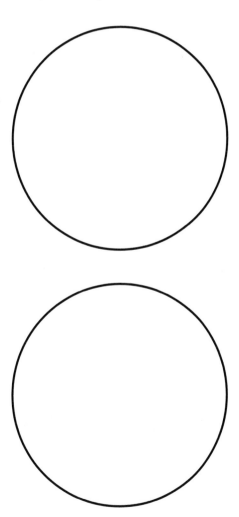

4.8 Exit Poll

Exit polling is the practice of questioning voters—who have just left the ballot booth—on how they voted on various political issues. When organizing the data, pollsters often categorize the responses according to the voters' races, ages, genders, and levels of income and education. Politicians can then use this information to analyze voting patterns and demographic trends.

Study the following tallies gathered by an exit polling of 100 voters—50 men and 50 women. Then use the data to answer the questions below.

Voters	Candidate A	Candidate B
Male	20	30
Female	35	15
White	25	12
Black	11	8
Hispanic	2	10
Asian	4	20
Other	7	1
18-29 years	14	6
30-44 years	10	9
45-59 years	11	18
60+ years	11	21
Under $15,000 income	1	5
$15,000-29,999 income	7	7
$30,000-49,999 income	12	10
$50,000-74,999 income	12	17
$75,000-99,999 income	10	9
$100,000+ income	8	2

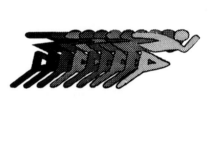

1. What percentage of all Candidate B's voters is female? _____

2. Among voters who earn at least $50,000, which candidate is more popular? _____

3. Which candidate is favored among non-Hispanic voters? _____

4. What percentage of the youngest voters chose Candidate A? _____

II. MAKING GOVERNMENT WORK

- Federal, State, and Local Powers
- The Structure of the Federal Government
- The Executive Branch
- Congress
- The Federal Judiciary
- The Legislative Process
- Elections
- The Media

Section 5

Federal, State, and Local Powers

5.1 Federalism

Modern federalism was invented in Philadelphia, Pennsylvania over 200 years ago by the authors of the U.S. Constitution. Until then, a *federal* country had been seen as a league or club of member states. Under the U.S. Constitution, each citizen is a citizen of two governments: *national* and state.

There is general agreement among experts that a functioning federal system, composed of a number of *regional* governments, must have a *democratic* and *pluralist* political system that provides opportunities for access and participation by citizens at both the national and *state* levels.

The basic objective of federalism is to reconcile *unity* and *diversity*. In particular, federalism has been adopted in various forms by many nations as a way to balance the interests of different *ethnic* and language groups, although this was not the purpose of the founders of U.S. federalism, where former British colonies covering a large territory with a vast unsettled frontier were joined together.

Countries currently and frequently classified as federal are: Australia, Canada, Brazil, Germany, India, Switzerland, and the United States.

Look up the following words in a dictionary. Select the definition that best fits the context in which the word is used in the above passage. Write the definition you selected.

federal _____

_____

national _____

_____

regional _____

_____

democratic _____

_____

pluralist _____

_____

state _____

_____

unity _____

_____

diversity _____

_____

ethnic _____

_____

5.2 Limits on the Powers of the States

Article I, Section 10 of the U.S. Constitution carefully limits the powers of the states and reserves certain powers for the federal government. Read this passage, then write in your own words a list of six actions that the states may *not* take according to the Constitution.

> *Article I. Section 10. 1. No State shall enter into any treaty, alliance, or confederation; grant letters of marque and reprisal; coin money; emit bills of credit; make anything but gold and silver coin a tender in payment of debts; pass any bill of attainder, ex post facto law, or law impairing the obligation of contracts, or grant any title of nobility.*
>
> *2. No State shall, without the consent of the Congress, lay any imposts or duties on imports or exports, except what may be absolutely necessary for executing its inspection laws; and the net produce of all duties and imposts, laid by any State on imports or exports, shall be for the use of the Treasury of the United States; and all such laws shall be subject to the revision and control of the Congress.*
>
> *3. No State shall, without the consent of Congress, lay any duty of tonnage, keep troops, or ships of war in time of peace, enter into any agreement or compact with another State, or with a foreign power, or engage in war, unless actually invaded, or in such imminent danger as will not admit of delay.*

Summary of six actions the states may *not* take:

1. _____
2. _____
3. _____
4. _____
5. _____
6. _____

Step Ahead!
Pick one of the restrictions listed above and explain what problems might arise if a state took the action that is prohibited.

_____

_____

_____

_____

5.3 Three Levels of Government

Using the information below, write a paragraph describing the functions of the three levels of government.

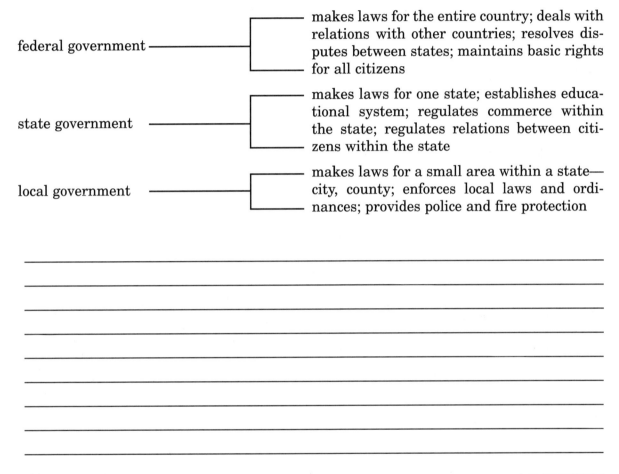

federal government ——————— makes laws for the entire country; deals with relations with other countries; resolves disputes between states; maintains basic rights for all citizens

state government ——————— makes laws for one state; establishes educational system; regulates commerce within the state; regulates relations between citizens within the state

local government ——————— makes laws for a small area within a state—city, county; enforces local laws and ordinances; provides police and fire protection

_____
_____
_____
_____
_____
_____
_____
_____
_____
_____
_____
_____
_____
_____

5.4 Three Branches of the Federal Government

Using the diagram below, write three paragraphs describing the functions of the three branches of the federal government. Write your paragraphs on another sheet of paper.

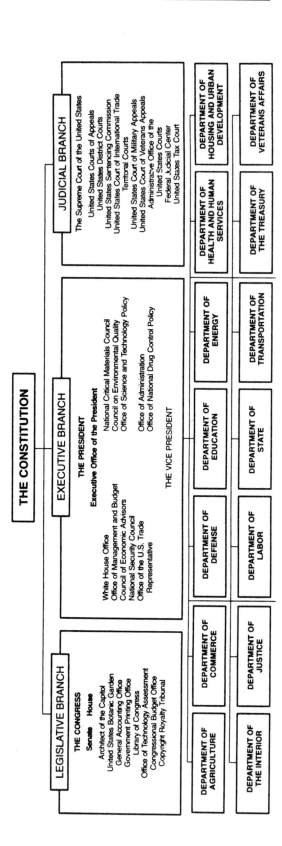

5.5 Three Branches of State Government

Using the diagram below, write three paragraphs describing the functions of each of the three branches of state government. Write your answers on another sheet of paper.

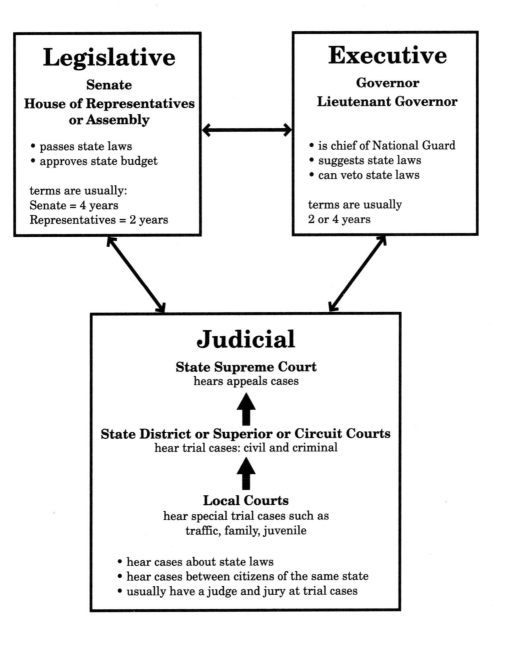

Legislative

Senate
House of Representatives
or Assembly

• passes state laws
• approves state budget

terms are usually:
Senate = 4 years
Representatives = 2 years

Executive

Governor
Lieutenant Governor

• is chief of National Guard
• suggests state laws
• can veto state laws

terms are usually
2 or 4 years

Judicial

State Supreme Court
hears appeals cases

State District or Superior or Circuit Courts
hear trial cases: civil and criminal

Local Courts
hear special trial cases such as
traffic, family, juvenile

• hear cases about state laws
• hear cases between citizens of the same state
• usually have a judge and jury at trial cases

5.6 Three Branches of Local Government

Local governments, unlike state and federal governments, do not have constitutions but usually receive a charter from the state government. Local governments may be organized on the basis of a city, county, town, or village. The executive and legislative posts are usually elected positions. Using the diagram below, write a paragraph about the branches of local government.

Executive
Mayor
The mayor is usually elected and is responsible for the day-to-day business of running the city.

Legislative
City Council
County Board
The council or board is usually elected by the citizens of the city or the county and is responsible for making laws and directing the affairs of the city or county.

Judicial
City Courts
County Courts
Local governments usually have a court system that handles local issues, such as traffic laws and small claims. Often these cases may be appealed to the state courts. Local judges are sometimes called justices of the peace or magistrates. Local courts often specialize in one area of law, such as traffic law or family law.

_____

_____

_____

_____

_____

_____

_____

5.7 Federal, State, and Local Responsibilities

Write the number of each need and duty listed on the left in the box of the level of government responsible for that duty. Some duties might be done by more than one level of government.

1. Collecting federal taxes
2. Issuing driver licenses
3. Collecting garbage
4. Regulating the sale of alcohol
5. Building schools
6. Regulating foreign trade
7. Providing police
8. Protecting national borders
9. Enforcing traffic laws
10. Building interstate highways
11. Issuing marriage licenses
12. Maintaining parks
13. Collecting property taxes
14. Building sewers
15. Providing old age benefits
16. Keeping birth records
17. Providing safe drinking water

FEDERAL

STATE

LOCAL

5.8 Duties of the President and Vice President

The President and the Vice President both exercise a great deal of power and fulfill a number of duties. Write the number of each duty listed in the proper box. Some duties might be done by both the President and Vice President!

1. Commander-in-Chief of military
2. Approves or vetoes laws
3. Advises Congress
4. Goes to meetings with advisors
5. Presides over Senate
6. Acts as President if President can't
7. Makes foreign policy
8. Grants pardons
9. Appoints ambassadors
10. Votes in the Senate if necessary
11. Appoints federal court judges
12. Delivers State of the Union address
13. Is the Chief Executive
14. Visits with foreign dignitaries

PRESIDENT

VICE PRESIDENT

Section 6

The Structure of the Federal Government

Name _____ Date _____ Class _____

6.1 Political Terms

How fluent are you with our country's political words and phrases? Can you spell some common political expressions? Do you understand their meanings?

Below are several "jumbled" political terms, along with their definitions. Use these definitions to unscramble the jumbles, then write a sentence using each term correctly.

1. DENTMENAM (A formal change to the Constitution)

   Word: _____

   Sentence: _____

   _____

2. PHIW (A political party leader elected in caucus)

   Word: _____

   Sentence: _____

   _____

3. TENSEA (The upper house of Congress)

   Word: _____

   Sentence: _____

   _____

4. LIVIC STRIBELIE (Basic freedoms guaranteed in the Constitution and Bill of Rights)

   Word: _____

   Sentence: _____

   _____

5. DEAMANT (A politician's authority to carry out a program based on election victory)

   Word: _____

   Sentence: _____

   _____

6.2 Check, Please!

In their desire to ensure that no one branch of the United States government could exceed the power and authority of another, the drafters of the Constitution established a complex system of "checks and balances." This arrangement calls for each of the three branches— legislative, executive, and judicial—to carry out its own responsibilities while at the same time holding a degree of influence over each other's power. For example, while a member of the Supreme Court can remain in office for life, it is the President who has the authority to nominate each Justice and Congress who must approve that nomination. Thus, "checks and balances" encourages cooperation within our government while providing for a fair distribution of power.

Using a check mark, identify which of the following legislative, executive, and judicial actions can be considered "checks" against the unlimited power of another government branch.

_____ 1. Congress can pass federal legislation

_____ 2. President can veto federal bills

_____ 3. Supreme Court can declare new laws unconstitutional

_____ 4. President can appoint federal judges

_____ 5. Senate can refuse to confirm presidential appointments

_____ 6. Congress can impeach federal judges

_____ 7. President can make foreign treaties

_____ 8. Congress can override a presidential veto

_____ 9. President can approve or veto federal bills

_____ 10. Supreme Court interprets the law

_____ 11. Congress can propose constitutional amendments to overturn judicial decisions

_____ 12. Congress can declare executive acts unconstitutional

6.3 Checks and Balances

Answer these questions about our system of checks and balances. Refer to the diagram below.

1. What checks does the President have over Congress? _____
   _____
   _____

2. How can Congress limit the President's power? _____
   _____
   _____

3. How can the courts influence Congress and the President? _____
   _____
   _____

LEGISLATIVE ⟵⟶ **EXECUTIVE**

passes laws
can override veto
must approve treaties
must approve appointments
can impeach President and judges
approves judges

can veto laws
makes treaties
appoints officials
appoints judges

JUDICIAL

can rule that a law is unconstitutional
can say Presidential action is unconstitutional

6.4 Power Plays

Using all seven of the terms defined below, write a paragraph about a bill passing into law. Use the back of this sheet if you need more space.

Override of a Veto: The process by which each chamber of Congress votes on a bill vetoed by the President. To pass a bill over the President's objections requires a two-thirds vote in each Chamber. Historically, Congress has overridden fewer than ten percent of all presidential vetoes.

Pocket Veto: The Constitution grants the President 10 days to review a measure passed by the Congress. If the President has not signed the bill after 10 days, it becomes law without his signature. However, if Congress adjourns during the 10-day period, the bill does not become law.

Presidential Signature: A proposed law passed by Congress must be presented to the President, who then has 10 days to approve or disapprove it. The President signs bills he supports, making them law. He vetoes a bill by returning it to the House in which it began, usually with a written message. Normally, bills he neither signs nor vetoes within 10 days become law without his signature.

Private Law: This is a private bill enacted into law. Private laws have restricted applicability, often addressing immigration and naturalization issues affecting individuals.

Public Law: This is a public bill or joint resolution that has passed both chambers and been enacted into law. Public laws have general applicability nationwide.

Statutes at Large: This is a chronological listing of the laws enacted each Congress. They are published in volumes numbered by Congress.

Veto: The procedure established under the Constitution by which the President refuses to approve a bill or joint resolution and thus prevents its enactment into law. A regular veto occurs when the President returns the legislation to the house in which it originated. The President usually returns a vetoed bill with a message indicating his reasons for rejecting the measure. The veto can be overridden only by a two-thirds vote in both the Senate and the House.

6.5 Legislative Terms

Write the letter of each definition next to the appropriate term.

act

    A. A permanent committee given jurisdiction over all legislation concerning a particular subject.

bill

    B. A by-law setting forth the procedure under which the House or Senate shall operate.

conference

    C. The head of the minority party in a chamber as elected by the members of the minority party in that chamber.

joint committee

    D. The official presiding officer in the Senate; whoever is serving as Vice President of the U.S.

majority leader

    E. A committee whose membership is divided equally between members of the House and Senate.

minority leader

    F. The head of the majority party in a chamber as elected by the members of the majority party in that chamber.

President of the Senate

    G. A meeting between delegations from the House and Senate, whose purpose is to reconcile differences between the House-passed version of a bill and the version passed by the Senate.

rule

    H. A piece of legislation that has passed both houses of Congress and been signed by the President (or passed over his veto) into law.

standing committee

    I. A piece of legislation that, if passed by both houses of Congress and signed by the President, becomes law.

6.6 Senators

The Senate is composed of 100 members—two from each state, irrespective of population or area—elected by the people under the provisions of the 17th Amendment to the Constitution. That amendment changed the former Constitutional method under which Senators were chosen by the respective state legislatures.

A Senator must be at least 30 years of age, have been a citizen of the United States for nine years, and, when elected, be a resident of the state for which he or she is chosen. The term of office is six years and one-third of the total membership of the Senate is elected every second year. The terms of both Senators from a particular state are so arranged that they do not terminate at the same time. Of the two Senators from a state serving at the same time, the one who was elected first—or if both were elected at the same time, the one elected for a full term—is referred to as the "senior" Senator from that state. The other is referred to as the "junior" Senator.

If a Senator dies or resigns during the term, the governor of the state must call a special election unless the state legislature has authorized the governor to appoint a successor until the next election, at which time a successor is elected for the balance of the term. Most of the state legislatures have granted their governors the power of appointment.

Each Senator has one vote.

Answer the following questions.

1. What are the qualifications required for becoming a Senator?

   _____

   _____

   _____

2. What do we mean when we refer to a "junior" or "senior" Senator?

   _____

   _____

   _____

3. What happens if a Senator dies during his or her term in office?

   _____

   _____

   _____

6.7 Representatives

The House of Representatives is composed of 435 members elected every two years from among the 50 states, apportioned to their total populations. The permanent number of 435 was established following the Thirteenth Decennial Census in 1910, as directed in Article I, Section 2 of the Constitution, and was increased temporarily to 437 for the 87th Congress, to provide for one Representative each for Alaska and Hawaii. It seems undesirable to make a considerable increase in the number of members, because a larger body—similar to the British House of Commons, consisting of 650 members—would be too unwieldy.

A Representative must be at least 25 years of age, have been a citizen of the United States for seven years, and, when elected, be a resident of the state in which he or she is chosen. If a Representative dies or resigns during the term, the governor of the state must call a special election for the choosing of a successor to serve for the unexpired portion of the term.

Each Representative has one vote. In addition to the Representatives from each of the States, there is a Resident Commissioner from the Commonwealth of Puerto Rico and Delegates from the District of Columbia, American Samoa, Guam, and the Virgin Islands. The Resident Commissioner and the Delegates have most of the prerogatives of Representatives, with the important exception of the right to vote on matters before the House.

Answer the following questions.

1. How many members are currently in the House of Representatives and how is this number determined? _____

_____

_____

2. What qualifications are required for members of the House? _____

_____

_____

3. What happens if a Representative dies during his or her term in office? _____

_____

_____

4. In addition to the Representatives from the 50 states, who participates in the House without voting? _____

_____

_____

6.8 Congress at Work

Under the provisions of Section 2 of the 20th Amendment to the Constitution, Congress must assemble at least once every year, at noon on the third day of January, unless by law they appoint a different day. A Congress lasts for two years, commencing in January of the year following the biennial election of Members, and is divided into two sessions.

Unlike some other parliamentary bodies, both the Senate and the House of Representatives have equal legislative functions and powers (except that only the House of Representatives may initiate revenue bills). The Constitution authorizes each House to determine the rules of its proceedings. Pursuant to that authority the House of Representatives adopts its rules on the opening day of each Congress. The Senate, which considers itself a continuing body, operates under standing rules that it amends from time to time.

The chief function of Congress is the making of laws. In addition, the Senate has the function of advising and consenting to treaties and to certain nominations by the President. In the matter of impeachments, the House of Representatives presents the charges—a function similar to that of a grand jury—and the Senate sits as a court to try the impeachment. Both Houses meet in joint session on the sixth day of January, unless by law they appoint a different day, following a presidential election, to count the electoral votes. If no candidate receives a majority of the total electoral votes, the House of Representatives, each state delegation having one vote, chooses the President from among the three candidates having the largest number of votes, and the Senate chooses the Vice President from the two candidates having the largest number of votes for that office.

Answer the following questions.

1. When does Congress meet? _____

_____

_____

2. Under what rules do the Senate and House operate? _____

_____

_____

_____

3. List at least six duties of the Senate and the House. _____

_____

_____

_____

_____

_____

6.9 When the Senate Meets

Advice and Consent: Under the Constitution, presidential nominations for executive and judicial posts take effect only when confirmed by the Senate, and international treaties become effective only when the Senate approves them by a two-thirds vote.

Confirmation: Informal term for the Senate giving "Advice and Consent" to a presidential nomination for an executive or judicial position.

Executive Business: Nominations and treaties; called executive business because these categories of business are received by the Senate from the President, rather than introduced by Senators.

Executive Session: A portion of the Senate's daily session in which it considers executive business.

Morning Business: Routine business that is supposed to occur during the first two hours of a new legislative day. This business includes receiving messages from the President and from the House of Representatives, reports from executive branch officials, petitions from citizens, committee reports, and the introduction of bills and submission of resolutions. In practice, the Senate often does this business instead by unanimous consent at other convenient points in the day.

Nomination: An appointment by the President to executive or judicial office that is subject to Senate confirmation.

Rider: Informal term for a nongermane amendment to a bill or an amendment to an appropriation bill that changes the permanent law governing a program funded by the bill.

Using *all* of the terms defined above, write a diary entry for one Senator from your state describing his or her work during one day.

_____

_____

_____

_____

_____

_____

_____

_____

6.10 On the Floor

Floor: Action "on the floor" is that which occurs as part of a formal session of the full Senate. An action "from the floor" is one taken by a Senator during a session of the Senate. A Senator who has been recognized to speak by the Chair is said to "have the floor."

Floor Amendment: An amendment offered by an individual Senator from the floor during consideration of a bill or other measure, in contrast to a committee amendment.

Point of Order: A claim made by a Senator from the floor that a rule of the Senate is being violated. If the Chair sustains the point of order, the action in violation of the rule is not permitted.

Recognize: The Chair permits a Senator to speak by recognizing him or her; the Senator then "has the floor." When time is controlled, a Senator must have time yielded to him or her before he or she can be recognized.

Motion to Table: A Senator may move to table any pending question. The motion is not debatable, and agreement to the motion is equivalent to defeating the question tabled. The motion is used to dispose quickly of questions the Senate does not wish to consider further.

Vote: Unless rules specify otherwise, the Senate may agree to any question by a majority of Senators voting, if a quorum is present. The Chair puts each question by voice vote unless the "yeas and nays" are requested, in which case a roll-call vote occurs.

Yield: When a Senator who has been recognized to speak "yields" to another, he or she permits the other to speak while the first Senator retains the floor. Technically, a Senator may yield to another only for a question.

Using *all* of the terms defined above, write a newspaper article describing the action in the Senate during the consideration of a bill.

6.11 Qualifications for Federal Office

Using the table below, write the offices for which these candidates are qualified.

1. Ramon Savez, age 45, born in Equador, U.S. citizen living in California for 14 years.

_____

2. Rosa Moridian, age 60, born in Hawaii, living in Hawaii all her life.

_____

3. Jimmy Carter, age 66, born in Georgia, living in Georgia, was U.S. President from 1977-1981.

_____

4. Ronald Reagan, age 84, born in Illinois, was U.S. President from 1981-1989.

_____

5. Harry Harrison, age 28, born in New Jersey, living in New Jersey all his life.

_____

6. Katherine Smaller, age 24, born in New York, living in New York all her life.

_____

	PRESIDENT	VICE-PRES	SENATOR	REPRESENTATIVE
AGE	35+	35+	30+	25+
CITIZEN	born in U.S.	born in U.S.	9+ years	7+ years
RESIDENCE	14+ years	14+ years	in state	in state
TERM	4 years	4 years	6 years	2 years
LIMIT	2 terms	none	none	none
NUMBER OF	1	1	100	435

6.12 Term Limits

Two hundred years before today's debate, Thomas Jefferson was considering the merits of what we now call "term limits." Read the following excerpt of a letter Jefferson wrote to his friend and fellow patriot Edmund Pendleton on August 26, 1776. Then, answer the questions below in your own words.

> "... So much for the wisdom of the Senate. To make them independent, I had proposed that they should hold their places for nine years, & then go out (one third every three years) & be incapable for ever of being re-elected to that house. My idea was that if they might be re-elected, they would be casting their eye forward to the period of election (however distant) & be currying favor with the electors, & consequently dependent on them. My reason for fixing them in office for a term of years rather than for life, was that they might have in idea that they were at a certain period to return into the mass of the people & become the governed instead of the governor..."

1. Why did Jefferson favor a nine-year term in office for Senators?

   _____

   _____

   _____

   _____

2. Why might it be a good idea for an elected official to have to leave politics and return to private life?

   _____

   _____

   _____

   _____

3. Do you agree or disagree with Jefferson's proposal to limit a politician's time in office? Why?

   _____

   _____

   _____

   _____

Section 7

The Executive Branch

7.1 Powers of the Presidency

Article II of the U.S. Constitution, shown below, sets out the powers of the Presidency. Read the passage, then list ten of the powers and responsibilities named in Article II.

U.S. Constitution, Article II

Section 2. The President shall be Commander in chief of the Army and Navy of the United States, and of the militia of the several States, when called into the actual service of the United States; he may require the opinion, in writing, of the principal officer in each of the executive departments, upon any subject relating to the duties of their respective offices, and he shall have power to grant reprieves and pardons for offenses against the United States, except in cases of impeachment.

He shall have power, by and with the advice and consent of the Senate, to make treaties, provided two-thirds of the senators present concur; and he shall nominate, and by and with the advice and consent of the Senate, shall appoint ambassadors, other public ministers and consuls, judges of the Supreme Court, and all other officers of the United States, whose appointments are not herein otherwise provided for, and which shall be established by law: but the Congress may by law vest the appointment of such inferior officers, as they think proper, in the President alone, in the courts of law, or in the heads of departments.

The President shall have power to fill up all vacancies that may happen during the recess of the Senate, by granting commissions which shall expire at the end of their next session.

Section 3. He shall from time to time give to the Congress information of the state of the Union, and recommend to their consideration such measures as he shall judge necessary and expedient; he may, on extraordinary occasions, convene both Houses, or either of them, and in case of disagreement between them with respect to the time of adjournment, he may adjourn them to such time as he shall think proper; he shall receive ambassadors and other public ministers; he shall take care that the laws be faithfully executed, and shall commission all the officers of the United States.

1. _____

2. _____

3. _____

4. _____

5. _____

6. _____

7. _____

8. _____

9. _____

10. _____

7.2. Veto Power

Article I, Section 7.2. of the Constitution, printed below, provides the President with veto power. Read this passage and summarize it in the space below. Then answer the questions.

Article I, Section 7.2. Every bill which shall have passed the House of Representatives and the Senate, shall, before it becomes a law, be presented to the President of the United States; if he approves he shall sign it, but if not he shall return it, with his objections, to that House in which it shall have originated, who shall enter the objections at large on their journal, and proceed to reconsider it. If after such reconsideration two thirds of that House shall agree to pass the bill, it shall be sent, together with the objections, to the other House, by which it shall likewise be reconsidered, and if approved by two thirds of that House, it shall become a law . . . .

_____

_____

_____

_____

_____

_____

_____

1. What is the purpose of the veto power? How does it contribute to the system of checks and balances?

_____

_____

_____

2. What other means does the President have for controlling the power of Congress?

_____

_____

_____

7.3 Presidential Prose

Franklin D. Roosevelt had his "kitchen cabinet." Theodore Roosevelt referred to the Executive Office as a "bully pulpit." Atop Harry S. Truman's desk was a sign announcing "The Buck Stops Here." What does this presidential jargon mean? Match the terms and definitions below to better understand the language of the presidency.

1. Executive privilege

2. White House

3. Bully Pulpit

4. State of the Union

5. Oval Office

6. Air Force One

7. Kitchen Cabinet

8. Pennsylvania

9. Executive Order

10. "The buck stops here"

_____ The Avenue on which the President lives

_____ The presidential jet

_____ Expression assigning ultimate responsibility to the president

_____ Informal group of presidential advisors

_____ Claim of presidential right to withhold certain information from Congress

_____ Annual presidential report to Congress

_____ Presidential directive not requiring congressional approval

_____ The official room in which the President works

_____ The President's home

_____ Using the position of the Presidency to provide moral leadership to the country

7.4 Dear Mr. President

October 15, 1860

Hon. A. Lincoln

Dear Sir:

My father has just come from the fair and brought home your picture.... I am a little girl only eleven years old, but want you should be President of the United States very much so I hope you won't think me very bold to write to such a great man as you are.... I have got 4 brothers and part of them will vote for you anyway and if you will let your whiskers grow I will try and get the rest of them to vote for you. You would look a great deal better for your face is so thin. All the ladies like whiskers and they would tease their husbands to vote for you and then you would be President.... Answer this letter right off. Good-bye.

Grace Bedell

Seven days later, Grace received an answer to her letter. Later that fall, Mr. Lincoln's train, en route from Springfield, Illinois to the swearing-in in Washington D.C., stopped near Grace's home in New York where the President-elect showed the little girl his now-famous beard.

The above story is true. While most of the letters written to our Chief Executive these days tend to be of a less personal nature, they continue to pour into the White House by the thousands, penned by citizens of all ages.

What would you discuss in a letter to the President? Have you any compelling thoughts about national security? An idea about revamping our educational system? A suggestion for how our country could better address voter apathy? On the back of this sheet, compose your own letter to the President. Look up how to address the Chief Executive and put your note in proper letter format. If you wish, later copy it onto another sheet of paper and send it off to the White House. Perhaps, as did Grace Bedell, you'll even receive a response!

7.5 Timeline: The American Presidency

How well do you know our presidents' places in history? Can you match America's milestones with its leaders? Twelve of our presidents, and their terms in office, are listed below. Using the corresponding letter next to their names, indicate on the time line next to the **P** the president under whose administration each of the major events, discoveries, or inventions listed below took place. (Hint: Some presidents may be used more than once.)

Presidents:

A. Rutherford B. Hayes (1877–81)

B. Woodrow Wilson (1913–1921)

C. Richard Nixon (1969–1974)

D. John Adams (1797–1801)

E. Abraham Lincoln (1861–1865)

F. James Madison (1809–1817)

G. Theodore Roosevelt (1901–1909)

H. Thomas Jefferson (1801–1809)

I. Calvin Coolidge (1923–1929)

J. Ronald Reagan (1981–1989)

K. Lyndon Johnson (1963–1969)

L. Franklin Roosevelt (1933–1945)

1800	1804	1812	1862	1879	1903	1908
Wash. D.C. becomes U.S. Capitol **P:** ___	Louisiana Purchase completed **P:** ___	War begins against Great Britain **P:** ___	Emancipation Proclamation is issued **P:** ___	Edison invents electric lightbulb **P:** ___	Wright Bros.' first successful flight **P:** ___	Henry Ford develops Model T auto **P:** ___

1917	1920	1924	1941	1964	1971	1982
U.S. declares War on Germany and enters WWI **P:** ___	19th Amendment gives women right to vote **P:** ___	Congress gives citizenship to Native Americans **P:** ___	Attack on Pearl Harbor; U.S. enters WWII **P:** ___	Civil Rights passes Congress, is signed into law **P:** ___	Act Voting age is lowered to eighteen **P:** ___	Vietnam War Memorial is dedicated **P:** ___

79

7.6 The Presidential Cabinet

The United States Cabinet is a group of presidential advisors, each of whom heads a government department. Appointed by the President and confirmed by the Senate, these men and women, known as "Secretaries," meet regularly and advise the president on special matters. Below are the current fifteen Cabinet positions, listed in order of their succession to the presidency. Choose the phrase at the right that best defines each position and write the corresponding number next to it.

1. Secretary of State   ____ Oversees U.S. armed forces

2. Secretary of the Treasury   ____ Oversees federal moneys and economic policy

3. Secretary of Defense   ____ Oversees work force issues

4. Attorney General   ____ Oversees social programs

5. Secretary of the Interior   ____ Oversees foreign affairs

6. Secretary of Agriculture   ____ Oversees farming matters

7. Secretary of Commerce   ____ Oversees public lands

8. Secretary of Labor   ____ Oversees the Department of Justice and all legal matters

9. Secretary of Health/Human Services   ____ Oversees trade relations and business issues

10. Secretary of Housing and Urban Development   ____ Oversees energy resources

11. Secretary of Transportation   ____ Oversees aviation, highways, railroads

12. Secretary of Energy   ____ Oversees public housing

13. Secretary of Education   ____ Oversees educational programs

14. Secretary of Veterans Affairs   ____ Oversees environmental issues

15. Secretary of the Environment   ____ Oversees veterans' programs

Step Ahead!
Give yourself one bonus point for each current Secretary you can name.

_____

_____

_____

7.7 The Power to Wage War

In the mid–nineteenth century, President Abraham Lincoln ordered a military draft, set up a blockade and fought the first few months of the Civil War without any formal Congressional knowledge or authorization. One hundred years later, President Richard Nixon waged a secret air war in Cambodia and ordered a covert bombing campaign against North Vietnam, again without calling Congress into session.

According to our Constitution, Congress alone has the authority to declare a legal state of war. However, it is the President who carries the title "Commander in Chief of the U.S. Army and Navy." Additionally, the President holds the authority to send out military forces without congressional authorization if he or she determines that a particular armed attack could so threaten the security of the United States that waiting for congressional response could prove risky to our country's safety.

This overlapping of authority, and the ambiguity of constitutional powers that are "implied" rather than specified, has led to considerable debate in our country over which branch of our government has final authority in determining when war can be waged.

In response to President Nixon's escalation of the war in southeast Asia, and in an effort to forestall any such future presidential actions, Congress proposed the War Powers Resolution Act. This measure stated that any time a President sends American armed forces into hostilities or dangerous situations, he or she must report it to Congress within 48 hours. Congress then has 60 days to either make an official declaration of war or pass a resolution of support. If Congress chooses to do neither, the President must withdraw the troops. Furthermore, at any time during that 60 day period, Congress can pass a resolution requiring the President to end the fighting. Although President Nixon vetoed the proposal, declaring it an unconstitutional infringement on his powers as Commander in Chief, Congress overrode his veto and in 1973 the War Powers Resolution was passed into law.

The debate did not end there, however. In the very next decade, President Ronald Reagan used military power in Libya, ordered the sinking of Iranian boats in the Persian Gulf, and authorized a peacekeeping force to be installed in Lebanon, all without consulting beforehand with Congress or obeying the provisions of the War Powers Act.

It seems likely that the struggle between Congress and the President over the right to wage war will continue. Where do you stand on the issue? Should the country's Chief Executive (and "Commander in Chief") be empowered to make decisions on his own? Or is it safer to rely on Congress to decide what's best for our national security? Choose one point of view and, using the back of this sheet, write a persuasive paragraph defending your position.

7.8 Federal Agencies— Alphabet Soup!

Federal agencies are often known by their *acronyms*—a word formed by the first letter of each word in a name. Draw a line from each acronym floating in the soup to the name it matches below. Trade papers with a partner and check each other's answers. Then test each other to see how many acronyms you can remember.

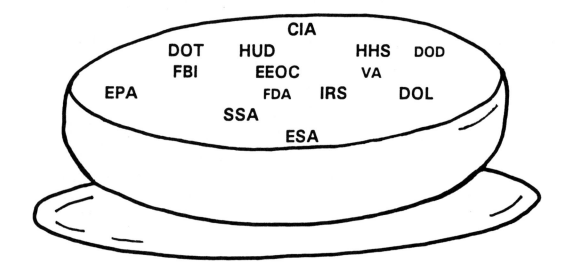

Central Intelligence Agency
Department of Defense
Internal Revenue Service
Food and Drug Administration
Health and Human Services
Veterans Administration
Equal Employment Opportunity
  Commission

Environmental Protection Agency
Department of Transportation
Employment Standards Administration
Department of Labor
Social Security Administration
Federal Bureau of Investigation
Housing and Urban Development

7.9 Foreign Affairs

| consul | coup d'etat | embassy | fact-finding trip | puppet government |
| junket | isolationism | imperialism | secretary of state | Security Council |

ACROSS

2. the house or office of an ambassador in the capital city of another country
4. a sudden overthrowing of a government
5. a trip to a foreign country to gather information on an overseas issue
9. the foreign policy of keeping to one's own domestic business or remaining neutral in international conflicts
11. a government that is controlled by another nation

DOWN

1. the transporting of a diplomat back and forth between cities that are negotiating
3. the council of the United States in charge of keeping peace with other nations
6. the person who is the chief advisor of foreign policies for the president
7. a fact finding trip taken by a politician which is paid for by the taxpayers but is often suspected to be more of a vacation than information-gathering
8. an official appointed to represent a foreign city's commercial interests
9. expanding a country's land area and authority through the acquiring of new territories and resources
10. a country's authority and control over its domestic affairs; self-government

7.10 Presidents of the First 100 Years

Use the dates below as your clues for filling in the names of the presidents in the puzzle. When you've finished, the dark spaces will describe the time period covered.

1. 1829–1837
2. 1837–1841
3. 1881
4. 1801–1809
5. 1889–1893
6. 1850–1853
7. 1809–1817
8. 1857–1861
9. 1853–1857
10. 1869–1877
11. 1789–1797
12. 1881–1885
13. 1841
14. 1849–1850

7.11 Presidents of the 20th Century

The dates below are your clues to the twentieth-century presidents whose names fill in the puzzle below. When you've finished, the dark spaces will tell you what the puzzle contains.

1. 1961–1963
2. Executive Office
3. Not all but
4. 1945–1953
5. Not mine but
6. 1981–1989
7. 1901–1909
8. 1977–1981
9. After nineteenth

10. 100 years.
11. 1913–1921
12. 1953–1961
13. 1993–present
14. Off minus one letter
15. 1933–1945
16. 1974–1977
17. 1963–1969

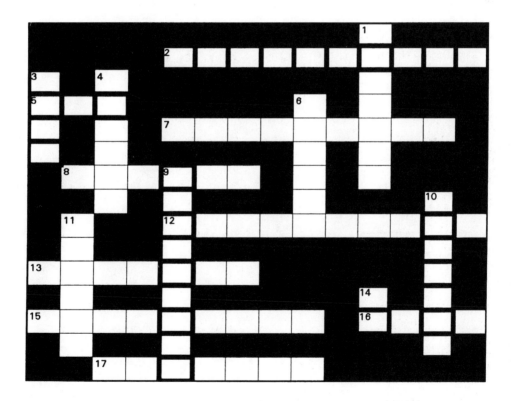

Section 8

Congress

8.1. The Powers of Congress—Part 1

Article I, Section 8 of the U.S. Constitution lists the powers granted to Congress. The first half of those powers are printed below. In the blank spaces provided, summarize each power in your own words. Use a dictionary if necessary.

Summary of the powers of Congress:

Section 8. The Congress shall have the power
1. To lay and collect taxes, duties, imposts and excises, to pay the debts and provide for the common defen[c]e and general welfare of the United States; but all duties, imposts and excises shall be uniform throughout the United States;
2. To borrow money on the credit of the United States;
3. To regulate commerce with foreign nations, and among the several States, and with the Indian tribes;
4. To establish a[n] uniform rule of naturalization, and uniform laws on the subject of bankruptcies throughout the United States;
5. To coin money, regulate the value thereof, and of foreign coin, and fix the standard of weights and measures;
6. To provide for the punishment of counterfeiting the securities and current coin of the United States;
7. To establish post offices and post roads;
8. To promote the progress of science and useful arts, by securing for limited times to authors and inventors the exclusive right to their respective writings and discoveries;
9. To constitute tribunals inferior to the Supreme Court; . . .

1. _____
2. _____
3. _____
4. _____
5. _____
6. _____
7. _____
8. _____
9. _____

8.2 The Powers of Congress— Part 2

Article I, Section 8 of the Constitution lists the powers granted to Congress. Half of those powers are printed below. In the blank spaces provided, summarize each power in your own terms. Use a dictionary if necessary.

Section 8. The Congress shall have the power

10. To define and punish piracies and felonies committed on the high seas, and offenses against the law of nations;
11. To declare war, grant letters of marque and reprisal, and make rules concerning captures on land and water;
12. To raise and support armies, but no appropriation of money to that use shall be for a longer term than two years;
13. To provide and maintain a navy;
14. To make rules for the government and regulation of the land and naval forces;
15. To provide for calling forth the militia to execute the laws of the Union, suppress insurrections and repel invasions;
16. To provide for organizing, arming, and disciplining the militia, and for governing such part of them as may be employed in the service of the United States, reserving to the States respectively, the appointment of the officers, and the authority of training the militia according to the discipline prescribed by Congress;
17. To exercise exclusive legislation in all cases whatsoever, over such district (not exceeding ten miles square) as may, by cession of particular States, and the acceptance of Congress, become the seat of the government of the United States, and to exercise like authority over all places purchased by the consent of the legislature of the State in which the same shall be, for the erection of forts, magazines, arsenals, dockyards, and other needful buildings;—And
18. To make all laws which shall be necessary and proper for carrying into execution the foregoing powers, and all other powers vested by this Constitution in the government of the United States, or in any department or officer thereof.

Summary of the powers of Congress:

10. _____
11. _____
12. _____
13. _____
14. _____
15. _____
16. _____
17. _____
18. _____

8.3. Congress—Reviewing the Basics

Congress meets in Washington, D.C. on the third day of January of each year. It usually remains in session until its business for the year is completed. The President may call a special session when he thinks it necessary. Each of the fifty states in the Union sends two Senators to the United States Senate, for a total of 100 Senators. The term of office is six years. One-third of the Senators go out of office every two years.

The number of Representatives from any state depends upon the population of the state. Each state is entitled to at least one Representative, no matter how small its population. The basis of representation is changed every ten years, following the taking of the United States census. When the Constitution was adopted the basis was one Representative for every 30,000 people. At present the basis is one Representative for every 410,481 people. A Representative serves two years.

The present House of Representatives has 435 members plus a Resident Commissioner from Puerto Rico. The latter has no vote but does take part in discussions and may request the House to consider problems that are of interest to his or her home area.

The Vice President of the United States presides over the Senate and is called the President of the Senate. When the Vice President is absent for any reason, the President pro tempore of the Senate presides over the Senate. The Vice President votes in the Senate only to break a tie.

The presiding officer of the House of Representatives is called the Speaker. The Speaker is one of the members of the House of Representatives, and is elected by his or her fellow members. As the Speaker is one of the Representatives, he or she can vote on all questions. The Speaker would succeed to the office of President of the United States if both the President and Vice President were unable to serve. A Speaker pro tempore is chosen by the Representatives to preside when the Speaker is absent.

1. How many Senators and Representatives serve in Congress? _____

2. What is the term of office for Senators? _____ Representatives? _____

3. How is the number of Representatives for each state determined?

   _____

4. How long is Congress in session each year? _____

5. Who leads the Senate? _____

6. Who leads the House? _____

7. If both the President and the Vice President are unable to perform the duties of their office, who becomes President? _____

8.4 Membership in the House

Membership of the House of Representatives is apportioned according to a state's population. In other words, each state is assigned a certain number of Representatives in the House based on the number of people living in that state. Use the information below to put the correct number of representatives inside each state on the map.

Alabama, 7; Alaska, 1; Arizona, 6; Arkansas, 4; California, 52; Colorado, 6; Connecticut, 6; Delaware, 1; Florida, 13; Georgia, 11; Hawaii, 2; Idaho, 2; Illinois, 20; Indiana, 19; Iowa, 5; Kansas, 4; Kentucky, 6; Louisiana, 7; Maine, 2; Maryland, 8; Massachusetts, 10; Michigan, 16; Minnesota, 8; Mississippi, 5; Missouri, 9; Montana, 1; Nebraska, 3; Nevada, 2; New Hampshire, 2; New Jersey, 13; New Mexico, 3; New York, 31; North Carolina, 12; North Dakota, 1; Ohio, 21; Oklahoma, 6; Oregon, 5; Pennsylvania, 21; Rhode Island, 2; South Carolina, 6; South Dakota, 1; Tennessee, 9; Texas, 30; Utah, 3; Vermont, 1; Virginia, 11; Washington, 9; West Virginia, 3; Wisconsin, 9; Wyoming, 1.

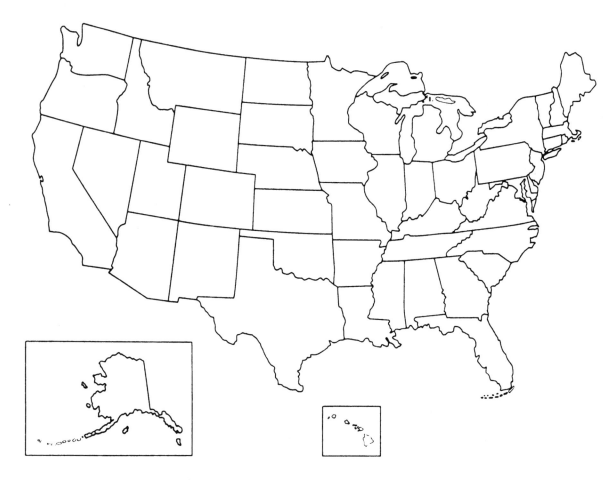

8.5 The Senate in the 19th Century

While the House in 1789 immediately opened its doors to the public, the Senate conducted its business in secret session for the first few years, when it met in New York and Philadelphia. However, public pressure encouraged the Senate to construct a visitors gallery, which opened in 1795. In 1800, when the federal government moved from Philadelphia to the newly created District of Columbia, both the House and Senate chambers provided public galleries.

By the 1830s, the Senate had attracted the nation's leading political figures and most gifted orators. Daniel Webster, Henry Clay, John C. Calhoun, and other towering figures made the old Senate chamber the chief forum for debating the great national issues of the day.

During these decades, the Senate tackled the issues of federal authority versus states' rights, and the spread of slavery into the territories. Valiant efforts to achieve compromise eventually failed, and the nation split apart in a bloody Civil War. Southern members resigned from the Senate as their states seceded, and the new Republican party became the majority of the sharply reduced Senate in 1861.

Following the war, those senators who favored vigorous reconstruction of the southern states clashed frequently with President Andrew Johnson, who adopted Abraham Lincoln's more lenient policies. Their clashes culminated in the impeachment trial of President Johnson, in the Senate chamber, where the president was spared from removal from office by a single vote.

A series of weak presidents followed Johnson throughout the remainder of the nineteenth century, allowing the Senate to become the strongest branch of the federal government. Senators argued that the executive should be subordinate to the legislature, and that the president's sole role was to enforce the laws enacted by Congress.

Source: The United States Senate, One Hundred Fourth Congress, S. PUB. 104-5. Prepared Under the Direction of the Senate Committee on Rules and Administration.

Answer the following questions.

1. When did the Senate first open its sessions to the public? _____

2. What issues preoccupied the Senate during the middle decades of the nineteenth century?

   _____

   _____

3. What happened to the Senate when the sourthern states seceded in the Civil War?

   _____

4. Describe the relationship between the Senate and the Executive Office in the later part of the nineteenth century.

   _____

   _____

8.6 The Senate in the 20th Century

By the beginning of the twentieth century, the energetic presidencies of Theodore Roosevelt and Woodrow Wilson challenged senatorial dominance, and the balance of power shifted toward the White House. Still, the Senate delivered Wilson a major blow at the end of his presidency by rejecting the Treaty of Versailles, which ended the First World War and created the League of Nations.

At the depths of the Great Depression of the 1930s, the Senate responded enthusiastically to President Franklin D. Roosevelt's New Deal program of recovery, relief, and reform. An unprecedented burst of legislative activity profoundly altered the size, shape, and scope of the federal government. By 1937, the Senate had broken with President Roosevelt over his proposal to "pack" the Supreme Court, and strong isolationist sentiments limited Roosevelt's international policies. The attack on Pearl Harbor in 1941 brought a sharp shift in public opinion, and senators rallied behind the war effort.

A major turning point in the Senate's history occurred with the passage of the 1946 Legislative Reorganization Act, which reshaped the committee system and provided the first professional staff for senators and committees. The Cold War brought an increase in legislation, with the expansion of the national defense program, foreign aid, and economic and military assistance to America's allies.

During the 1950s the Senate engaged in sharp debates over civil rights policies, which stimulated lengthy filibusters, but eventually resulted in passage of the landmark Civil Rights Act of 1964 and Voting Rights Act of 1965. The Senate also divided over American involvement in the war in Vietnam. Although senators overwhelmingly approved the Gulf of Tonkin Resolution in 1964, they later disagreed over its application, and voted for its repeal. Senate concern over increased presidential powers in foreign affairs led to the passage of the War Powers Act of 1973, requiring Congressional notification and approval whenever American troops are sent into combat.

The Watergate burglary and irregularities of the presidential campaign in 1972 led to a Senate investigation chaired by Senator Sam Ervin of North Carolina. Testimony and evidence gathered by Ervin's committee eventually led to the resignation of Richard Nixon as president. Subsequently the Senate has striven to maintain a balance with the presidency, supporting presidential initiatives while maintaining vigilant oversight over the operations of the executive branch. This is the system of checks and balances which the framers of the Constitution had envisioned, and which has endured for over 200 years of American representative democracy.

Source: The United States Senate, One Hundred Fourth Congress, S. PUB. 104-5. Prepared Under the Direction of the Senate Committee on Rules and Administration.

Answer the following questions.

1. Name three important occasions when the Senate clashed with the President.

_____

_____

2. What led to the creation of the War Powers Act? _____

_____

©1999 by The Center for Applied Research in Education

8.7 Congressional Crossword

Test your knowledge of the legislative branch. Answer the clues to the crossword using the words and phrases given in the box. When the puzzle is complete, 14 Across will tell you where all the action takes place.

Congress	Representative	Act	Watchdog	Appropriations	Cloture	Rider	Whip	Senator
Speaker	Impeachment	Bill	Filibuster	Joint Committee	Statute	Floor	Pocket	Veto

Across

4. Our law-making branch of government
6. Monies set aside to pay for approved government projects
8. Where the President can "put" a bill for 10 days; if Congress adjourns during that time, the bill is "silently" forgotten
10. The President's "response" to a bill he does not wish to approve
16. A provision added, but not relevant, to a piece of legislation
17. A law passed by the Legislature
19. A meeting of the House and Senate

Down

1. A member of Congress who represents a population area of a state
2. The place where Congresspeople sit and vote
3. A party leadership post in Congress
5. One of two members of Congress from each state
7. Formal proceedings to remove a public official from office
9. Continuous speechifying by a Senator to prevent action from being taken on a piece of legislation
11. A vote taken to end 9-Down
12. A proposed law
13. A congressional committee that oversees government spending
15. The Presiding Officer of the House of Representatives
18. A bill that has become law

8.8 The Committee System

Due to the high volume and complexity of its work, Congress divides its tasks among approximately 250 committees and subcommittees. The House and Senate each has its own committee system, which are similar. Within chamber guidelines, however, each committee adopts its own rules.

Standing committees generally have legislative jurisdiction and most operate with subcommittees that handle a committee's work in specific areas. Select and joint committees are chiefly for oversight or housekeeping tasks.

The chair of each committee and a majority of its members come from the majority party. The chair primarily controls a committee's business. Each party is predominantly responsible for assigning its members to committees, and each committee distributes its members among its subcommittees. There are limits on the number and types of panels any one member may serve on and chair.

Committees receive varying levels of operating funds and employ varying numbers of aides. Each hires and fires its own staff. Several thousand measures are referred to committees during each Congress. Committees select a small percentage for consideration, and those not addressed often receive no further action. Determining the fate of measures and, in effect, helping to set a chamber's agenda make committees powerful.

When a committee or subcommittee favors a measure, it usually takes four actions. First, it asks relevant executive agencies for written comments on the measure. Second, it holds hearings to gather information and views from noncommittee experts. Third, a committee meets to perfect the measure through amendments, and noncommittee members sometimes attempt to influence the language. Fourth, when language is agreed upon, the committee sends the measure back to the chamber, usually along with a written report describing its purposes and provisions and the work of the committee thereon.

The influence of committees over measures extends to their enactment into law. A committee that considers a measure will manage the full chamber's deliberation on it. Also, its members will be appointed to any conference committee created to reconcile the two chambers' differing versions of a measure.

Source: The Committee System in the U.S. Congress, Congressional Research Service, Library of Congress.

©1999 by The Center for Applied Research in Education

Answer the following questions.

1. Describe the different types of committees and their work. _____

_____

_____

2. Name the four actions committees take when the committee favors a measure.

_____

_____

3. Why are committees powerful? _____

_____

_____

8.9 "Talk the Talk"—Senate Committees

A great deal of the work of the Senate goes on in the Senate Committees. You are the Chair of an important committee. Using at least eight of the ten terms defined below, write a paragraph about the work of your committee in the space provided. Use the back of this sheet if you need more space.

Chair: The presiding officer of a committee or subcommittee.

Committee: Subsidiary organization of the Senate established for the purpose of considering legislation, and conducting hearings and investigations.

Hearing: A meeting of a committee or subcommittee—generally open to the public—to take testimony in order to gather information and opinions on proposed legislation, to conduct an investigation, or review the operation or other aspects of a Federal agency or program.

Joint Committee: Committees including membership from both houses of Congress.

Markup: The process by which congressional committees and subcommittees debate, amend, and rewrite proposed legislation.

Oversight: Committee review of the activities of a Federal agency or program.

Referral: After a bill or resolution is introduced, it is normally referred to the committee having jurisdiction over the subject of the bill.

Standing Committee: Permanent committees established under the standing rules of the Senate and specializing in the consideration of particular subject areas. There are currently 16 standing committees.

Select or Special Committee: A committee established by the Senate for a limited time period to perform a particular study or investigation.

Subcommittee: Subunit of a committee established for the purpose of dividing the committee's workload.

8.10 Senate Standing Committees

Find at least fifteen of the standing committees hidden in the puzzle below.

Senate Standing Committees
Agriculture, Nutrition, and Forestry
Appropriations
Armed Services
Banking, Housing, and Urban Affairs
Budget
Commerce, Science, and Transportation
Energy and Natural Resources
Environment and Public Works
Finance
Foreign Relations
Governmental Affairs
Judiciary
Labor and Human Resources

Rules and Administration
Small Business
Veterans' Affairs

Special, Select, and Other Committees
Committee on Indian Affairs
Select Committee on Ethics
Select Committee on Intelligence
Special Committee on Aging

Joint Committees of the Congress
Joint Economic Committee
Joint Committee on the Library of Congress
Joint Committee on Printing
Joint Committee on Taxation

```
E T H I C S D D G I J S W T F I N A N C E
J A S R A A F F A S N A R E T E V C A S E
U S R O B A L O N K M P P L R U L E S N J
D D D M O P R R R O B A L O P L P M N Z
I Q U E E O G G E N V I R O M E N T N I
C W S U D D C R G I E R U T L U C I R G A
I B U D G E T P O U I G N O I T A X A T G
A P O R B M E M O M I N S E L U R A N D T
R C D S P R I N T I N G B A N K I N G I E
Y B M C D A O I V M O P I E L M M V C A G
J I A P P R O P R I A T I O N S O I N S D
A G I N G P P O P C O M M E R C E S C I U
R P S C I M O N O C E N E R G Y O N T O B
```

8.11 Senate Leadership

The Vice President of the United States presides over the Senate and is called the President of the Senate. When the Vice President is absent for any reason, the President Pro Tempore presides over the Senate. The Vice President can vote only in case of a tie in the Senate. When the Vice President votes on a tie, it is always to pass the measure; he does not vote against a measure. If it is a tie and the Vice President does not vote, the measure is lost, automatically.

Label the diagram below to show these key Senate leadership positions: Vice President; President Pro Tempore; Majority Leader; Minority Leader; Majority Secretary; Minority Secretary; Assistant Majority Leader; Assistant Minority Leader.

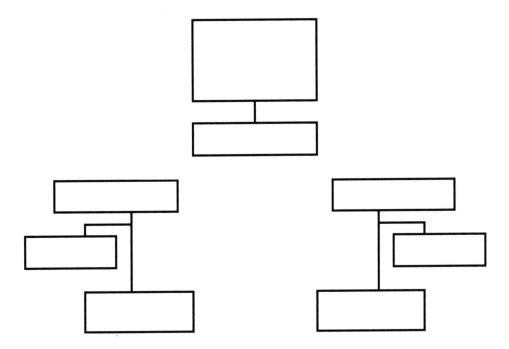

Section 9

The Federal Judiciary

9.1 The Federal Judicial Branch

The government of the United States is a dual one—federal and state. The federal government has three separate branches: the legislative branch, the executive branch, and the judicial branch.

The Constitution ensures the judicial branch's equality with and independence from the legislative and executive branches. Although federal judges are appointed by the President with the advice and consent of the Senate and the funds for the operation of the courts are appropriated by Congress, the independence of the U.S. courts is provided for in three ways:

1. Under the Constitution, these courts can be called upon to exercise only judicial powers and to perform only judicial work. Judicial powers and judicial work involve the application and interpretation of the law in the decision of real differences—cases and controversies. The courts cannot be called upon to make laws, which is the function of the legislative branch, or be expected to enforce and execute laws, which is the function of the executive branch.

2. Federal judges are appointed for life. In the language of the Constitution, they " . . . hold their Offices during good Behavio[u]r"; that is, they serve as long as they desire to, and they can be removed from office against their will only through " . . . Impeachment for, and Conviction of, Treason, Bribery, or other high Crimes and Misdemeanors. . . ."

3. The Constitution provides that the compensation of federal judges " . . . shall not be diminished during their Continuance in Office. . . ." Neither the President nor Congress may reduce the salary of a federal judge.

These three provisions are designed to assure federal judges of independence from outside influence so that their decisions can be completely impartial and based only on the laws and facts of the cases.

Answer the following questions.

1. How are federal judges appointed? _____

_____

2. Under the Constitution, what is the function of the federal courts? _____

_____

3. How long do federal judges serve? _____

_____

4. How is the independence of the courts preserved? _____

_____

_____

_____

9.2 Structure of the Federal Courts

The structure of the federal court system has varied a great deal throughout the history of the nation. The Constitution merely provides that the judicial power of the United States " . . . be vested in one supreme Court, and in such inferior Courts as the Congress may from time to time ordain and establish. . . ." Thus, the only indispensable court is the Supreme Court. Congress has established and abolished other U.S. courts as national needs have changed over time.

If the federal court system is viewed as a pyramid, at the top is the Supreme Court of the U.S., the highest court. On the next level are the 13 U.S. Courts of Appeals and the Court of Military Appeals. On the following level are the 94 U.S. district courts and the specialized courts, such as the Tax Court, the Court of Federal Claims, the Court of Veterans Appeals, and the Court of International Trade. There are various routes a case may take to a federal court. Some cases may originate in a U.S. district court, while others will come from a state court or federal agency.

This pyramid-like organization of the courts serves two purposes. First, the courts of appeals can correct errors that have been made in the decisions of trial courts. Second, the Supreme Court can ensure the uniformity of decisions by reviewing cases in which constitutional issues have been decided or in which two or more lower courts have reached different results.

Label the parts of the pyramid with the names of the federal courts.

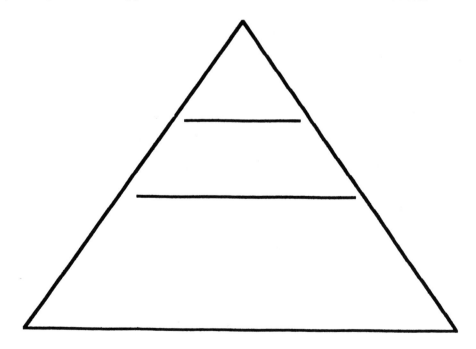

©1999 by The Center for Applied Research in Education

9.3 The Chief Justices

Read the chart about the Chief Justices of the U.S. Supreme Court, then answer the questions below.

Justice	Years on Court	President Who Nominated	Party
John Jay	1789–1795	George Washington	F
John Rutledge*	1795	George Washington	F
Oliver Ellsworth	1796–1800	George Washington	F
John Marshall	1801–1835	John Adams	F
Roger B. Taney	1836–1864	Andrew Jackson	D
Salmon P. Chase	1864–1873	Abraham Lincoln	R
Morrison R. Waite	1874–1888	Ulysses S. Grant	R
Melville W. Fuller	1888–1910	Grover Cleveland	D
Edward D. White**	1910–1921	William H. Taft	D
William H. Taft	1921–1930	Warren G. Harding	R
Charles E. Hughes	1930–1940	Herbert Hoover	R
Harlan F. Stone	1941–1946	Franklin D. Roosevelt	D
Frederick M. Vinson	1946–1953	Harry S. Truman	D
Earl Warren	1953–1969	Dwight D. Eisenhower	R
Warren E. Burger	1969–1986	Richard M. Nixon	R
William H. Rehnquist**	1986–	Ronald Reagan	R

*Appointed to replace John Jay; served without confirmation Aug. 12–Dec. 15, 1795, while Congress was in recess. Senate refused to confirm his nomination.
**Former associate justice.
D = Democrat; F = Federalist; R = Republican.

1. Who served as Chief Justice for the longest time? _____

2. What is the average number of years served by the Chief Justices? _____

3. What percentage of the Chief Justices have been Democrats? _____

4. How many women have served as Chief Justice? _____

9.4 "And Justice for All . . ."

Across

1. John Adams' Secretary of State, he later held the longest tenure of any Chief Justice so far
5. "Seating" on the Supreme Court
7. Nominated to the Court by President Eisenhower in the l950s, he later chaired the Commission of Inquiry into the assassination of President Kennedy
9. What the "E" stands for in E.R.A.
10. What the "v." stands for in the title of court cases
14. A legal dispute brought before the Court
15. A president has to _____ (recommend) a candidate for Justice
17. Our first Chief Justice
18. Lawyers must be admitted to this to gain their license
19. The earliest Justices wore these 18th-century hair accessories
22. The decision a Justice makes
25. The only President to become Chief Justice
26. To bring a case against in court
27. Cases are decided by this type of vote
29. Total number of Justices on the Supreme Court

Down

2. The current Chief Justice
3. A pronoun for all but two present-day Justices
4. What attorneys "practice"
5. Nominated by President Nixon, he served as Chief Justice from 1969–86
6. Where **19 Across** were worn
8. A recent law school graduate who assists a Justice
11. This government body must approve a President's Supreme Court nominee
12. The Supreme Court convenes each year in this fall month
13. The Senate has to _____ (approve) a President's choice for Justice
16. First name of **7 Across**
17. First name of **17 across** (also first name of Presidents Adams (both), Tyler, and Kennedy)
20. What the Justices "do" on **5 Across**
21. What each star stands for on the American flag
23. Our country, abbrev.
24. The Court will _____ (or announce) a ruling
27. Until 1981, all Supreme Court Justices were these
28. Patrick Henry's famous quote: "Give me liberty ___ give me death"

9.5 Today's Court

Using the profiles provided here, answer the questions below.

WILLIAM M. REHNQUIST (Age: 72)
Appointed by: President Richard Nixon in 1971, and elevated to the position of chief justice by President Ronald Reagan in 1986.
Background: Practiced law in Phoenix before going to work for the Nixon administration as assistant attorney general for the Justice Department.

JOHN PAUL STEVENS (Age: 77)
Appointed by: President Gerald Ford in 1975.
Background: Practiced antitrust law in Chicago before being appointed to the Seventh U.S. Circuit Court of Appeals by President Nixon.

SANDRA DAY O'CONNOR (Age: 67)
Appointed by: President Ronald Reagan in 1981.
Background: Practiced law in California and then Arizona. Served as Republican state senator in Arizona, and later sat on the Arizona Court of Appeals.

ANTONIN SCALIA (Age: 61)
Appointed by: President Reagan in 1986.
Background: Served as general counsel in Nixon administration, and assistant attorney general in the Ford administration. Appointed to U.S. Court of Appeals for the District of Columbia by President Reagan.

ANTHONY M. KENNEDY (Age: 61)
Appointed by: President Reagan in 1988.
Background: Practiced law in San Francisco, later appointed to U.S. Court of Appeals for the Ninth Circuit by President Ford.

DAVID H. SOUTER (Age: 58)
Appointed by: President George Bush in 1990.
Background: Assistant attorney general and deputy attorney general in New Hampshire. Served as associate justice of New Hampshire's highest court, and appointed to the First Circuit U.S. Court of Appeals by President Bush.

CLARENCE THOMAS (Age: 49)
Appointed by: President Bush in 1991.
Background: Assistant secretary of civil rights in the Education Department under President Reagan, and head of the Equal Employment Opportunity Commission. Appointed to U.S. Court of Appeals for the District of Columbia by President Bush.

RUTH BADER GINSBURG (Age: 64)
Appointed by: President William Clinton in 1993.
Background: Law professor at Rutgers University Law School in Newark, where she assisted the New Jersey American Civil Liberties Union and later the national ACLU. Law professor at Columbia Law School. Appointed to U.S. Court of Appeals for the District of Columbia by President Jimmy Carter.

STEPHEN G. BREYER (Age: 59)
Appointed by: President Clinton in 1994.
Background: Professor at Harvard Law School. Served as assistant special prosecutor in the Watergate Investigation, and worked for the Senate Judiciary Committee. Appointed to U.S. Court of Appeals.

1. What is the average age? _____

2. What percentage of the justices are women? _____

3. On the back of this sheet name three characteristics or experiences the justices have in common.

9.6 "And the Ruling Is..."

The United States Supreme Court has the responsibility to interpret our Constitution and to determine whether the laws passed in our country agree with the freedoms and rights the Constitution guarantees. The Chief Justice and the eight Associate Justices "hear" cases that are "argued" before them. The decision is then put to a vote. The greater proportion of alike votes becomes the Court's final and official ruling, known as the "majority opinion." The opposing (but outnumbered) viewpoint is called the "minority opinion."

One of the issues the Supreme Court often faces concerns First Amendment freedoms. Although freedoms of speech and religion are guaranteed in our Bill of Rights, it is not always easy to sort out their applications in real life. Consider the issue of saluting the American flag. At one point, many school systems in our country required students to salute the flag as a daily ritual, symbolizing loyalty. In the early 1930s, two students at a public school in Minersville, Pennsylvania refused to participate in the salute, since "bowing down" before symbols was against their Jehovah's Witness religion. As a result, they were expelled from school. Their parents took their case to court, claiming that their Constitutional rights had been violated. The ensuing publicity branded Jehovah's Witnesses as disloyal Americans and many began to be persecuted nationwide. Ultimately, the issue reached the Supreme Court not once, but twice. A 1940 decision ruled in favor of states' rights to require demonstrated loyalty, while a decision three years later sided with the rights of citizens not to be forced by the state to "say" something that violated their beliefs.

What do you think? In the space below, take both sides of the case. Issue your own majority and minority rulings, one in favor of the state, one in favor of the students. Be sure to include the reasoning behind your opinions.

Majority Ruling:

_____

_____

_____

_____

_____

Minority Ruling:

_____

_____

_____

_____

_____

9.7 Courts of Appeals

The intermediate appellate courts in the federal judicial system are the courts of appeals. Twelve of these courts have jurisdiction over cases from certain geographic areas. The Court of Appeals for the Federal Circuit has national jurisdiction over specific types of cases.

The U.S. Court of Appeals for the Federal Circuit and the 12 regional courts of appeals are often referred to as circuit courts. That is because early in the nation's history, the judges of the first courts of appeals visited each of the courts in one region in a particular sequence, traveling by horseback and riding "circuit." These courts of appeals review matters from the district courts of their geographical regions, the U.S. Tax Court, and from certain federal administrative agencies. A disappointed party in a district court usually has the right to have the case reviewed in the court of appeals for the circuit.

The First through Eleventh Circuits each include three or more states. The U.S. Court of Appeals for the District of Columbia hears cases arising in the District of Columbia and has appellate jurisdiction assigned by Congress in legislation concerning many departments of the federal government.

As in the district courts, the judges who sit on the courts of appeals are appointed for life by the President with the advice and consent of the Senate. Each court of appeals consists of six or more judges, depending on the caseload of the courts. The judge who has served on the court the longest and who is under 65 years of age is designated as the chief judge, and performs administrative duties in addition to hearing cases. The chief judge serves for a maximum term of seven years. There are 167 judges on the 12 regional courts of appeals.

Answer the following questions.

1. Why are the courts of appeals sometimes called "circuit courts"?

_____

_____

2. How are courts of appeals judges appointed and how long do they serve?

_____

_____

3. Which cases go to the courts of appeals?

_____

_____

9.8 Find the Eleven Circuits

Using the map below, outline the region for each of the U.S. Circuit Courts and write the number of each circuit in the region.

First Circuit
ME, MA, NH, RI,
Puerto Rico

Second Circuit
CT, NY, VT

Third Circuit
DE, NJ, PA,
Virgin Islands

Fourth Circuit
MD, NC, SC,
VA, WV

Fifth Circuit
LA, MS, TX

Sixth Circuit
KY, MI, OH, TN

Seventh Circuit
IL, IN, WI

Eighth Circuit
AR, IA, MN, MO,
NE, ND, SD

Ninth Circuit
AK, AZ, CA, HI,
ID, MT, NV, OR,
WA, Guam,
N. Mariana Islands

Tenth Circuit
CO, KS, NM,
OK, UT, WY

Eleventh Circuit
AL, FL, GA

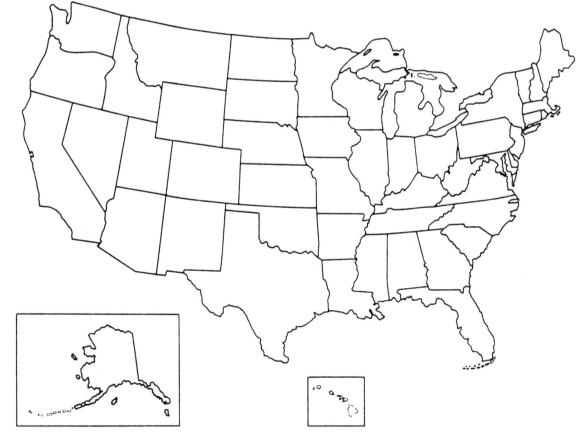

9.9 District Courts

Most federal cases are initially tried and decided in the U.S. district courts, the federal courts of general trial jurisdiction. There are 94 district courts in the 50 states, the District of Columbia, the Commonwealth of Puerto Rico, and the territories of Guam, the U.S. Virgin Islands, and the Northern Mariana Islands. A district may itself be divided into divisions and may have several places where the court hears cases. Each district court also has a bankruptcy unit.

With the exception of the three territorial courts, all district court judges are appointed for life by the President with the advice and consent of the Senate. Congress authorizes judgeships for each district based in large part on the caseload. In each district, the judge who has served on the court the longest and who is under 65 years of age is designated as the chief judge. The chief judge has administrative duties in addition to a caseload. There are 649 district court judges.

The federal district courts are the real workhorses of the federal judicial system. Appointment to a federal judgeship is considered an honor. The Constitution does not specify the qualifications or characteristics a person should have to become a federal judge. The President is free to choose anyone for appointment, but the selection must be approved by the Senate.

In the space below, make your own appointment to a federal court and provide a detailed explanation of why you believe this person would make a good federal judge. The appointment may be someone you know, or a fictional character based on what you think would be the ideal person for the job. Remember that these judges serve for life and represent the front line in defending our most cherished rights and liberties.

My nominee is: _____

_____

_____

_____

_____

_____

_____

_____

_____

_____

_____

_____

9.10 Spell "Subpoena"

Civil court cases have a language of their own. Study the spelling and the definitions of the words below. Then team up with a classmate and test each other.

affidavit: A written statement of facts confirmed by the oath of the party making it, before a notary or officer having authority to administer oaths.

appellate: About appeals; an appellate court has the power to review the judgment of another lower court or tribunal.

counterclaim: A claim that a defendant makes against a plaintiff.

deposition: An oral statement made before an officer authorized by law to administer oaths. Such statements are often taken to examine potential witnesses, to obtain discovery, or to be used later in trial.

injunction: An order of the court prohibiting (or compelling) the performance of a specific act to prevent irreparable damage or injury.

interrogatories: Written questions asked by one party of an opposing party, who must answer them in writing under oath; a discovery device in a lawsuit.

jurisdiction: The legal authority of a court to hear and decide a case, or the geographic area over which the court has authority to decide cases.

jurisprudence: The study of law and the structure of the legal system.

plaintiff: The person who files the complaint in a civil lawsuit.

procedure: The rules for the conduct of a lawsuit; there are rules of civil, criminal, evidence, bankruptcy, and appellate procedure.

subpoena: A command to a witness to appear and give testimony.

Section 10

The Legislative Process

10.1 A Bill Becomes Law

Use this diagram to write a paragraph about how a bill becomes a law. Use another sheet of paper for your answer.

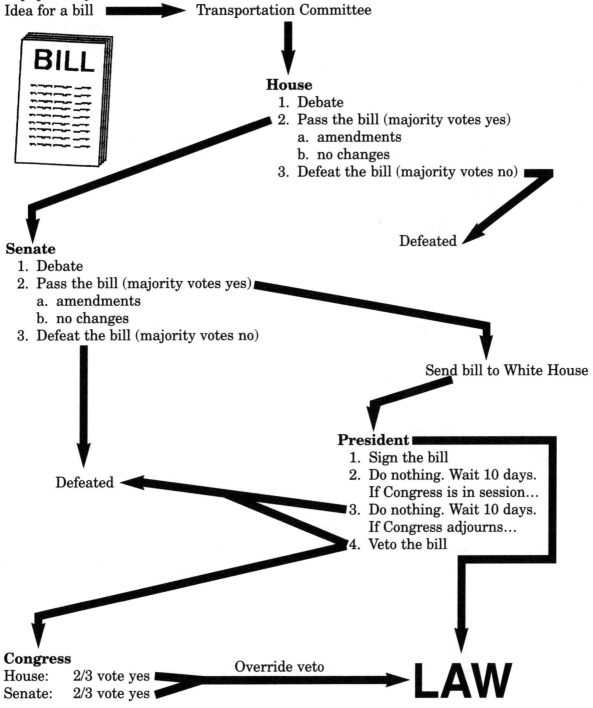

Idea for a bill ➡ Transportation Committee

BILL

House
1. Debate
2. Pass the bill (majority votes yes)
   a. amendments
   b. no changes
3. Defeat the bill (majority votes no)

Defeated

Senate
1. Debate
2. Pass the bill (majority votes yes)
   a. amendments
   b. no changes
3. Defeat the bill (majority votes no)

Send bill to White House

President
1. Sign the bill
2. Do nothing. Wait 10 days.
   If Congress is in session…
3. Do nothing. Wait 10 days.
   If Congress adjourns…
4. Veto the bill

Defeated

Congress
House: 2/3 vote yes
Senate: 2/3 vote yes

Override veto

LAW

10.2 Three Ways to Pass a Bill

A proposed law is called a bill. There are three ways in
which bills may become laws.

• **First Way:** A bill must pass both houses of Congress
by a majority vote. It must then be sent to the
President. If the President signs the bill, it becomes a law.

• **Second Way:** A bill must pass both houses by a majority vote and be sent to the
President. If the President vetoes the bill, he sends it back to the house in which it start-
ed. If both houses pass it again by a two-thirds majority vote, it becomes a law without the
President's signature.

• **Third Way:** A bill must pass both houses by a majority vote and be sent to the President.
If the President keeps it ten days (Sundays excepted), it becomes a law without his signature, unless Congress adjourns before the ten days are up.

Congress sometimes passes laws that are needed for a short time only, and sometimes
passes laws that prove unsatisfactory. The Constitution provides that all laws passed by
Congress may be repealed or changed by Congress.

In your own words, describe the three ways that a bill may become a law.

_____

_____

_____

_____

_____

_____

_____

_____

_____

_____

_____

_____

_____

_____

_____

10.3 Congressional Incumbents

In most congressional elections, incumbents run for reelection, and they usually win. Since World War II, an average of 92 percent of all incumbent representatives and 75 percent of incumbent senators running for reelection have been returned to office. Short of a major scandal or huge mistake, it is nearly impossible to topple a House incumbent, and nearly as difficult to dislodge a Senator.

Incumbents have resources that ensure visibility and promote support: through speeches, statements, press releases, press coverage, newsletters and mailings, staff assistance, and constituency services. The average House member enjoys perquisites valued at well over $1 million over a two-year term. Senators' resources are valued at between $4 million and $7 million. Although incumbents need less money than their challengers, they receive more from outside sources that rightly view them as better investments than their opponents. Incumbents capture nine out of every ten dollars given by political action committees (PACs) to congressional candidates. Most incumbents, in fact, finish their campaign with a surplus.

Answer the following questions.

1. How likely are incumbents to be re-elected? _____

_____

2. Name some of the resources incumbents can draw from to ensure reelection.

_____

_____

_____

3. Why are outside sources more likely to contribute to incumbents?

_____

_____

4. What do you think about the advantages that incumbents have over their opponents?

_____

_____

5. What are the advantages and disadvantages of making it easy for incumbents to stay in office? _____

_____

_____

_____

10.4 Congressional Staffs

Staff aides extend senators' and representatives' constituent outreach. About 12,000 people work in members' offices. Senators' staffs range in size from 13 to 71, depending on the state's population; the average is about 36. Representatives' staffs average about 17. Constituent relations are their most time-consuming job. Members of Congress have from one to six local offices in key home-state locations; increasingly, casework and voter contacts are handled there.

Although staff members obviously cannot vote on legislation, their imprint is on every step in getting a bill passed. Legislators are asked to debate and vote on a wide range of complex issues, and they need staff to conduct research and provide expertise that one person alone simply could not master.

A total of 18,000 people work for the House and Senate, and another 3,000 handle security, maintenance, and other support services. In addition, 3,000 employees work at four legislative service agencies: the Congressional Research Service of the Library of Congress, the Congressional Budget Office, the Office of Technology Assessment, and the General Accounting Office. Legislative branch appropriations total more than $1.7 billion. Most of that goes to pay salaries.

Congressional employees come from a mix of backgrounds, but most are young and well-educated. Some outlast the legislator who originally hired them; they simply get a job with someone else. Some become politicians themselves. President Lyndon B. Johnson began his career as a congressional aide and was later elected to Congress where he served for 24 years before becoming President.

Answer the following questions.

1. Describe the size and the costs of staff for the Senate and the House.

_____

_____

_____

_____

_____

2. Some critics argue that congressional staff have too much power. What do you think? What are the alternatives? _____

_____

_____

_____

_____

_____

10.5 Congressional Committees

Congress has retained an active legislative role by delegating its workload to committees and subcommittee that write, revise, and oversee laws, programs, and agencies. Most bills and resolutions are referred to the relevant committee of jurisdiction. It is very difficult, especially in the House, to bypass a committee that refuses to act upon a measure. "Congressional government is committee government," wrote Woodrow Wilson (*Congressional Government*, 1885). "Congress in session is Congress on display, but Congress in committee is Congress at work."

House and Senate committee structures are complicated. The Senate has 20 committees, and these have 87 subcommittees. The House has 27 committees with 152 subcommittees. There are also four joint committees (with eight subcommittees), not to mention temporary panels, boards, and commissions.

Most standing committees are authorizing committees: they draft the substance of policies and oversee executive agencies' implementation of laws. There are also appropriations committees that draft bills empowering agencies to spend money for programs; revenue committees draft revenue bills to pay for the programs.

Committees usually exert decisive control over legislative proposals: nine out of every ten measures referred to committee go no further in the legislative process. Promising bills may be accorded staff research and public hearings, which give executive officials, lobbyists, and citizens a chance to speak publicly on the issue. If the bill has enough support, the committee will hold meetings to revise the text ("mark-ups") and may eventually report the measure to the full chamber.

Each committee is a unique mixture of members, viewpoints, and decision-making styles. They differ in levels of conflict, partisanship, or public visibility.

In your own words, describe the committee system.

_____

_____

_____

_____

_____

_____

_____

_____

_____

_____

10.6 The Lobbyists

lobbyist   bloc
delegate   backer
lobby

Fill in the crossword puzzle with words from the box.

ACROSS

1. a representative of a constituency at a convention

3. a person who gives a political candidate financial support

4. an organization that tries to influence an elected official's decision on important legislation or the attempt to do so

DOWN

2. a person who tries to influence the decision of a politician on an upcoming vote

5. representatives with a certain interest in common

Now that you know the meanings of the words in the box, write a short paragraph using all five of them.

_____

_____

_____

_____

_____

10.7 Talking About Legislation

Study the definitions below, then team up with a partner and test each other on the meanings.

Act: Legislation that has passed both chambers of Congress in identical form, been signed into law by the President, or passed over his veto, thus becoming law.

Bill: The principal vehicle employed by lawmakers for introducing their proposals. Bills are designated S. 1, S. 2, and so on depending on the order in which they are introduced. They address either matters of general interest ("public bills") or narrow interest ("private bills"), such as immigration cases and individual claims against the Federal government.

"Christmas Tree" Bill: A bill on the Senate floor that attracts many, often unrelated, floor amendments. The amendments which adorn the bill may provide special benefits to various groups or interests.

Companion Bill or Measure: Similar or identical legislation which is introduced in the Senate and House. House and Senate lawmakers who share similar views on legislation may introduce a companion bill in their respective chambers to promote simultaneous consideration of the measure.

Enacted: Once legislation has passed both chambers of Congress in identical form, been signed into law by the President, become law without his signature, or passed over his veto, the legislation is enacted.

Joint Resolution: A legislative measure that requires the approval of both chambers and, with one exception, is submitted (just as a bill) to the President for possible signature into law.

"Must Pass" Bill: A vitally important measure that Congress must enact, such as annual money bills to fund operations of the government. Because of their must-pass quality, these measures often attract "riders" (unrelated policy provisos).

10.8 First Steps

"All legislative Powers herein granted shall be vested in a Congress of the United States, which shall consist of a Senate and House of Representatives."
Article I, Section 1, of the United States Constitution

The chief function of Congress is the making of laws. The legislative process comprises a number of steps. Read the steps described below, then write your own summary of the four initial steps in passing legislation on the back of this sheet.

1. Introducing Legislation.
The work of Congress is initiated by the introduction of a proposal in one of four principal forms: the bill, the joint resolution, the concurrent resolution, and the simple resolution. A bill is the form used for most legislation. A bill originating in the House of Representatives is designated by the letters "H.R.," signifying "House of Representatives," followed by a number that it retains throughout all its parliamentary stages. Bills are presented to the President for action when approved in identical form by both the House of Representatives and the Senate.

2. Referral to Committee
Any member in the House of Representatives may introduce a bill at any time while the House is in session by simply placing it in the "hopper" provided for the purpose at the side of the Clerk's desk in the House Chamber. The sponsor's signature must appear on the bill. A public bill may have an unlimited number of co-sponsoring members. The bill is assigned its legislative number by the Clerk and referred to the appropriate committee by the Speaker, with the assistance of the Parliamentarian. The bill is then printed in its introduced form. An important phase of the legislative process is the action taken by committees. It is during committee action that the most intense consideration is given to the proposed measures; this is also the time when the people are given their opportunity to be heard. Each piece of legislation is referred to the committee that has jurisdiction over the area affected by the measure.

3. Consideration by Committee
Usually the first step in this process is a public hearing, where the committee members hear witnesses representing various viewpoints on the measure. After hearings are completed, the bill is considered in a session that is popularly known as the "mark-up" session. Members of the committee study the viewpoints presented in detail. Amendments may be offered to the bill, and the committee members vote to accept or reject these changes.

4. Committee Action
At the conclusion of deliberation, a vote of committee or subcommittee members is taken to determine what action to take on the measure. It can be reported, with or without amendment, or tabled, which means no further action on it will occur. If the committee has approved extensive amendments, it may decide to report a new bill incorporating all the amendments. This is known as a "clean bill," which will have a new number. If the committee votes to report a bill, the Committee Report is written. This report describes the purpose and scope of the measure and the reasons for recommended approval. House Report numbers are prefixed with "H.Rpt." and then a number indicating the Congress.

©1999 by The Center for Applied Research in Education

10.9 Final Steps

The legislative process comprises a number of steps, beginning with introducing a bill and committee consideration of the bill. Once the bill leaves committee, it still must go through a number of steps before it becomes a law. Read the steps described below, then—on another sheet of paper—write your own summary of the final steps in passing legislation.

1. House Floor Consideration

Consideration of a measure by the full House can be either a simple or very complex operation. In general a measure is ready for consideration by the full House after it has been reported by a committee. Under certain circumstances, it may be brought to the floor directly. The consideration of a measure may be governed by a "rule." A rule is itself a simple resolution, which must be passed by the House, that sets out the particulars of debate for a specific bill—how much time will be allowed for debate, whether amendments can be offered, and other matters. Debate time for a measure is normally divided between proponents and opponents. Each side yields time to those members who wish to speak on the bill. When amendments are offered, these are also debated and voted upon. After all debate is concluded and amendments decided upon, the House is ready to vote on final passage.

2. Resolving Differences

After a measure passes in the House, it goes to the Senate for consideration. A bill must pass both bodies in the same form before it can be presented to the President for signature into law. If the Senate changes the language of the measure, it must return to the House for concurrence or additional changes. This back-and-forth negotiation may occur on the House floor, with the House accepting or rejecting Senate amendments or complete Senate text. Often a conference committee will be appointed with both House and Senate members. This group will resolve the differences in committee and report the identical measure back to both bodies for a vote. Conference committees also issue reports outlining the final version of the bill.

3. Final Step

Votes on final passage, as well as all other votes in the House, may be taken by the electronic voting system that registers each individual member's response. These votes are referred to as Yea/Nay votes or recorded votes, and are available in House Votes by Bill number, roll-call vote number, or words describing the reason for the vote. Votes in the House may also be by voice vote, and no record of individual responses is available. After a measure has been passed in identical form by both the House and Senate, it is considered "enrolled." It is sent to the President who may sign the measure into law, veto it and return it to Congress, let it become law without signature, or, at the end of a session, pocket-veto it.

10.10 Quorum Calls and Roll-Call Votes

The Constitution requires that a quorum, or a majority of all Senators, be present to conduct business on the floor. Even though Senators have many responsibilities that frequently keep them from the floor, the Senate presumes that a quorum is present unless a quorum call demonstrates that it is not. A Senator who has been recognized may suggest the lack of a quorum at almost any time; a clerk then begins to call the roll of Senators. If a majority of Senators do not appear and respond to their names, the Senate can only adjourn or recess, or attempt to secure the attendance of additional Senators.

The Constitution also provides that one-fifth of the Senators on the floor (assuming that a quorum is present) can demand a roll-call vote. Since the smallest possible quorum is 51 Senators, the support of at least 11 Senators is required to order a roll-call vote. A Senator who has been recognized can ask for "the yeas and nays" at any time the Senate is considering a motion, amendment, bill, or other question. If a roll call is ordered, that is how the Senate will vote on the question whenever the time for the vote arrives. Thus, the Senate may order a roll-call vote on an amendment as soon as it is offered, but the vote itself may not take place for several hours or more, when Senators no longer wish to debate the amendment.

The alternative to a roll-call vote usually is a voice vote in which the Senators favoring the bill or amendment (or whatever question is to be decided) vote "aye" in unison, followed by those voting "no." Although a voice vote does not create a public record of how each Senator voted, it is an equally valid and conclusive way for the Senate to reach a decision.

Answer the following questions.

1. What is a quorum? _____

_____

2. How many Senators must be present for a quorum? _____

3. How does the clerk check for a quorum? _____

_____

4. What is a roll-call vote? _____

_____

5. What is a voice vote? _____

_____

10.11 Filibusters and Cloture

The *dearth* of debate limitations in Senate rules creates the possibility of *filibusters*. Individual Senators or minority groups of Senators who *adamantly* oppose a bill or amendment may speak against it at great length, in the hope of changing their *colleagues'* minds, winning support for amendments that meet their *objections,* or convincing the Senate to withdraw the bill or amendment from further consideration on the floor. Opposing Senators can also delay final floor action by offering numerous amendments and motions, insisting that amendments be read in full, demanding roll-call votes on amendments and motions, and using a variety of other devices.

The only formal procedure that Senate rules provide for breaking filibusters is to invoke *cloture*. However, cloture cannot be voted until two days after it is proposed, and a simple majority of the Senate is insufficient to *invoke* cloture. Cloture requires the support of three-fifths of the Senators duly chosen and sworn, or a minimum of 60 votes (unless the matter being considered changes the standing rules, in which case cloture requires a vote of two-thirds of the Senators present and voting). For this reason alone, cloture can be difficult to invoke and almost always requires some *bipartisan* support. In addition, some Senators are *reluctant* to vote for cloture, even if they support the legislation being *jeopardized* by the filibuster, precisely because the right of extended debate is such an *integral* element of Senate history and *procedure.*

In the spaces below, define the twelve words underlined in the passage. Use a dictionary if you are unsure of the meanings.

1. _____

2. _____

3. _____

4. _____

5. _____

6. _____

7. _____

8. _____

9. _____

10. _____

11. _____

12. _____

Section 11

Elections

11.1 Voting in the General Election

Use this copy of an actual voting ballot from the 1996 election to cast your vote for President, Vice President, Senator, and Representative. Follow the instructions for voting. Use your pencil to mark an X where it should appear. Then collect all the ballots and tabulate the results for your class.

INSTRUCTIONS FOR VOTING

1 PRESS THE BLACK SQUARE ■ TO THE RIGHT OF THE CANDIDATE OF YOUR CHOICE; A **GREEN X** WILL APPEAR SIGNIFYING YOUR SELECTION.

2 IF YOU WISH TO CAST A WRITE-IN VOTE, GO TO THE PERSONAL CHOICE COLUMN. IN THE PERSONAL CHOICE COLUMN, PRESS THE BLACK SQUARE ■ ACROSS FROM THE OFFICE YOU WISH TO WRITE-IN. A BLINKING GREEN X WILL APPEAR. GO DOWN TO THE KEYBOARD AND TYPE IN THE WRITE-IN NAME. AFTER YOU HAVE COMPLETED YOUR SELECTION, PRESS THE ENTER KEY ON THE PANEL. DO NOT PRESS THE CAST VOTE BUTTON UNTIL ALL OTHER CHOICES ARE COMPLETED. (EACH WRITE-IN IS A SEPARATE ENTRY)

3 TO VOTE IN FAVOR OF A PROPOSITION OR PROPOSAL, PRESS THE BLACK SQUARE ■ TO THE RIGHT OF THE WORD "YES." TO VOTE AGAINST THE PROPOSITION OR PROPOSAL, PRESS THE BLACK SQUARE ■ TO THE RIGHT OF THE WORD "NO". A **GREEN X** WILL APPEAR NEXT TO YOUR SELECTION.

4 <u>TO CHANGE ANY SELECTION</u> PRESS THE BLACK SQUARE ■ AGAIN. THE **GREEN X** WILL DISAPPEAR AND YOU MAY MAKE A NEW SELECTION.

5 AFTER YOU HAVE COMPLETED ALL YOUR SELECTIONS, THEN PRESS THE CAST VOTE BUTTON [CAST VOTE] LOCATED IN THE LOWER RIGHT HAND CORNER OF THE MACHINE. THIS ELECTRONICALLY RECORDS ALL YOUR VOTES.

6 PART THE CURTAINS AND EXIT THE VOTING BOOTH.

PERSONAL CHOICE	GENERAL ELECTION 5th Congressional District November 5, 1996	REPUBLICAN Column 1	DEMOCRAT Column 2	NOMINATION BY PETITION Column 3	NOMINATION BY PETITION Column 4
1 □■	Presidential Electors for President and Vice President of the United States (VOTE FOR ONE)	BOB **DOLE** JACK **KEMP** □■	BILL **CLINTON** AL **GORE** □■	Reform Party ROSS **PEROT** NO NOMINATION MADE □■	Workers World Party MONICA **MOOREHEAD** GLORIA **LA RIVA** □■
2 □■		□■	□■	Libertarian Party HARRY **BROWNE** JO **JORGENSEN** □■	Socialist Equality Party JEROME **WHITE** FRED **MAZELIS** □■
3 □■		□■	□■	Green Party RALPH **NADER** MADELYN R. **HOFFMAN** □■	Socialist Workers Party JAMES **HARRIS** LAURA **GARZA** □■
4 □■	Member of the United States Senate (VOTE FOR ONE)	DICK **ZIMMER** □■	ROBERT G. **TORRICELLI** □■	Socialist Workers Party OLGA L. **RODRIGUEZ** □■	Green Coalition Party PAUL A. **WOOMER** □■
5 □■		□■	□■	Independent Peoples Coalition WILBURT **KORNEGAY** □■	Natural Law Party MARY JO **CHRISTIAN** □■
6 □■		□■	□■	Protecting Freedom STEVEN J. **BAELI** □■	NJ Conservative Party RICHARD J. **PEZZULLO** □■
7 □■	Member of the House of Representatives (VOTE FOR ONE)	MARGE **ROUKEMA** □■	BILL **AUER** □■	Natural Law Party HELEN **HAMILTON** □■	NJ Conservative Party LORRAINE L. **LA NEVE** □■
8 □■		□■	□■	Libertarian Party DAN **KARLAN** □■	Undauntable Stalwart Allegiance E. GREGORY **KRESGE** □■

11.2 How the Electoral College Works

The electoral college remains a mystery to most people. Read this explanation, then write your own summary of the steps involved in selecting a president. Here's how the electoral college works:

Each State is allocated a number of Electors equal to the number of its U.S. Senators (always 2) plus the number of its U.S. Representatives (which may change each decade according to the size of each state's population as determined in the census).

The political parties (or independent candidates) in each state submit to the state's chief election official a list of individuals pledged to their candidate for president and equal in number to the state's electoral vote. Usually, the major political parties select these individuals either in their state party conventions or through appointment by their state party leaders while third parties and independent candidates merely designate theirs.

After their caucuses and primaries, the major parties nominate their candidates for president and vice president in their national conventions traditionally held in the summer preceding the election. Third parties and independent candidates follow different procedures according to the individual state laws. The names of the duly nominated candidates are then officially submitted to each state's chief election official so that they might appear on the general election ballot.

On the Tuesday following the first Monday of November in years divisible by four, the people in each state cast their ballots for the party slate of Electors representing their choice for president and vice president. Whichever party slate wins the most popular votes in the state becomes that state's Electors—so that, in effect, whichever presidential ticket gets the most popular votes in a state wins all the Electors of that state. (The two exceptions to this are Maine and Nebraska where two Electors are chosen by statewide popular vote and the remainder by the popular vote within each Congressional district.)

On the Monday following the second Wednesday of December each state's Electors meet in their respective state capitals and cast their electoral votes—one for president and one for vice president. In order to prevent Electors from voting only for "favorite sons" of their home state, at least one of their votes must be for a person from outside their state. The electoral votes are then sealed and transmitted from each state to the President of the Senate who, on the following January 6, opens and reads them before both houses of the Congress.

The candidate for president with the most electoral votes, provided that it is an absolute majority (one over half of the total), is declared president. Similarly, the vice presidential candidate with the absolute majority of electoral votes is declared vice president.

In the event no one obtains an absolute majority of electoral votes for president, the U.S. House of Representatives (as the chamber closer to the people) selects the president from among the top three contenders with each State casting only one vote and an absolute majority of the States being required to elect. Similarly, if no one obtains an absolute majority for vice president, then the U.S. Senate makes the selection from among the top two contenders for that office. At noon on January 20, the duly elected president and vice president are sworn into office.

©1999 by The Center for Applied Research in Education

11.3 Voting in the Land of OhNo

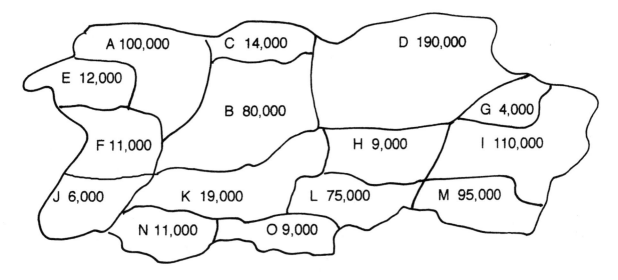

This is the newly created nation of OhNo. The map shows OhNo's 15 states and the population of each state. Under OhNo's new constitution, each state is worth five points and the candidate who wins the most votes in a state wins that state. The candidate with the greatest number of points becomes president.

In its first presidential election, three candidates are running: Mr. HoHo, Ms. HeHe, and Mr. MeTo.

Describe three problems that may arise in this election.

1. _____

   _____

2. _____

   _____

3. _____

   _____

11.4 Election Results in OhNo

OhNo's northern and eastern coastal waters have been polluted by heavy ocean dumping by the neighboring island of Stinkie. Presidential candidate HoHo promises to cut off imports with Stinkie unless it stops the dumping. OhNo's steel industry, the major employer in the southwest, is dependent on ores imported from Stinkie. Candidate HeHe lives in state G, and promises to protect steel jobs.

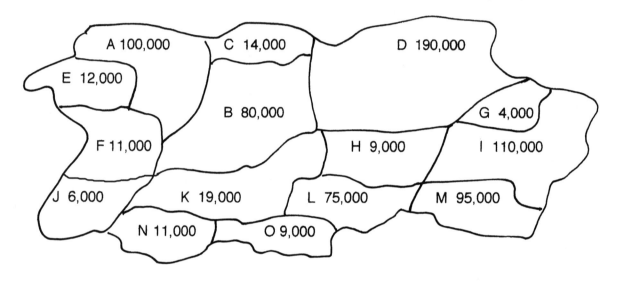

In the presidential election, each state is worth five points and the candidate who wins the most votes in a state wins that state. The candidate with the greatest number of points becomes president.

Answer the following questions.

Which states are likely to support HoHo? _____ How many voters live in these states? _____ What percentage of the national popular vote do they represent? _____ How many points can HoHo win with these states? _____ HeHe receives a majority of the votes in states E, F, J, K, N, and O. How many points does he win? _____ Who wins the election? _____

Step Ahead!
How could you redesign the election process in OhNo to make it more "fair"? Write your answer on the back of this sheet.

11.5 International Voter Turnout

This chart shows actual voter turnout rates for recent elections in selected countries. Read the chart, then answer the questions below.

Country	Year	Type of Election	% Turnout of Eligible Voters
Algeria	1995	Presidential	75.69
Argentina	1995	Presidential	80.9
Australia	1996	Parliamentary	96.3
Austria	1995	Parliamentary	82.74
Belgium	1995	Parliamentary	91.15
Bulgaria	1996	Presidential	49.79
Canada	1993	Prime Min.	73
Croatia	1995	Legislative	68.79
Cyprus	1996	Legislative	90.13
Czech Republic	1996	Legislative	76.29
Ecuador	1996	Presidential	73
Germany	1994	Parliamentary	71
Ghana	1996	Presidential	78.21
Greece	1996	Parliamentary	76.34
Japan	1995	Parliamentary	44.5
Nicaragua	1996	Presidential	76.38
Russia	1996	Presidential	69.56
Slovenia	1996	Parliamentary	73.67
Sweden	1994	Parliamentary	87.3
Taiwan	1996	Presidential	75.2
Turkey	1995	Parliamentary	85.2
United States	1996	Presidential	65.97
Zambia	1996	Presidential	58.23
Zimbabwe	1995	Parliamentary	31.8

Source: International Foundation for Election Systems (IFES).

1. Which three countries have the highest voter turnout rates? _____

_____

2. Which three have the lowest? _____

_____

3. List five factors that may affect voter turnout. _____

_____

_____

_____

133

11.6 Polling the Populace

Politicians often rely on information gathered from public opinion polls. By asking specific questions on a variety of topics, elected officials can better understand how their voters feel about certain issues. Polling results can indicate whether an administration has been adequately addressing specific problems, whether a political campaign should change course, or whether an incumbent's approval rating is high enough to predict a victory at the next election.

Learn to conduct your own poll. First, choose a topic. It can be something "light" as in the sample below, or a subject of more serious or newsworthy importance. Using the sample as your guide, write down your polling question on the back of this sheet, making sure to include at least four possible responses from which to choose. Next, survey your classmates and tally their responses. Finally, design a bar graph interpreting your results.

SAMPLE

Question: When choosing to listen to music, do your prefer: rap, rock, jazz, country, classical or other?

Tally:

<u>Rap</u>	<u>Rock</u>	<u>Jazz</u>	<u>Country</u>	<u>Classical</u>	<u>Other</u>
lll	llll	llll	ll	lll	ll

Bar Graph:

©1999 by The Center for Applied Research in Education

11.7 Election Update

"And, now, we bring you an up-to-the-minute analysis of yesterday's elections. With nearly all votes counted, it appears that Governor-elect Smith, last year's dark-horse candidate, has hitched a ride on the President's coattails right into a landslide victory. As was predicted in a straw vote taken of the electorate last week, all his opponent's mudslinging failed to slow Mr. Smith's popularity. By turning down the incumbent's bid for re-election, Mr. Smith's constituents demonstrated the strong popularity of the new majority party's platform. Returns nationwide indicate straight ticket voting took place in several states, where party affiliation virtually guaranteed shoo-in victories for slates of candidates running at all political levels. Well, folks, it appears a lot of rubber chicken was consumed in vain this election year!"

What is this man saying? See if you can match the following election terms with the definitions below:

A. Coattails   B. Constituent   C. Darkhorse   D. Electorate
E. Incumbent   F. Landslide   G. Mudslinging   H. Platform
I. Referendum   J. Returns   K. Rubber Chicken L. Shoo-in
M. Straight Ticket N. Straw Vote   O. Slate

____ A party's statement of policy and political views

____ Leveling offensive accusations between candidates

____ A candidate whose name is unfamiliar to the public

____ Voting for the candidates of only one party

____ Slang term for meals consumed on the campaign trail

____ A candidate whose election is nearly guaranteed

____ A person currently holding an elective office

____ An election where the winner receives a very large percentage of the popular vote

____ The voting public

____ Election results

____ A list of candidates

____ A public vote on an issue

____ An opinion poll

____ A voter represented by a particular politician

____ When a popular nominee helps other members of the party win election

11.8 Left of Center or Right of Left?

Terms describing political beliefs are commonplace in our media today. Sometimes they are used negatively to label a political opponent ("right wing reactionary," "far out liberal"). Other times, they are simply used to describe where one stands on various political issues ("fiscal conservative," "social centrist"). But what exactly do these ideological phrases mean? Below are six political terms. See how well you can match these terms to the beliefs that follow. (**Hint:** Some terms will be used more than once and some beliefs can match more than one term.)

1. Radical
    2. Liberal
        3. Centrist/Moderate
        4. Conservative
5. Reactionary

_____ Favors a tax system that places the greater burden on large corporations and wealthy individuals

_____ Strongly opposes federal involvement in promoting social welfare

_____ Argues for a strong national defense program

_____ Strives to completely overcome social inequities

_____ Supports active federal social welfare programs

_____ Advocates greater empowerment of state and local governments

_____ Believes change is necessary but should occur slowly

_____ Advocates return to economic and social conditions of earlier times

_____ Favors extreme change in the political system

©1999 by The Center for Applied Research in Education

11.9 The Third P*A*R*T*Y

Historically, the United States government has always functioned within a two-party political system (although the names and platforms of the two dominant parties have changed periodically over the past 200 years). Some Americans have always felt, however, that although each party strives to accommodate a wide range of ideologies, a two-party system cannot adequately represent all political points of view. This is where "third parties" have often come in.

Third parties are generally formed in one of three ways: to secure the nomination of a particular candidate; to rally a group of people around a particular cause; or to unite a group of citizens who have similar ideas about government or society. But while some third-party issues initially viewed as radical have often gone on to be embraced by the major political parties and even adopted as public policy (the national income tax, secret ballots, abolition, women's suffrage, and the minimum wage, to name a few), no third-party candidate for president has ever been elected or advanced further than the 18.9% showing of Ross Perot in the 1992 elections.

Today, Americans are very undecided about the desirability of third-party candidates. Although the Constitution makes no mention of political parties (and, in fact, George Washington himself hated them), our two-party tradition has certainly added stability to our government. If a third-party candidate were to be elected President, certain laws would need to be changed and the balance and structure of political power in Washington would be radically altered. With this in mind, some voters, eager to cast a "protest vote" against mainstream party politics and hopeful of truly impacting the political system, avidly promote their third-party nominee. Others, however supportive of political change, are either reluctant to "throw away" their vote on a candidate with no chance of winning or are hesitant to upset a stable political system.

Where do you stand? Does the Republican or Democrat party adequately reflect your political beliefs? Would you vote for a third-party presidential candidate in order to effect change, even if that meant risking our two-party system? Would you support a third-party nominee even if you knew that by doing so, you might be "throwing away" your vote? Below and on the back of this sheet, write a paragraph or two describing your views on third-party candidates.

_____

_____

_____

_____

_____

_____

11.10 Who Wins?

Year	President	Party	Year	President	Party
1900	William McKinley (OH) and Theodore Roosevelt (NY)	Republican	1948	Harry S. Truman (MO) and Alben Barkley (KY)	Democratic
1904	Theodore Roosevelt (NY) and Charles Fairbanks (IN)	Republican	1952	Dwight D. Eisenhower (KS) and Richard M. Nixon (CA)	Republican
1908	William H. Taft (OH) and James Sherman (NY)	Republican	1956	Dwight D. Eisenhower (KS) and Richard M. Nixon (CA)	Republican
1912	Woodrow Wilson (NJ) and Thomas Marshall (IN)	Democratic	1960	John F. Kennedy (MA) and Lyndon Johnson (TX)	Democratic
1916	Woodrow Wilson (NJ) and Thomas Marshall (IN)	Democratic	1964	Lyndon Johnson (TX) and Hubert H. Humphrey (MN)	Democratic
1920	Warren G. Harding (OH) and Calvin Coolidge (MA)	Republican	1968	Richard M. Nixon (CA) and Spiro T. Agnew (MD)	Republican
1924	Calvin Coolidge (MA) and Charles Dawes (OH)	Republican	1972	Richard M. Nixon (CA) and Spiro T. Agnew (MD)	Republican
1928	Herbert C. Hoover (IA) and Charles Curtis (KS)	Republican	1976	Jimmy Carter (GA) and Walter Mondale (MN)	Democratic
1932	Franklin D. Roosevelt (NY) and John Nance Garner (TX)	Democratic	1980	Ronald Reagan (CA) and George Bush (TX)	Republican
1936	Franklin D. Roosevelt (NY) and John Nance Garner (TX)	Democratic	1984	Ronald Reagan (CA) and George Bush (TX)	Republican
1940	Franklin D. Roosevelt (NY) and Henry A. Wallace (IA)	Democratic	1988	George Bush (TX) and Dan Quayle (IN)	Republican
1944	Franklin D. Roosevelt (NY) and Harry S. Truman (MO)	Democratic	1992	Bill Clinton (AR) and Al Gore, Jr. (TN)	Democratic
			1996	Bill Clinton (AR) and Al Gore, Jr. (TN)	Democratic

All of the twentieth-century presidents are listed above. Answer these questions:

1. How many presidents were elected to more than one term? _____ What percentage of all twentieth-century presidents does this represent? _____

2. How many vice presidents eventually were elected president? _____

3. How many elections did the Republicans win? _____ What percentage? _____

4. How many elections did the Democrats win? _____ What percentage? _____

5. What was the greatest number of consecutive years that one party maintained control over the presidency? _____

6. Which state has had the greatest number of presidents in the twentieth century?

   _____

7. Which states have had no presidents or vice presidents elected in the twentieth century?

_____

_____

_____

11.11 Campaign Contributions

Political Action Committee Contributions 1985–86 and 1995–96		
Committee Type	**Number of Committees**	**Contributions to Candidates**
Corporate		
1985–86	1,906	$49,566,619
1995–96	1,836	78,194,723
Labor		
1985–86	417	31,038,885
1995–96	58	47,980,492
Nonconnected		
1985–86	1,270	19,410,358
1995–96	1,259	23,960,110

Answer the following questions according to the chart above.

1. How much did the contributions from each of the three types of committees increase during the ten-year period?

_____

2. How much did the number of committees decrease for each of the three types?

_____

3. What is the average amount of contributions per committee for each of the three types of committees?

_____

4. Has this been increasing or decreasing over the years?

_____

Section 12

The Media

12.1 In My Opinion . . .

As Americans we enjoy the freedom to express ourselves. On any subject, from such weighty topics as bilingual education or affirmative action to less serious issues like designer fashions or the latest TV shows, we enthusiastically present our opinions and offer our solutions. The editorial page of the local newspaper is one place to air these public expressions, in letters to the editor that often begin with lines such as: "I am in complete disagreement with . . ." or "I wholeheartedly support . . ." or "I am responding with outrage to . . ." or "I applaud the mayor's decision to. . . ."

Now it's your turn to share your thoughts. Choose any topic, whether it's a national concern or a local issue, and in the space below, write your own "Letter to the Editor." Be sure to express the problem or issue clearly and use specifics to back up your solution. (You might even try sending a copy of this letter to your own newspaper to see if it gets published!)

_____

_____

_____

_____

_____

_____

_____

_____

_____

_____

_____

_____

_____

_____

_____

_____

_____

_____

(Continue on the back of this sheet if you need more space.)

Article 1

> The Danish mom arrested for leaving her baby daughter in a stroller outside an East Village restaurant while she dined inside sued the city yesterday for $20 million.
>
> "Stroller Mom" Annette Sorensen charged the city with false arrest and claimed that cops and child-welfare officials acted "maliciously" when they took her daughter away on May 10 last year.
>
> The child now suffers "emotional problems, a certain amount of fear of separation from her mother," said Sorensen's lawyer, Michael Carey.
>
> Sorensen, 31, an actress who lives with 2-year-old Liv in Copenhagen, was arrested after other diners at the Dallas BBQ Restaurant on Second Avenue complained to cops that the baby was left outside, unattended.

Article 2

> Last May, Anette Sorensen, a Danish tourist visiting New York City, was arrested for leaving her infant daughter in a stroller outside a Lower East Side restaurant where she and the child's father were dining. Ms. Sorensen was charged with endangering the welfare of a child, the child was placed in foster care for a few days, and city officials scolded the mother for ignoring American customs.
>
> Apparently she learned her lesson. On Monday, she followed another kind of American custom: she filed a lawsuit against the city.
>
> The $20 million lawsuit, which was filed in Federal District Court in Manhattan, says that Ms. Sorensen, 31, was arrested without cause, subjected to malicious prosecution and deprived of her constitutional rights.
>
> "What we hope to achieve by this is to make Anette and her daughter whole for the enormous pain and suffering that they've been put through," said Michael Q. Carey, a Manhattan lawyer who is representing Ms. Sorensen and her 2-year-old daughter, Liv.
>
> A spokesman for the city's Corporation Counsel said that the city had not been served with the lawsuit and could not comment.

12.2 Just the Facts?

The slogan that appears on the first page of every copy of *The New York Times* reads "All the News That's Fit to Print." A noble thought, but who gets to determine which news **is** fit to print and which news isn't? No matter how hard they may try to be impartial in their news coverage, each newspaper publisher brings to his or her paper a set of individual viewpoints. These perspectives are most clearly reflected and presented on the paper's editorial page.

The articles shown here cover the same news story. They were published on the same day in the same city, but by two different newspapers. Read them, then answer these questions:

1. Is one article written from a more "dispassionate" viewpoint than the other? How is this evident to you?

   _____

   _____

   _____

   _____

2. Does one article use more informal language than the other? Cite two examples of words that appear in both articles but are used differently in each. Why might a journalist choose one style over another?

   _____

   _____

   _____

   _____

   _____

   _____

   _____

12.3 Campaign News

Read the news report below about a presidential debate and fill in the blanks using the following underlined words.

<u>bandwagon:</u> a popular issue on which politicians jump so they will be seen as part of the majority

<u>mudslinging:</u> insults and unsubstantiated allegations traded back and forth between politicians

<u>red herring:</u> an issue raised to distract the public's attention from a more important issue

<u>deep six:</u> to get rid of or throw away something, often hoping that it will never be discovered

<u>rhetoric:</u> a speech, argument, or debate that is persuasive and widely used by politicians

<u>smear campaign:</u> a political campaign in which a candidate constantly insults another candidate

    Last night the presidential debate was held. It was a complete

_____ with constant _____ between

President Harper and Senator George Hunter. President Harper brought up many

_____s in an attempt to take the focus off the scandals he had

_____ed many years before the campaign. Both candidates jumped

on the _____ whenever possible to gain points in the polls.

President Harper used some effective and impressive _____

which helped him maintain his small lead over Senator Hunter. This year's campaign is

certainly a close one.

12.4 Colorful Reporting

Find the underlined words below in the puzzle and circle them. Then work with a partner to quiz each other on the meanings of the words.

Q	W	E	R	T	Y	U	I	O	P	A	S	D	F	G	H	J	K	L	Z
X	P	U	N	D	I	T	C	V	B	N	M	Q	W	T	E	R	T	Y	U
I	O	O	P	A	S	N	D	F	G	H	J	K	L	N	Z	X	C	V	B
N	M	Q	L	W	E	A	R	T	Y	U	I	O	A	U	P	A	S	D	F
G	H	J	K	I	L	C	Z	X	C	V	B	M	N	H	M	Q	W	E	R
T	Y	F	U	I	T	O	P	A	S	D	E	G	H	J	K	L	Z	X	
C	V	E	B	N	M	I	Q	W	E	C	R	T	Y	C	U	I	O	P	A
S	D	N	F	G	H	J	C	K	N	L	Z	X	C	T	V	B	N	M	Q
W	E	C	R	T	Y	U	I	A	O	P	A	S	D	I	F	G	H	J	K
Z	X	E	C	V	B	N	V	M	L	Q	W	E	R	W	T	Y	U	I	O
P	A	M	A	D	F	D	S	G	H	F	J	L	K	Z	X	V	C	B	N
M	Q	E	H	W	A	E	T	R	Y	U	O	I	K	I	O	O	P	A	S
D	F	N	A	G	H	J	K	L	Z	E	X	O	C	V	B	N	M	Z	X
Q	W	D	H	E	E	R	O	T	M	Y	U	I	T	H	E	H	I	L	L
A	D	I	U	F	H	O	O	E	A	J	H	K	L	B	Z	X	C	V	B
N	M	N	O	Q	W	E	C	R	T	Y	U	I	P	O	A	A	S	D	F
G	H	G	R	O	U	N	D	S	W	E	L	L	H	K	L	L	Z	X	C
V	B	N	B	N	E	M	Q	E	R	T	Y	U	I	O	P	A	L	S	D
F	G	H	J	F	K	L	Z	X	C	V	B	N	M	Q	E	W	R	T	Y
U	I	S	D	H	L	I	O	A	R	E	K	A	R	D	U	M	C	V	B

advance man: the person in charge of scheduling speeches, conferences, etc., for the candidate

brouhaha: an uproar or uprising, usually because of a controversy

cant: pet words and phrases used by a politician

fence mending: reestablishing ties with local contacts, such as with local politicians or the media

groundswell: a rapidly growing wave of popular opinion

the Hill: Capitol Hill or the legislative branch of government

muckraker: a reporter who tries to uncover corruption and incompetence within the government

political football: any issue or topic used or "grabbed" by a politician for partisan gain

pundit: a broadcaster who is educated in politics and elections and works as an analyzer and observer

witch hunt: an investigation with much fingerpointing

12.5 Cover the President

Imagine that you are a reporter covering the President's latest speech. At the speech you took the notes below on what the President said. Go over you notes and then, on a separate sheet of paper, write a newspaper article on the speech. The tips below your notes will help you.

Notes:

President is pleased with country's progress

wants to lower taxes & increase education funding

economy is best in 20 years

stock market has reached new highs

however, there are people in major cities that are homeless & hungry

need to help them

illegal drugs are still a problem too

we need to help the poor, stop drug trade & make schools better

Tips

1. Answer *who?, what?, where?, when?, why?,* and *how?* before writing your article. Look for the answers to each question in your notes. Be sure to include them all in your article.
2. A "lead" is one sentence in an article that tells what the article is about, gives the most important information, and draws in the reader. Most good news articles have "leads," and yours should, too.
3. When you've written your article, check it over to make sure it includes a "lead" and the answers to the questions in tip #1. Also check for mistakes and make any necessary changes. Then write your final copy.
4. Write a headline at the top of your article. It should be short, about seven words or less, and worded to get the reader's attention. Like the "lead," it should give some information about the story as well.
5. Now your article is complete. Share it with the class and compare it with your classmates' articles.

12.6 Media Talk

Complete the crossword puzzle below with words from the box.

press agent	libel
slant	wire service
sacred cow	investigative journalism
mouthpiece	press kit
tabloid	press pass
press release	

©1999 by The Center for Applied Research in Education

Across

1. a written statement provided to reporters
2. journalism based on extensive researching, investigating and interviewing
7. a news service such as Associated Press or United Press International
10. materials for the media, such as pictures or information given to reporters and papers

Down

1. an agent of publicity
3. an untrue accusation that is published
4. a person or institution that is favored by the media and that is rarely investigated by the press
5. an officer of public relations
6. a half-sized newspaper containing sensational pictures and articles
8. the viewpoint of a story or a perspective
9. an ID card that confirms the person who holds it is a member of the press, giving that person free access or admission to a certain event

12.7 Hacks and Banners

Fill in the blanks in the paragraph with the underlined words below. Compare your answers with a classmate's.

bury a story: to put a news story on an inside page of a newspaper
byline: the name of the person who wrote the story, which appears at the beginning of an article
dateline: at the beginning of an article, the word or words that indicate where the story took place. It also is used to indicate when it took place
correspondent: a person who reports from remote places
editorial: a column in a newspaper in which personal opinions can be expressed
editorializing: the insertion of the personal opinion of the reporter
fluff: a particularly empty or unoriginal story or article
hack: a writer or reporter who is more interested in making money than in writing a good story
kill: to cancel a newspaper article before it is published
banner: a large headline that takes up the entire width of the page at the top
rag: the nickname for a newspaper that has a poor reputation
muckraker: a reporter who finds information on corruption and scandals

Our Newspaper

The newspaper I work for is terrible! Everyone calls it a _____, and with its bad reputation I guess I can't blame them. Nobody likes the paper because all the stories are the usual _____, nothing really exciting like the other papers. We don't have any _____s, so our stories don't expose any government corruption, and we don't have any _____s, so our stories are only local and never about events in far away places. We do, however, have a lot of _____s. Practically everyone who works here doesn't care about good stories, only money! The writers never do any _____ in order to express how they feel about the issues. We don't even have _____s in which writers and readers can show their views on different topics! This is because the boss is trying to make the paper shorter. Many stories get _____ed before publication because they are too long. The only long stories go on the front page. Those have to be big so a _____ can be at the top of the page. But these gigantic headlines can take up a lot of space, so the editor has to _____ every now and then to make room on the front page. The boss is cutting down the newspaper so much now that we're not even sure if he'll keep _____s and _____s!

©1999 by The Center for Applied Research in Education

12.8 To the Editor

Citizens can remove politicians by voting for the opposing candidate in the next election and campaigning for or contributing money to the opposing candidate. They can attempt to influence a politician's behavior by writing letters to the politician, calling his or her office, or demonstrating with groups. Citizens can also write a letter to the editor. Read the letter below, then answer the questions.

1. What is the main point

   of this letter? _____

   _____

   _____

   _____

   _____

   _____

2. Which statements are facts? Which

   are opinions? _____

   _____

   _____

   _____

   _____

   _____

> To the Editor:
>
> As a committed and lifelong Republican, I take strong exception to the reprehensible remarks by Trent Lott, the Senate majority leader, who called homosexuality a "sin" (news article, June 16).
>
> His vile words were intended to be divisive and to appease the far-right fringe of the party. He hit home on both counts and, shamefully, nothing positive is the result. Mr. Lott has unnecessarily alienated productive, morally balanced and patriotic people, both homosexual and heterosexual.
>
> Most Americans know that gay people are not in need of pity, concern or counseling. Mr. Lott's unfounded stance focuses attention on nonproblems when there are so many real social issues crying out for our attention and his leadership.

©1999 by The Center for Applied Research in Education

3. What is the author's purpose in writing this editorial? _____

_____

_____

_____

_____

4. Is this an effective letter? Why? How would you improve it? _____

_____

_____

_____

_____

III. ECONOMIC PARTICIPATION

- Taxes and Spending
- Budgets, Debts, and Deficits
- Federal Economic Policy
- Inflation, Employment, and Wages
- Corporate America
- Participating in Wall Street

Section 13

Taxes and Spending

13.1 Taxes

All governments must tax their citizens to function. But who gets taxed and how much they pay are two of the most difficult questions governments must answer. Different countries answer these questions in very different ways. In the most heavily taxed nation, Sweden, taxes are equal to 54 percent of the country's entire gross domestic product (GDP). But in the least heavily taxed nations of Africa, the governments take in less than 2.6 percent of GDP in taxes.

Generally, the poorer the nation, the smaller its tax base, and, consequently, the less revenue the government will have at its disposal. The average tax burden across all nations is approximately 30 percent of GDP.

Democracy creates greater demands for public spending, but it also gives citizens who oppose taxes more power to resist tax increases. Most citizens want both more public spending and tax cuts at the same time. This is a fundamental dilemma that no nation has yet resolved.

Most advanced countries rely on the four types of taxes: personal income tax, corporate profits taxes, value added taxes (VAT), and social insurance contributions. These taxes are preferred because they are very broad based—virtually everyone pays them and they generate a great deal of revenue even with relatively low rates. These taxes are also useful because revenues from them increase automatically with inflation and economic growth. The United States relies mostly on progressive income taxes and social security taxes and has no national VAT.

Answer the following questions.

1. Name at least three ways in which taxes may vary from country to country.

   _____

   _____

   _____

2. What is the fundamental dilemma that all democratic nations face when they deal with taxes and spending?

   _____

   _____

3. Name the four basic types of taxes that are commonly used in advanced countries.

   _____

   _____

13.2 Who Pays?

The U.S. government collects taxes from a number of sources to fund federal government spending. Use the table below to answer the following questions:

1. How much did the federal government collect from individual income taxes in 1998?

   _____

   _____

2. How much did the federal government collect in corporate income taxes in 1998? __

   _____

3. What percentage of the total government receipts came from individual income taxes in 1998? _____

4. What percentage of the total government receipts came from corporate income taxes in 1998? _____

Step Ahead!

Using the information in the table, describe one or more trends in government tax receipts. _____

   _____

   _____

   _____

THE U.S. BUDGET
Receipts by Source
(In millions of dollars)

Fiscal Year	Individual income taxes	Corporate income taxes	Social insurance taxes and contributions	Excise taxes	Other	Total receipts
1987	$392,557	$ 83,926	$303,318	$32,457	$42,137	$ 854,396
1990	466,884	93,507	380,047	35,345	56,186	1,031,969
1996	656,417	171,824	509,414	54,014	61,393	1,453,062
1997	732,900	187,100	538,500	55,900	63,200	1,577,700
1998	748,600	192,600	564,800	55,300	70,200	1,631,600

Source: Office of Management and Budget.

13.3 Tax Time!

Welcome to the world of income taxes. On or before April 15 of each year, anyone who earns more than a small amount of money must report their income and pay any taxes due to the U.S. Internal Revenue Service. Filling out and mailing income tax forms and paying taxes is the way that people living in the U.S. pay for the services provided by the government. The form below is the first part of an actual federal income tax form. Use real information or create your own to fill in the blanks.

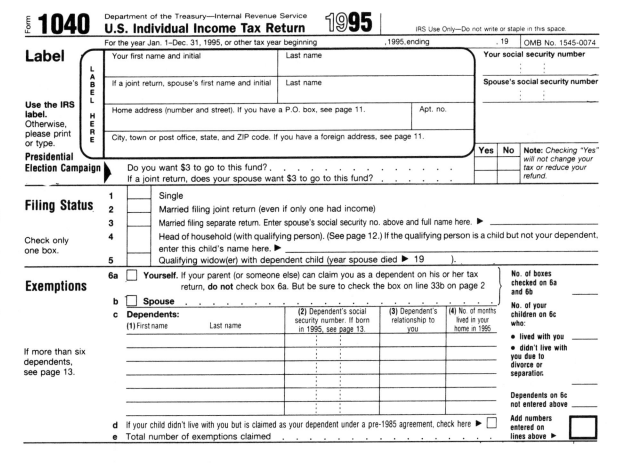

13.4 Where Does It All Go?

Federal government spending in 1998 reached a total of $1,689,900,000,000! Using the information in the table below, answer the following questions.

1. List the five items on which the government spent the most money in 1998, beginning with the most expensive:

_____   _____

_____   _____

_____

2. What percentage of total spending goes to these five items? _____

3. List four items for which spending has declined over the five years shown in the table.

_____   _____

_____   _____

Step Ahead!

Using the information in the table, draw a graph that represents some aspect of government spending over the five years shown in the table.

Spending
(In millions of dollars)

	1987	1990	1996	1997*	1998*
National defense	$281,999	$299,331	$265,748	$268,400	$266,400
International affairs	11,648	13,764	13,496	14,000	14,600
General space, science, technology	9,216	14,444	16,709	17,100	16,500
Energy	4,115	3,341	2,836	2,000	2,300
Natural resources and environment	13,363	17,080	21,614	23,200	23,400
Agriculture	26,606	11,958	9,159	10,000	11,900
Commerce and housing credit	6,435	67,600	-10,646	-11,200	2,400
Transportation	26,222	29,485	39,565	39,700	40,200
Community and regional development	5,051	8,498	10,685	12,700	12,100
Education, training, employment, and social services	29,724	38,755	52,001	52,900	56,500
Health	39,967	57,716	119,378	126,400	139,200
Medicare	75,120	98,102	174,225	191,400	199,500
Income security	123,282	147,076	225,989	232,800	244,200
Social security	207,353	248,623	349,676	366,200	383,100
Veterans benefits and services	26,750	29,058	36,985	40,200	41,300
Administration of justice	7,553	9,993	17,548	20,100	24,800
General government	7,565	10,734	11,892	13,200	13,200
Net interest	138,652	184,221	241,090	245,700	248,400
Undistributed offsetting receipts	-36,455	-36,615	-37,620	-49,700	-48,500
Total outlays	1,004,164	1,253,163	1,560,330	1,615,000	1,689,900
Deficit	-149,769	-221,194	-107,268	-37,300	-58,300

*Estimate.
Source: Office of Management and Budget

158

13.5 How Much Do You Owe?

When you file your income tax returns each year, you must refer to a tax table distributed by the Internal Revenue Service to determine how much tax money you owe the federal government. An actual tax table is shown below. Use it to determine the taxes owed by each of the people described here.

1. Single mother, head of household, with a taxable income of $32,012. _____

2. Married, filing with your spouse, with a taxable income of $39,949. _____

3. Single, with a taxable income of $35,246. _____

4. Married, filing separately, with a taxable income of $35,246. _____

5. Single, with a taxable income of $39,875. _____

1997 Tax Table—Continued

32,000

If line 38 (taxable income) is— At least	But less than	Single	Married filing jointly	Married filing separately	Head of a household
32,000	32,050	5,763	4,804	6,289	4,804
32,050	32,100	5,777	4,811	6,303	4,811
32,100	32,150	5,791	4,819	6,317	4,819
32,150	32,200	5,805	4,826	6,331	4,826
32,200	32,250	5,819	4,834	6,345	4,834
32,250	32,300	5,833	4,841	6,359	4,841
32,300	32,350	5,847	4,849	6,373	4,849
32,350	32,400	5,861	4,856	6,387	4,856
32,400	32,450	5,875	4,864	6,401	4,864
32,450	32,500	5,889	4,871	6,415	4,871
32,500	32,550	5,903	4,879	6,429	4,879
32,550	32,600	5,917	4,886	6,443	4,886
32,600	32,650	5,931	4,894	6,457	4,894
32,650	32,700	5,945	4,901	6,471	4,901
32,700	32,750	5,959	4,909	6,485	4,909
32,750	32,800	5,973	4,916	6,499	4,916
32,800	32,850	5,987	4,924	6,513	4,924
32,850	32,900	6,001	4,931	6,527	4,931
32,900	32,950	6,015	4,939	6,541	4,939
32,950	33,000	6,029	4,946	6,555	4,946

35,000

At least	But less than	Single	Married filing jointly	Married filing separately	Head of a household
35,000	35,050	6,603	5,254	7,129	5,511
35,050	35,100	6,617	5,261	7,143	5,525
35,100	35,150	6,631	5,269	7,157	5,539
35,150	35,200	6,645	5,276	7,171	5,553
35,200	35,250	6,659	5,284	7,185	5,567
35,250	35,300	6,673	5,291	7,199	5,581
35,300	35,350	6,687	5,299	7,213	5,595
35,350	35,400	6,701	5,306	7,227	5,609
35,400	35,450	6,715	5,314	7,241	5,623
35,450	35,500	6,729	5,321	7,255	5,637
35,500	35,550	6,743	5,329	7,269	5,651
35,550	35,600	6,757	5,336	7,283	5,665
35,600	35,650	6,771	5,344	7,297	5,679
35,650	35,700	6,785	5,351	7,311	5,693
35,700	35,750	6,799	5,359	7,325	5,707
35,750	35,800	6,813	5,366	7,339	5,721
35,800	35,850	6,827	5,374	7,353	5,735
35,850	35,900	6,841	5,381	7,367	5,749
35,900	35,950	6,855	5,389	7,381	5,763
35,950	36,000	6,869	5,396	7,395	5,777

38,000

At least	But less than	Single	Married filing jointly	Married filing separately	Head of a household
38,000	38,050	7,443	5,704	7,969	6,351
38,050	38,100	7,457	5,711	7,983	6,365
38,100	38,150	7,471	5,719	7,997	6,379
38,150	38,200	7,485	5,726	8,011	6,393
38,200	38,250	7,499	5,734	8,025	6,407
38,250	38,300	7,513	5,741	8,039	6,421
38,300	38,350	7,527	5,749	8,053	6,435
38,350	38,400	7,541	5,756	8,067	6,449
38,400	38,450	7,555	5,764	8,081	6,463
38,450	38,500	7,569	5,771	8,095	6,477
38,500	38,550	7,583	5,779	8,109	6,491
38,550	38,600	7,597	5,786	8,123	6,505
38,600	38,650	7,611	5,794	8,137	6,519
38,650	38,700	7,625	5,801	8,151	6,533
38,700	38,750	7,639	5,809	8,165	6,547
38,750	38,800	7,653	5,816	8,179	6,561
38,800	38,850	7,667	5,824	8,193	6,575
38,850	38,900	7,681	5,831	8,207	6,589
38,900	38,950	7,695	5,839	8,221	6,603
38,950	39,000	7,709	5,846	8,235	6,617

33,000

At least	But less than	Single	Married filing jointly	Married filing separately	Head of a household
33,000	33,050	6,043	4,954	6,569	4,954
33,050	33,100	6,057	4,961	6,583	4,965
33,100	33,150	6,071	4,969	6,597	4,979
33,150	33,200	6,085	4,976	6,611	4,993
33,200	33,250	6,099	4,984	6,625	5,007
33,250	33,300	6,113	4,991	6,639	5,021
33,300	33,350	6,127	4,999	6,653	5,035
33,350	33,400	6,141	5,006	6,667	5,049
33,400	33,450	6,155	5,014	6,681	5,063
33,450	33,500	6,169	5,021	6,695	5,077
33,500	33,550	6,183	5,029	6,709	5,091
33,550	33,600	6,197	5,036	6,723	5,105
33,600	33,650	6,211	5,044	6,737	5,119
33,650	33,700	6,225	5,051	6,751	5,133
33,700	33,750	6,239	5,059	6,765	5,147
33,750	33,800	6,253	5,066	6,779	5,161
33,800	33,850	6,267	5,074	6,793	5,175
33,850	33,900	6,281	5,081	6,807	5,189
33,900	33,950	6,295	5,089	6,821	5,203
33,950	34,000	6,309	5,096	6,835	5,217

36,000

At least	But less than	Single	Married filing jointly	Married filing separately	Head of a household
36,000	36,050	6,883	5,404	7,409	5,791
36,050	36,100	6,897	5,411	7,423	5,805
36,100	36,150	6,911	5,419	7,437	5,819
36,150	36,200	6,925	5,426	7,451	5,833
36,200	36,250	6,939	5,434	7,465	5,847
36,250	36,300	6,953	5,441	7,479	5,861
36,300	36,350	6,967	5,449	7,493	5,875
36,350	36,400	6,981	5,456	7,507	5,889
36,400	36,450	6,995	5,464	7,521	5,903
36,450	36,500	7,009	5,471	7,535	5,917
36,500	36,550	7,023	5,479	7,549	5,931
36,550	36,600	7,037	5,486	7,563	5,945
36,600	36,650	7,051	5,494	7,577	5,959
36,650	36,700	7,065	5,501	7,591	5,973
36,700	36,750	7,079	5,509	7,605	5,987
36,750	36,800	7,093	5,516	7,619	6,001
36,800	36,850	7,107	5,524	7,633	6,015
36,850	36,900	7,121	5,531	7,647	6,029
36,900	36,950	7,135	5,539	7,661	6,043
36,950	37,000	7,149	5,546	7,675	6,057

39,000

At least	But less than	Single	Married filing jointly	Married filing separately	Head of a household
39,000	39,050	7,723	5,854	8,249	6,631
39,050	39,100	7,737	5,861	8,263	6,645
39,100	39,150	7,751	5,869	8,277	6,659
39,150	39,200	7,765	5,876	8,291	6,673
39,200	39,250	7,779	5,884	8,305	6,687
39,250	39,300	7,793	5,891	8,319	6,701
39,300	39,350	7,807	5,899	8,333	6,715
39,350	39,400	7,821	5,906	8,347	6,729
39,400	39,450	7,835	5,914	8,361	6,743
39,450	39,500	7,849	5,921	8,375	6,757
39,500	39,550	7,863	5,929	8,389	6,771
39,550	39,600	7,877	5,936	8,403	6,785
39,600	39,650	7,891	5,944	8,417	6,799
39,650	39,700	7,905	5,951	8,431	6,813
39,700	39,750	7,919	5,959	8,445	6,827
39,750	39,800	7,933	5,966	8,459	6,841
39,800	39,850	7,947	5,974	8,473	6,855
39,850	39,900	7,961	5,981	8,487	6,869
39,900	39,950	7,975	5,989	8,501	6,883
39,950	40,000	7,989	5,996	8,515	6,897

13.6 Using Opportunity Sets

If you want to buy some books and you have $100 to spend, you may face a choice between buying paperbacks or hardcover books. You can use an *opportunity set* to help make your decision. An opportunity set is simply the group of options available to you. If paperbacks cost $10 each and hardbacks cost $20, your opportunity set looks like this:

paperbacks	hardcovers
0	5
2	4
4	3
6	2
8	1
10	0

You can buy 5 hardcover books, or 4 hardcovers and 2 paperbacks, or 3 hardcovers and 4 paperbacks, and so on. In each case, the total spent is $100.

Governments also face choices that involve a group of options and various tradeoffs. One of the most basic choices is between defense programs and social programs. If defense programs cost $20 billion each and social programs cost $10 billion each—and the budget is $100 billion—the opportunity set might look like this:

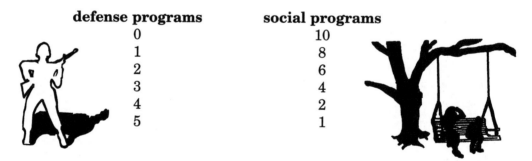

defense programs	social programs
0	10
1	8
2	6
3	4
4	2
5	1

Using the back of this sheet, pick two sets and discuss the possible consequences of each set.

Name _____   Date _____   Class _____

13.7 Tax-Free Day

Each year a private organization called the Tax Foundation estimates the number of days the average American must work to pay all of his or her federal, state, and local taxes. The map shows the first "tax-free" day for each state and the state's ranking compared with other states. Refer to the map to answer the following questions.

1. In which state do citizens work the most number of days to pay their tax bill?

_____

2. In which state do citizens work the fewest number of days to pay their tax bill?

_____

3. Create a bar graph comparing the tax-free days for the ten states with the highest taxes.

©1999 by The Center for Applied Research in Education

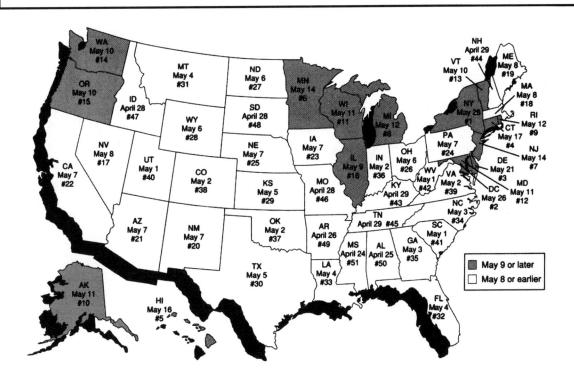

WA May 10 #14
OR May 10 #15
ID April 28 #47
MT May 4 #31
ND May 6 #27
MN May 14 #6
WI May 11 #11
MI May 12 #8
NH April 29 #44
VT May 10 #13
ME May 8 #19
MA May 8 #18
NY May 26 #1
RI May 12 #9
CT May 17 #9
NV May 8 #17
UT May 1 #40
WY May 6 #28
SD April 28 #48
IA May 7 #23
NE May 7 #25
IL May 9 #16
IN May 2 #36
OH May 6 #26
PA May 7 #24
NJ May 14 #7
DE May 21 #3
CA May 7 #22
CO May 2 #38
KS May 5 #29
MO April 28 #46
KY April 29 #43
WV May 1 #42
VA May 2 #39
MD May 11 #12
DC May 26 #2
AZ May 7 #21
NM May 7 #20
OK May 2 #37
AR April 26 #49
TN April 29 #45
NC May 3 #34
SC May 1 #41
AK May 11 #10
HI May 16 #5
TX May 5 #30
LA May 4 #33
MS April 24 #51
AL April 25 #50
GA May 3 #35
FL May 4 #32

■ May 9 or later
□ May 8 or earlier

161

13.8 Sharing the Burden

Different countries have different laws that determine who will shoulder the burden of tax payments. The table below shows the approximate percent distribution of tax receipts by type of tax. Use the information in the table to create pie charts in the circles provided below.

	Individual income taxes	Corporate income taxes	Social security contributions	Taxes on goods and services
U.S.	36.2	8.1	28.8	16.7
Japan	24.0	22.9	28.6	12.9
U.K.	26.6	10.6	18.1	31.4

1. Tax Receipts in the U.S. Percent distribution by type of tax.

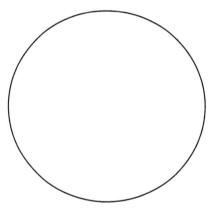

2. Tax Receipts in Japan. Percent distribution by type of tax.

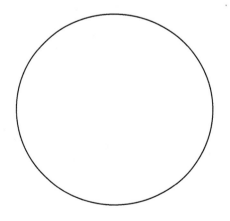

©1999 by The Center for Applied Research in Education

Section 14

Budgets, Debts, and Deficits

14.1 Budget Matters

Using at least six of the eight terms defined below, write a paragraph describing a bill expanding Social Security benefits to younger retirees.

appropriation bill: a piece of legislation that provides authority for federal agencies to spend money for specific purposes

authorization bill: a piece of legislation that establishes or continues the operation of a federal program or agency

budget authority: permission given to federal agencies by Congress, allowing them to enter into spending agreements

budget resolution: a planning guide used by Congress that sets out guidelines for spending

debt: the total accumulation of all deficits

deficit: the shortfall that occurs when the government spends more than it takes in during a fiscal year

entitlement program: a program that requires the federal government to make payments to people who meet certain eligibility requirements, such as Social Security, Medicare, and unemployment benefits

expenditures: payments made by the federal government

14.2 Balancing the Budget

Use the information in the graph and the definitions of terms to write a paragraph describing trends in the federal budget from 1945 to 1996. Be sure to include all seven terms in your paragraph.

Balanced Budget: A budget in which receipts equal outlays.

Deficit: The amount by which outlays exceed receipts in a given fiscal period. (A surplus would be the amount by which receipts exceed outlays.)

Fiscal Year: The fiscal year for the federal government begins on October 1

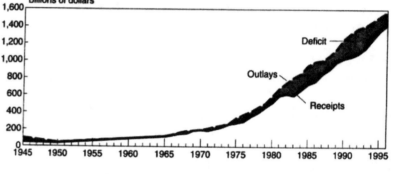

Federal Budget Summary: 1945 to 1996

and ends on September 30. The fiscal year is designated by the calendar year in which it ends; for example, fiscal year 1996 begins on October 1, 1995 and ends on September 30, 1996.

Outlays: Outlays are payments made (generally through the issuance of checks or disbursement of cash) to cover obligations. Outlays during a fiscal year may be for payment of obligations incurred in prior years or in the same year.

Public Debt: Cumulative amounts borrowed by the Treasury Department or the Federal Financing Bank from the public or from another fund or account.

Receipts: Collections from the public and from payments by participants in certain social insurance and other federal programs. These collections consist primarily of tax revenues and social insurance premiums. Total receipts are compared with total outlays in calculating the budget surplus or deficit.

Trust Funds: Funds collected and used by the federal government for carrying out specific purposes and programs according to terms of a trust agreement or statute, such as the Social Security trust funds.

_____

_____

_____

_____

_____

_____

14.3 Social Security

The Great Depression of the 1930s dramatized the fact that many American workers were financially dependent on factors beyond their own control. The Social Security Act, signed into law by President Franklin Delano Roosevelt in 1935, helped to alleviate this situation.

The Social Security system provides "a minimum floor of protection" for three groups of people: retired workers, disabled workers, and families who face a loss of income due to the death of a family wage earner. The system is designed so that there is a clear link between how much a worker pays into the system and how much he or she will receive in benefits. Basically, high-wage earners get more; low-wage earners get less. At the same time, the Social Security benefit formula is weighted in favor of low-wage earners, who have fewer resources to save or invest during their working years. Social Security retirement benefits replace approximately 60 percent of the pre-retirement earnings of a low-wage earner, 42 percent of an average-wage earner, and 26 percent of a high-wage earner.

Basically, the Social Security program is a way of providing a base of economic security in today's society. It allows older Americans to live independently. Social Security also provides a valuable package of disability and survivors insurance to workers over their working lifetimes.

Retired workers can receive Social Security benefits as early as age 62. The age for full benefits will gradually rise in the next century, until it reaches age 67 in 2027 for people born in 1960 or later. Social Security has always been part of a "three-legged stool" that could solidly support a comfortable retirement. The other two legs of the stool are pension income and savings/investments.

Virtually all American workers pay Social Security taxes. If you work and you take a look at your pay stub—the part that shows how much is taken out for various taxes and benefits each pay period—you'll see deductions for Social Security and Medicare. On some pay stubs it's called FICA, which stands for Federal Insurance Contributions Act, the law that authorized payroll deductions for Social Security. The tax rate of 7.65 percent covers both Social Security and Medicare. Employers match a worker's Social Security tax payment.

Answer the following questions.

1. What is the purpose of the Social Security system? _____

_____

2. List the three groups of people who might receive Social Security benefits.

_____

_____

3. What determines the amount of benefits that will be paid? _____

_____

4. Who pays Social Security taxes and how much do they pay? _____

_____

14.4 Federal Spending

The table shows federal outlays by branch of government for 1990-1996. Read the information, then use the data to complete the graphs below.

Federal Outlays, by Branch and Detailed Function: 1990 to 1996
In millions of dollars.

BRANCH AND FUNCTION	1990	1992	1993	1994	1995	1996, est.
Total outlays	1,252,515	1,380,856	1,408,675	1,460,841	1,519,133	1,572,411
Legislative branch.	2,241	2,677	2,406	2,552	2,625	2,695
The Judiciary	1,646	2,308	2,628	2,677	2,910	3,297
Funds appropriated to President [1]	10,087	11,113	11,526	10,511	11,161	10,445
Departments:						
Agriculture	46,012	56,437	63,144	60,753	56,665	54,840
Commerce	3,734	2,567	2,798	2,915	3,401	3,789
Defense-Military	289,755	286,632	278,574	268,646	259,556	254,325
Defense-Civil	24,975	28,270	29,266	30,407	31,669	32,255
Education	23,109	26,047	30,290	24,699	31,322	30,404
Energy	12,084	15,523	16,942	17,839	17,617	14,678
Health and Human Services	175,531	231,560	253,835	278,901	303,081	327,429
Housing and Urban Development	20,167	24,470	25,181	25,845	29,044	26,432
Interior	5,790	6,539	6,784	6,900	7,405	6,939
Justice	6,507	9,802	10,170	10,005	10,788	12,964
Labor [2]	25,215	47,078	44,651	37,047	32,090	34,404
State	3,979	5,007	5,384	5,718	5,344	5,500
Transportation.	28,650	32,491	34,457	37,228	38,777	38,994
Treasury	255,172	292,987	298,804	307,577	348,579	364,956
Veterans Affairs.	28,998	33,897	35,487	37,401	37,771	37,606
Independent agencies:						
Environmental Protection Agency	5,108	5,950	5,930	5,855	6,351	6,329
General Services Administration	-123	469	743	334	707	469
NASA [3]	12,429	13,961	14,305	13,695	13,378	14,190
Office of Personnel Management	31,949	35,596	36,794	38,596	41,276	42,374
Small Business Administration	692	546	785	779	677	957
Other independent agencies	72,808	18,007	-11,428	10,281	4,199	9,503
Undistributed offsetting receipts.	-98,930	-117,111	-119,711	-123,469	-137,628	-139,866

Source: U.S. Department of Commerce.

1. Percentage of total outlays going to each of the three branches of government, 1990 and 1996

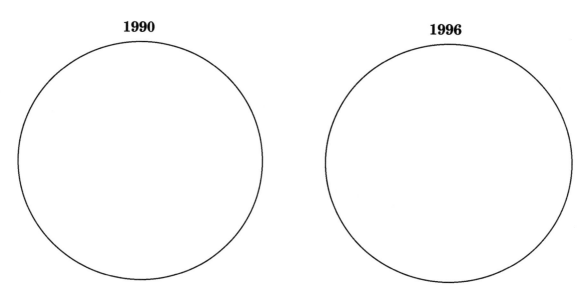

1990   **1996**

2. Outlays for the fifteen departments, 1996

14.5 Where Do Deficits Come From?

The table shows federal government receipts, outlays, and the annual surplus or deficit, in millions of dollars, for the years 1945–1996. Use data from five-year intervals to create line graphs in the boxes.

YEAR	Receipts	OUTLAYS				Surplus or deficit (-)
		Total	Human resources	National defense	Percent of GDP	
1945	45,159	92,712	1,859	82,965	43.7	-47,553
1950	39,443	42,562	14,221	13,724	16.0	-3,119
1955	65,451	68,444	14,908	42,729	17.8	-2,993
1960	92,492	92,191	26,184	48,130	18.3	301
1965	116,817	118,228	36,576	50,620	17.6	-1,411
1970	192,807	195,649	75,349	81,692	19.9	-2,842
1972	207,309	230,681	107,211	79,174	20.1	-23,373
1973	230,799	245,707	119,522	76,681	19.3	-14,908
1974	263,224	269,359	135,783	79,347	19.2	-6,135
1975	279,090	332,332	173,245	86,509	22.0	-53,242
1976	298,060	371,792	203,594	89,619	22.1	-73,732
1976	81,232	95,975	52,065	22,269	21.6	-14,744
1977	355,559	409,218	221,895	97,241	21.3	-53,659
1978	399,561	458,746	242,329	104,495	21.3	-59,186
1979	463,302	504,032	267,574	116,342	20.7	-40,729
1980	517,112	590,947	313,374	133,995	22.3	-73,835
1981	599,272	678,249	362,022	157,513	22.9	-78,976
1982	617,766	745,755	388,681	185,309	23.9	-127,989
1983	600,562	808,380	426,003	209,903	24.4	-207,818
1984	666,457	851,846	432,042	227,413	23.1	-185,388
1985	734,057	946,391	471,822	252,748	23.9	-212,334
1986	769,091	990,336	481,594	273,375	23.5	-221,245
1987	854,143	1,003,911	502,196	281,999	22.5	-149,769
1988	908,954	1,064,140	533,404	290,361	22.1	-155,187
1989	990,691	1,143,172	568,668	303,559	22.1	-152,481
1990	1,031,321	1,252,515	619,329	299,331	22.8	-221,194
1991	1,054,272	1,323,631	689,666	273,292	23.3	-269,359
1992	1,090,453	1,380,856	772,440	298,350	23.3	-290,403
1993	1,153,535	1,408,675	827,535	291,086	22.5	-255,140
1994	1,257,737	1,460,841	869,414	281,642	22.0	-203,104
1995	1,355,213	1,519,133	923,769	272,066	21.7	-163,920
1996, est. . .	1,426,775	1,572,411	969,942	265,556	21.4	-145,636

Source: U.S. Department of Commerce.

1. Receipts and total outlays, 1945–1996

2. Government spending as a percent of GDP

14.6 What Does a Budget Do?

The federal budget is:

• a plan for how the government spends its citizens' tax money. What activities are funded? How much does it spend for defense, national parks, the FBI, Medicare, and meat and fish inspection?

• a plan for how the government pays for its activities. How much revenue does it raise through different kinds of taxes—income taxes, excise taxes, and social insurance payroll taxes?

• a plan for government borrowing. If spending is greater than revenues, the government runs a deficit. To finance deficits, the government has to borrow money. Government borrowing adds to the national debt.

• something that affects the nation's economy. Some types of spending—such as improvements in education and support for science and technology—increase productivity and raise incomes in the future.

• something that is affected by the nation's economy. When the economy is doing well, people are earning more and unemployment is low. In this atmosphere, revenues increase and the deficit shrinks.

• an historical record. The budget reports on how the government has spent money in the past, and how that spending was financed.

The budget is set for one fiscal year. The 1999 budget is a document that embodies the President's budget proposal to Congress for fiscal 1999, the fiscal year that begins on October 1, 1998. This budget was the first proposed balanced budget in nearly three decades.

Total government spending accounts for about one-third of the national economy. Federal spending is about two-thirds of this amount, or 20 percent of GDP.

The federal budget, of course, is not the only budget that affects the economy. The budgets of state and local governments have an impact as well. While federal government spending was about 20 percent of the Gross Domestic Product (or GDP, which measures the size of the economy) in 1997, state and local governments spending was about another nine percent.

State and local governments are independent of the federal government, and they have their own sources of revenue (taxes and borrowing). But the federal government supplements state and local revenues by making grants to them. Of the $971 billion that state and local governments spent in 1997, $221 billion came from federal grants.

Answer the following questions.

1. What is the purpose of the federal budget?

_____

_____

2. What happens if spending exceeds revenues?

_____

_____

3. How does government spending affect the national economy?

_____

_____

4. How is federal spending related to state and local government spending?

_____

_____

©1999 by The Center for Applied Research in Education

14.7. Understanding Deficits

Put simply, a deficit occurs when spending exceeds revenues in any year—just as a surplus occurs when revenues exceed spending. Generally, to finance our deficits, the Treasury borrows money. The debt is the sum total of our deficits, minus our surpluses, over the years.

The deficit is not a new phenomenon; the government incurred its first in 1792, and it generated 70 annual deficits between 1900 and 1997. Deficits began increasing dramatically in the 1980s, but have declined. President Bill Clinton's budget reached a balance in 1999.

Why have deficits become such a perennial problem for budget decisionmakers? Because spending has been growing faster than revenues. Revenues have stayed relatively constant, at around 17 to 20 percent of GDP, since the 1960s. In that time, however, outlays have grown from about 17 percent of GDP in 1965 to up to nearly 24 percent in 1983 before falling to 20 percent today. Much of the spending growth has come in Social Security, Medicare, Medicaid, and interest payments. Between 1965 and 1997, spending on Social Security, Medicare, Medicaid, and interest as a percentage of GDP grew, while spending on defense fell.

The deficit forces the government to borrow money in the private capital markets. That borrowing competes with (1) borrowing by businesses that want to build factories and machines that make workers more productive and raise incomes, and (2) borrowing by families who hope to buy new homes, cars, and other goods. The competition for funds tends to produce higher interest rates.

Deficits increase the federal debt and, with it, the government's obligation to pay interest. The more it must pay in interest, the less it has available to spend on education, law enforcement, and other important services, or the more it must collect in taxes—forever after. The government will spend 14 percent of its budget to pay interest in 1999.

The federal interest burden grew substantially in the 1980s, both in actual dollars and as a percentage of federal income tax revenues. By 1999, net interest spending will be nearly as much as the government will spend on national defense, although it is declining as a percent of the budget with the President's balanced budget in 1999.

Answer the following questions.

1. What is a deficit?

_____

2. Why have deficits become a constant feature of the U.S. budget?

_____

_____

_____

3. Why are deficits a problem?

_____

_____

_____

_____

14.8 Deficits and Debt

If the government incurs a deficit, it must borrow from the public. Federal borrowing involves the sale, to the public, of notes and bonds of varying sizes and time periods. The cumulative amount of borrowing from the public—i.e., the debt held by the public—is the most important measure of federal debt because it is what the government has borrowed in the private markets over the years, and it determines how much the government pays in interest to the public.

Debt held by the public was $3.8 trillion at the end of 1997—roughly the net effect of deficits and surpluses over the last 200 years. Debt held by the public does not include debt the government owes itself—the total of all trust fund surpluses and deficits over the years, like the Social Security surpluses, that the law says must be invested in federal securities.

The sum of debt held by the public and debt the government owes itself is called Gross Federal Debt. At the end of 1997, it totaled $5.4 trillion.

Another measure of federal debt is debt subject to legal limit, which is similar to Gross Federal Debt. When the government reaches the limit, it loses its authority to borrow more to finance its spending; then, the President and Congress must enact a law to increase the limit.

The government's ability to finance its debt is tied to the size and strength of the economy, or Gross Domestic Product (GDP). Debt held by the public was 47 percent of GDP at the end of 1997. As a percentage of GDP, debt held by the public was highest at the end of World War II, at 109 percent, then fell to 24 percent in 1974 before gradually rising to a peak in the middle 1990s.

That decline, from 109 to 24 percent, occurred because the economy grew faster than the debt accumulated; debt held by the public rose from $242 billion to $344 billion in those years, but the economy grew faster.

Individuals and institutions in the United States hold two-thirds of debt held by the public. The rest is held in foreign countries.

Answer the following questions.

1. What is the federal debt? _____

_____

2. To whom is the money owed? _____

3. How large is the debt? _____

4. How is the strength of the economy related to the debt? _____

_____

_____

14.9 Deficit Reduction Efforts

Read the information below about deficit reduction. Then write your own summary of deficit reduction efforts on the back of this sheet.

©1999 by The Center for Applied Research in Education

Ever since the deficit soared in the early 1980s, successive Presidents and Congresses have tried to cut it. Until recently, they met with only limited success.

In the early 1980s, President Ronald Reagan and Congress agreed on a large tax cut, but could not agree about cutting spending; the President wanted to cut domestic spending more than Congress, while Congress sought fewer defense funds than the President wanted. By 1985, both sides were ready for drastic measures. That year, they enacted the Balanced Budget and Emergency Deficit Control Act, better known as Gramm–Rudman–Hollings (GRH). It set annual deficit targets for five years, declining to a balanced budget in 1991. If necessary, GRH required across-the-board cuts in programs to comply with the deficit targets.

Faced with the prospect of huge spending cuts in 1987, however, the President and Congress amended the law, postponing a balanced budget until 1993. By 1990, President George Bush and Congress enacted spending cuts and tax increases that were designed to cut the accumulated deficits by about $500 billion over five years. They also enacted the Budget Enforcement Act (BEA). Rather than set annual deficit targets, the BEA was designed to limit discretionary spending while ensuring that any new entitlement programs or tax cuts did not make the deficit worse.

For what it was designed to do, the law worked. It did, in fact, limit discretionary spending and force proponents of new entitlements and tax cuts to find ways to finance them. But the deficit, which government and private experts said would fall, actually rose. Why? Because the recession of the early 1990s reduced individual and corporate tax revenues and increased spending that is tied to economic fluctuations. Federal health-care spending also continued to grow rapidly.

In 1993, President Bill Clinton and Congress made another effort to cut the deficit. They enacted a five-year deficit reduction package of spending cuts and higher revenues. The law was designed to cut the accumulated deficits from 1994 to 1998 by about $500 billion. Clearly, the President's deficit reduction efforts have paid off. The deficit fell from $290 billion in 1992 to $22 billion in 1997, and by nearly 95 percent as a share of GDP, to 0.3 percent.

Although the 1993 plan had exceeded all expectations in reducing the deficit, the task of reaching balance would require one final push. That came with the historic 1997 Balanced Budget Act (BBA). Originally designed to balance the budget by 2002, the BBA actually allowed the President to balance the budget three years ahead of schedule, in 1999.

14.10 Creating a Budget

Read the following account of the budget process. Then write a list of numbered steps for creating a budget.

The President and Congress both play major roles in developing the federal budget. The law requires that, by the first Monday in February, the President submit to Congress his proposed federal budget for the next fiscal year, which begins October 1. The White House's Office of Management and Budget (OMB) prepares the budget proposal, after receiving direction from the President and consulting with his senior advisors and officials from Cabinet departments and other agencies.

Through the budget process, the President and Congress decide how much to spend and tax in any one fiscal year. More specifically, they decide how much to spend on each activity, ensure that the government spends no more and spends it only for that activity, and report on that spending at the end of each budget cycle. Only after the Congress passes, and the President signs, the required spending bills has the government created its actual budget.

Congress first must pass a "budget resolution"—a framework within which the members will make their decisions about spending and taxes. It includes targets for total spending, total revenues, the deficit, and allocations within the spending target for the two types of spending—discretionary and mandatory.

• Discretionary spending, which accounts for 33 percent of all federal spending, is what the President and Congress must decide to spend for the next year through the 13 annual appropriations bills. It includes money for such activities as the FBI and the Coast Guard, for housing and education, for space exploration and highway construction, and for defense and foreign aid.

• Mandatory spending, which accounts for 67 percent of all spending, is authorized by permanent laws, not by the 13 annual appropriations bills. It includes entitlements—such as Social Security and veterans' benefits. It also includes interest on the national debt. The President and Congress can change the law in order to change the spending on entitlements and other mandatory programs—but they don't have to.

For discretionary programs, Congress and the President must act each year to provide spending authority. For mandatory programs, they may act in order to change the spending that current laws require.

Currently, the law imposes a limit, or "cap," through 2002 on total annual discretionary spending. Within the cap, however, the President and Congress can, and often do, change the spending levels from year to year for the thousands of individual federal spending programs.

Once Congress passes the budget resolution, it turns its attention to passing the 13 annual appropriations bills and, if it chooses, "authorizing" bills to change the laws governing mandatory spending and revenues. Finally, Congress must reach some agreement with the President about the changes it has made.

Section 15

Federal Economic Policy

15.1 Policy Terms

Write the number of each definition on the line next to the correct term.

_____ **Deficit financing**

_____ **Deregulation**

_____ **Fiscal policy**

_____ **Income policy**

_____ **Laissez-faire policy**

_____ **National debt**

_____ **Nationalization**

_____ **Privatization**

_____ **Supply-side approach**

1. A government policy of nonintervention in economic activities characteristic of free-market economies.

2. The sale of state-owned industries to private investors.

3. Removal of protective controls from business activities in order to promote competition.

4. Strategic overspending of public funds by a government in order to pump money into a depressed economy and create new jobs. This is financed by borrowing.

5. Government policy related to raising revenue through taxation, public-sector borrowing, and government expenditures.

6. Government policy of controlling salary increases as a way of curbing inflations.

7. The process of bringing an industry under state ownership.

8. The money borrowed by a government and not yet repaid.

9. Economic approach based on the theory that the most effective way of increasing output is through the removal of tax disincentives to induce people to work harder and leave more money available for investment.

15.2 Trade Talk

Study the terms defined below, then write your own story about trade using all of the defined terms.

balance of trade: The difference between the value of imports and exports. A country that imports more than it exports has an "unfavorable" balance of trade.

currency devaluation: A nation's money is devalued when its government deliberately reduces its value in relation to the currencies of other nations.

Export–Import Bank of the U.S.: The Ex–Im Bank assists in financing, insuring, and guaranteeing of certain aspects of the import–export business, with the general goal of encouraging international trade with the U.S.

International Monetary Fund: The IMF makes loans and provides other services intended to stabilize world currencies and foster orderly and balanced trade.

most-favored nation: A status bestowed by the U.S. on trading partners with which it has a good relationship.

Organization for Economic Cooperation and Development: Founded in 1961 to replace the Organization for European Economic Cooperation, which was set up in connection with the Marshall Plan, the OECD is a forum for its members to coordinate economic policies.

Organization of Petroleum Exporting Countries: Established in 1960 to link countries whose main source of export earnings is petroleum, OPEC helps determine oil production and prices.

tariff: A tax levied on imported goods that makes them more expensive and less appealing to consumers.

World Bank: An organization created to make loans primarily in developing countries, with the stipulation that the country's government must guarantee the loan.

_____
_____
_____
_____
_____
_____
_____
_____
_____
_____

(Use the back of this sheet if you need more space.)

15.3 Trade Deficits

A trade deficit is the difference between the value of a nation's imports and exports. In 1997, the U.S. imported $113.7 billion more than it exported—it ran a deficit in trade. The table shows the U.S. trade deficit from 1987–1997. In the box provided create a line graph showing the deficit. Be sure to provide labels and a title for the graph. Then write a summary of the trends shown in the graph.

$ billions

1987	$153.4
1988	115.9
1989	92.3
1990	81.2
1991	31.0
1992	39.2
1993	72.0
1994	104.4
1995	105.6
1996	111.0
1997	113.7

Source: U.S. Department of Commerce.

15.4 Terms of Trade

Study the words below until you are familiar with their meanings. Then find them in the puzzle. The words may be vertical, horizontal, upside down, backwards, or diagonal. Circle each item when you find it. You will find some terms more than once.

Balance of payments: The difference between a country's income and outgoings over a period of time.

Devaluation: Reduction in the value of a currency.

Embargo: An order from a government to halt exports and/or imports.

European Monetary System: Organization set up in 1979 by members of the European Economic Community (EEC) with the aim of stabilizing and harmonizing European currencies.

Free trade area: A loose grouping of countries within which tariffs and barriers to trade are removed.

Import controls: Controls limiting the number of imports entering a country, such as import quotas and tariffs.

Quotas: A restriction placed on imports or exports, usually to protect fledgling industries, to conserve raw materials that are in short supply, or to maintain higher price levels.

Tariff: Tax or duty levied on imported or exported goods.

```
D D P L J I M P O R T C O N T R O L S N I P
T A R I F F F R E E T R A D E A R E A G O P
A S E B A L A N C E O F P A Y M E N T S D I
R M N M G F D D C M S A T O U Q S A T X R D
I B N G B T W D C S B D E V A L U A T I O N
F K L H D A S E U P I A F F I R A T G O T R
F X K H N B R A E E R R B A L A N C E O F S
Q U O T A S S G T G S I G P A Y M E N T S I
O K P U Y R W Y O N B O O B C D E R E W G H
M E T S Y S Y R A T E N O M N A E P O R U E
```

©1999 by The Center for Applied Research in Education

15.5 Antitrust Laws

There are three major federal antitrust laws: The Sherman Antitrust Act, the Clayton Act and the Federal Trade Commission Act.

The *Sherman Antitrust Act,* passed in 1890, is the principal law expressing a national commitment to a free market economy in which competition free from private and governmental restraints leads to the best results for the consumers. Congress felt so strongly about this law that there was only one dissenting vote to the Act. The Sherman Act outlaws all contracts, combinations, and conspiracies that unreasonably restrain interstate trade. This includes agreements among competitors to fix prices, rig bids, and control customers.

The *Clayton Act* is a civil statute that was passed in 1914 and significantly amended in 1950. The Clayton Act prohibits mergers or acquisitions that are likely to lessen competition. Under the Act, the government challenges those mergers that a careful economic analysis shows are likely to increase prices to consumers.

The *Federal Trade Commission Act* prohibits unfair methods of competition in interstate commerce. It also created the Federal Trade Commission to police violations of the Act.

There are three main ways in which the federal antitrust laws are enforced: criminal and civil enforcement actions brought by the Antitrust Division of the Department of Justice, civil enforcement actions brought by the Federal Trade Commission, and lawsuits brought by private parties asserting damage claims.

Most states also have antitrust laws closely paralleling the federal antitrust laws. The state laws generally apply to violations that occur wholly in one state. These state laws are enforced similarly to federal laws through the office of each state attorney general.

Answer the following questions.

1. What is the purpose of antitrust laws? _____

_____

_____

2. Name the three main antitrust laws. _____

_____

_____

3. Summarize the provisions of the Sherman Act and the Clayton Act. _____

_____

_____

4. Give an example of an action that would be illegal under the antitrust laws. _____

_____

_____

15.6 Regulating Relationships— Child Labor

Part of a nation's economic policy includes regulating relationships between people: employers and employees, buyers and sellers, importers and exporters. The United States has a number of laws regulating the relationship between employers and employees. One of the laws that affects almost all employers and employees is the Fair Labor Standards Act (FLSA), which establishes minimum wage, overtime pay, and child labor standards.

One of the most important provisions of the FLSA is the minimum wage law, which requires employers to pay a minimum wage. Congress passes laws to increase the minimum wage from time to time. The minimum wage was set at $5.15 per hour in 1997.

Another important provision of the FLSA requires employers to pay overtime pay at a rate of not less than one and one-half times the regular rate of pay for hours beyond 40 hours of work in a workweek.

The child labor provisions of the FLSA are designed to protect children from employment in jobs that interfere with their education or may be harmful to their health or well-being. The provisions include restrictions on hours of work for minors under 16 and lists of hazardous occupations that the Secretary of Labor finds to be too dangerous for minors to perform. Generally, youths are not allowed to work in mining, manufacturing, or in jobs that require the use of potentially dangerous machinery or exposure to dangerous working conditions.

Basically, the law says that youths 18 years and older may perform any job for unlimited hours. Youths 16 and 17 may perform any nonhazardous job for unlimited hours. Youths 14 and 15 years old may work outside school hours in nonhazardous jobs, but they may not work more than 3 hours on a school day, 18 hours in a school week. Fourteen is the minimum age for most nonfarm work. However, at any age, youths may deliver newspapers, perform in entertainment productions, or work for their parents in nonhazardous jobs.

The federal government's Department of Labor investigates violations of the FLSA and enforces the provisions of the Act to protect employees.

Summarize the child labor provisions of the FLSA.

_____

_____

_____

_____

_____

_____

_____

15.7 Tracking Enforcement

An important provision of the Fair Labor Standards Act (FLSA) requires employers to pay overtime pay at a rate of not less than one and one-half times the regular rate of pay for hours beyond 40 hours of work in a workweek. The federal government's Department of Labor investigates violations of the FLSA and enforces the provisions of the Act to protect employees from employers who fail to pay overtime.

The table below shows the number of violations of the overtime pay provisions in ten industries in 1995, the number of employees affected by the violations, and the amount of overtime pay that was owed to those employees. Read the table, then create a graph to illustrate the information.

FLSA Overtime Violations 1995
Top Ten Industries

Industry	Number of actions	Number of employees	Amount
All industries	44,158	180,724	$119,919,861
Business services	4,953	20,191	$9,585,886
Health services	2,457	16,596	$7,707,097
Construction	2,823	13,588	$10,852,108
Eating and drinking	5,902	10,039	$4,139,287
Local government	740	9,876	$14,423,736
Transportation equipment	194	7,694	$7,660,588
Garment	1,463	6,099	$1,532,822
Social services	1,624	7,096	$2,131,743
State government	262	5,394	$6,412,677
Amusement/recreation	644	4,808	$2,741,053

Source: U.S. Department of Labor, Employment Standards Administration.

15.8 Policy Debates

The terms listed below always surface in any broad debate about economic policy. Find them in the puzzle and circle them.

cost of living
cost-push inflation
currency
deflation

inflation
demand-pull
hyperinflation
inflation

monetarism
money supply
retail price index
stagflation

L	D	K	N	C	E	G	C	W	R	M	N	F	K	P	T	E	N	E	R
B	R	E	J	T	G	M	O	G	E	Y	U	G	F	K	E	B	K	I	L
O	H	C	S	E	Y	K	S	J	D	C	B	S	N	K	M	G	R	Y	A
J	X	G	I	R	B	L	T	S	U	G	E	Y	W	J	K	O	S	N	P
Q	D	E	M	A	N	D	P	U	L	L	I	N	F	L	A	T	I	O	N
I	W	L	E	Y	J	P	U	K	B	S	E	K	G	D	K	E	E	D	Z
N	C	A	C	F	E	H	S	M	K	O	Y	U	X	E	G	T	K	H	N
F	U	K	G	S	U	O	H	S	I	K	J	D	V	Q	E	T	U	Y	S
L	R	H	S	T	K	I	I	Y	R	W	G	J	I	O	T	E	P	S	K
A	R	L	S	X	F	S	N	P	L	K	M	V	S	Y	I	J	G	R	S
T	E	R	K	E	B	L	F	N	D	X	S	A	U	E	L	P	I	Y	H
I	N	R	T	I	J	N	L	C	D	Z	U	S	S	B	T	U	S	D	F
O	C	L	P	W	D	G	A	J	B	J	I	O	L	P	J	D	H	L	I
N	Y	E	F	C	O	S	T	O	F	L	I	V	I	N	G	T	S	Z	A
Y	N	H	Y	P	E	R	I	N	F	L	A	T	I	O	N	U	T	G	A
L	L	K	B	G	T	Y	O	O	Y	E	W	Y	K	Y	A	D	A	F	V
S	D	F	G	H	H	J	N	W	E	R	Y	U	Y	M	K	E	G	C	F
K	N	S	Q	E	T	S	M	G	U	K	K	A	B	V	F	F	F	A	I
D	I	L	F	V	J	S	O	E	A	J	C	X	G	S	Y	L	L	U	W
M	Z	A	V	E	U	O	N	K	I	E	T	F	G	R	U	A	A	H	S
G	E	J	K	M	B	D	E	S	W	J	R	Q	A	Z	G	T	T	J	K
X	T	U	I	W	D	H	T	D	K	L	V	N	K	U	T	I	I	U	I
B	J	G	K	O	R	E	A	S	E	K	L	P	J	R	D	O	O	H	G
R	E	T	A	I	L	P	R	I	C	E	I	N	D	E	X	N	N	X	D
K	H	A	Z	A	D	K	I	M	S	X	F	G	K	U	H	S	D	E	R
J	C	M	O	N	E	Y	S	U	P	P	L	Y	D	J	Y	I	E	V	Z
K	J	N	F	S	A	W	M	R	T	U	L	M	X	Z	A	I	Y	K	M

15.9 Policy Reports

Draft a speech to Congress on economic policy concerning the budget and the federal deficit. Use all of the terms defined below, and underline the terms in your speech.

Balanced Budget
A balanced budget occurs when total revenues equal total outlays for a fiscal year.

Balanced Budget and Emergency Deficit Control Act of 1985 (Gramm-Rudman-Hollings, or GRH)
The Balanced Budget and Emergency Deficit Control Act of 1985 was designed to end deficit spending. It set annual deficit targets for five years, declining to a balanced budget in 1991. If necessary, it required across-the-board cuts in programs to comply with the deficit targets. It was never fully implemented.

Budget Enforcement Act (BEA) of 1990
The BEA is the law that was designed to limit discretionary spending while ensuring that any new entitlement program or tax cuts did not make the deficit worse. It set annual limits on total discretionary spending and created "pay-as-you-go" rules for any changes in entitlements and taxes.

"Cap"
A "cap" is a legal limit on annual discretionary spending.

Deficit
The deficit is the difference produced when spending exceeds revenues in a fiscal year.

Gross Domestic Product (GDP)
GDP is the standard measurement of the size of the economy. It is the total production of goods and services within the United States.

"Pay-As-You-Go"
Set forth by the BEA, "pay-as-you-go" refers to requirements that new spending proposals on entitlements or tax cuts must be offset by cuts in other entitlements or by other tax increases, to ensure that the deficit does not rise.

15.10 Policy in the Press

Printed below is an actual press release from the White House announcing a new Executive Order. Read the press release, then write a story for the evening news.

White House
Office of the Press Secretary
_____

For Immediate Release March 13, 1998

PRESIDENT CLINTON SIGNS EXECUTIVE ORDER
ESTABLISHING NATIONAL TASK FORCE ON
EMPLOYMENT OF PEOPLE WITH DISABILITIES

The President today signed an Executive Order establishing a National Task Force on Employment of Adults with Disabilities that will create a coordinated and aggressive national policy to bring working-age individuals with disabilities into gainful employment at a rate approaching that of the general adult population.

"Since 1993, we have created 15 million new jobs. But the unemployment rate among people with disabilities is far too high, and that is why I'm so pleased to sign today an executive order that will design a strategy to make equality of opportunity, full participation, inclusion, and economic self-sufficiency realities for all 30 million working-age Americans with disabilities," declared President Clinton.

Charged with developing and recommending to the President a federal policy to reduce employment barriers for persons with disabilities, the Task Force will submit four reports, the first by November 15, 1998, and the last on July 26, 2002, the 10th anniversary of the initial implementation of the employment provisions of the Americans with Disabilities Act. Alexis M. Herman, Secretary of Labor, will Chair the Task Force. Tony Coelho, Chairman of the President's Committee on Employment of People with Disabilities, will serve as Vice-Chair.

Key components of the Task Force's directive include analyzing existing programs and policies to determine what changes, modifications and innovations may be necessary to remove barriers to work; developing and recommending options to address the barrier of health insurance coverage; analyzing youth programs related to employment and the outcomes of those programs for young people with disabilities; and evaluating whether federal studies related to employment and training can and should include a statistically significant sample of adults with disabilities.

15.11 Finding Solutions

Part of policy making involves finding solutions to problems in the economy and the work world. Below is an actual statement from the U.S. Department of Labor that describes a real problem—teen safety on the job. Read the statement, then propose a solution—new legislation or more safety regulations, for example—to reduce teen workplace injuries.

This summer, more than 3 million teens under 18 will work at summer jobs. For the majority of teens, work will be a rewarding experience. However, a sizable number of teens will risk being injured or killed on the job. Statistics show that each year:

- 70 teens are killed on the job, about one every 5 days.
- 210,000 working teens are injured.
- 70,000 teens are injured seriously enough to require hospital emergency room treatment.

Adolescent workers are protected by two laws enforced by the Department of Labor, the Fair Labor Standards Act (FLSA) and the Occupational Safety and Health Act. However, enforcement efforts can only go so far.

Most teens (51 percent) work in the retail industry, which includes fast-food outlets and food stores. An additional 34 percent work in the service industry, including health, education, and entertainment/recreation.

Fifty-four percent of teen occupational injuries occur in the retail industry, followed by the service industry (20 percent), agriculture (7 percent), and manufacturing (4 percent). Some tasks and tools associated with a large number of injuries include:

- driving a car
- driving heavy equipment, especially tractors
- using power tools, especially meat slicers

Teens are killed at work, most often, while driving or traveling as passengers in motor vehicles. Machine-related accidents, electrocution, homicide, and falls also account for many deaths. A study has determined that the risk of injury/death for workers age 16 and 17 was 5.1 per 100,000 full-time equivalent workers, compared with 6.0 for adult workers over age 18. This is of particular concern when you take into consideration the fact that as a whole teens work fewer hours than adult employees.

A possible solution:

_____

_____

_____

_____

_____

_____

15.12 The State of the Union

New economic policy is often announced in the President's annual State of the Union address. Read the excerpts from President Bill Clinton's 1998 State of the Union speech printed below, and then write a summary of the new economic policies proposed.

January 27, 1998
STATE OF THE UNION ADDRESS
BY THE PRESIDENT
Hall of the House
United States Capitol
9:12 P.M. EST

THE PRESIDENT: Mr. Speaker, Mr. Vice President, members of the 105th Congress, distinguished guests, my fellow Americans:

For 209 years it has been the President's duty to report to you on the state of the Union. Because of the hard work and high purpose of the American people, these are good times for America. We have more than 14 million new jobs; the lowest unemployment in 24 years; the lowest core inflation in 30 years; incomes are rising; and we have the highest home ownership in history. Crime has dropped for a record five years in a row. And the welfare rolls are at their lowest levels in 27 years. Our leadership in the world is unrivaled. Ladies and gentlemen, the state of our Union is strong.

We must not go back to unwise spending or untargeted tax cuts that risk reopening the deficit. But whether the issue is tax cuts or spending, I ask all of you to meet this test: Approve only those priorities that can actually be accomplished without adding a dime to the deficit.

Now, if we balance the budget for next year, it is projected that we'll then have a sizeable surplus in the years that immediately follow. What should we do with this projected surplus? I have a simple four-word answer: Save Social Security first. Tonight, I propose that we reserve 100 percent of the surplus—that's every penny of any surplus—until we have taken all the necessary measures to strengthen the Social Security system for the 21st century.

In an economy that honors opportunity, all Americans must be able to reap the rewards of prosperity. Because these times are good, we can afford to take one simple, sensible step to help millions of workers struggling to provide for their families: We should raise the minimum wage.

I also have something to say to every family listening to us tonight: Your children can go on to college. If you know a child from a poor family, tell her not to give up—she can go on to college. If you know a young couple struggling with bills, worried they won't be able to send their children to college, tell them not to give up—their children can go on to college. If you know somebody who's caught in a dead-end job and afraid he can't afford the classes necessary to get better jobs for the rest of his life, tell him not to give up—he can go on to college. Because of the things that have been done, we can make college as universal in the 21st century as high school is today. And, my friends, that will change the face and future of America. . . .

©1999 by The Center for Applied Research in Education

Section 16

Inflation, Employment, and Wages

16.1 Macroeconomic Terms

As a member of the President's Council of Economic Advisors, you have been asked to brief the President on the state of the economy, including developments in the auto industry and the steel industry. Write a paragraph for your briefing. You can create any conditions you choose, but use all of the terms defined below. Underline the terms as you use them. Use the back of the sheet if you need more space.

_____

_____

_____

_____

_____

_____

_____

_____

_____

_____

Capital goods: Goods purchased to be used in production.

Consumer goods: Goods produced and purchased for final use.

Depression: A decline in business activity and the economy, characterized by low purchasing power, high unemployment, and an excess of supply over demand.

Expansion: A rise in business activity, characterized by strong purchasing power, good productivity growth, low unemployment, and strong economic growth.

Gross domestic product (GDP): The value of all goods and services produced within a country's boundaries over a given period, including foreign-owned operations within the country.

Gross national product (GNP): The value of all goods and services produced by firms owned by nationals of that country, even if they are based abroad.

Labor: Human resources available for use in the process of production.

National income: The total of all income earned in a country over a given period.

Productive resources: Components or elements used in production, including natural resources, technology, the work force, and capital.

Productivity: Rate and efficiency of work in industrial production, usually measured as output per person.

Recession: A downturn in economic activity, often defined as a decline in the GDP for two consecutive quarters.

Supply and demand A fundamental approach to economic theory that analyzes and compares the supply of goods with demand for those goods.

16.2 Money and Inflation

Write the number of each definition on the line next to the correct term. Then study the definitions until you have mastered all the terms.

_____ Hyperinflation

_____ Deflation

_____ Monetarism

_____ Inflation

_____ Currency

_____ Stagflation

_____ Cost of living

_____ Money supply

_____ Cost-push inflation

_____ Demand-pull inflation

_____ Consumer price index

1. The cost of goods and services required to attain a reasonable standard of living.

2. Monthly index of the retail prices of certain goods, taken as an indicator of the cost of living.

3. Inflation as a result of increases in production costs.

4. Monetary unit in use in a specific country, such as the U.S. dollar, the French franc, or the Spanish peso.

5. A reduction in the amount of money available in a country resulting in lower levels of economic activity, industrial output, employment, and decreasing prices. The opposite of inflation.

6. Inflation caused by excess demand, such as during a boom.

7. Dramatic and uncontrollable increase in prices, usually accompanied by political instability.

8. Rate at which prices are increasing.

9. Regulation of an economy by controlling the amount of money in circulation. A major influence on U.S. and U.K. economics in the 1980s.

10. The amount of money in circulation at a given time including bills, coins, and bank deposits used for everyday payments.

11. State where high inflation is accompanied by stagnating or declining output and rising unemployment.

©1999 by The Center for Applied Research in Education

16.3 Evaluating Labor Markets

You've worked hard to make it into medical school, and now it's time to decide for which special area of medicine you'll train. Before you do, however, you need to know how easy or difficult it may be to get a job in that specialty. You need information about the **labor market** for that job.

Labor markets are simply the places where employers shop when they want to hire new employees and where workers go to find a new employer. In any labor market, there may be many workers looking for jobs and few employers interested in hiring them. In this case, the **supply** of labor is greater than the **demand** for labor.

Within each labor market, the supply of workers and the demand for them varies from place to place and from job to job. The overall demand for physicians, for example, is good. But the chart below shows that doctors with some specialties are having a harder time finding jobs than others. Look at the data, then answer the questions.

Specialty	Median salary	Percent without a full-time position
Pathology (general disease)	$190,000	10.8%
Plastic surgery	227,000	9.9%
Anesthesiology (anesthesia)	241,000	6.5%
Pulmonary disease (lungs)	171,000	6.2%
Orthopedic surgery (bones)	302,000	5.9%
Otolaryngology (ears, nose and throat)	220,000	1.5%
Geriatric medicine	128,000	1.5%
Psychiatry	132,000	1.3%
Obstetrics and gynecology	215,000	1.2%
Urology (urinary system)	213,000	0%

Source: U.S. Department of Labor.

You would like to be a plastic surgeon, but the **unemployment rate** is_____. Instead, you select _____ because *all* of the doctors in that specialty have found jobs. The difference in the **median salary** is only $_____. Your friend decides to go into _____ because it offers the highest salary of the specialties where the demand for doctors is very high. She was interested in pathology, but more than one out of every _____ pathologists are unable to find work.

16.4 Participation Rates

One of the most important factors in any economy is the rate at which adults participate in the economy by holding jobs. This *participation rate* expresses the percentage of people within a particular group who are either employed or actively seeking work. As you can see from the data below, the percentage of women participating in the U.S. work force has changed dramatically over the past fifty years. Draw a graph showing the change in the box provided. Then write a short paragraph describing the trend and why you think the change occurred.

Women in the Work Force 1945–1995

Year	Percent of All Adult Women in Work Force
1945	20.0%
1950	23.8
1955	27.7
1960	30.5
1965	34.7
1970	40.8
1975	44.4
1980	50.1
1985	54.2
1990	57.5
1995	58.9

Source: U.S. Department of Labor.

16.5 Inflation and Purchasing Power

Inflation is a rise in the price of goods and services that does not stem from an improvement or change in the goods and services. In periods of inflation, people pay more money for the same goods. The Consumer Price Index (CPI) is the most widely used measure of inflation in the U.S. When economists talk about inflation, they usually refer to the amount of increase in the CPI from year to year—the annual percent change. Study the data in the table. Then graph the data in the box provided, and write a paragraph describing trends in inflation from 1977–1997.

The Consumer Price Index—Annual Percent Change 1977–1997

Year	Percent
1977	6.5
1978	7.6
1979	11.3
1980	13.5
1981	10.3
1982	6.2
1983	3.2
1984	4.3
1985	3.6
1986	1.9
1987	3.6
1988	4.1
1989	4.8
1990	5.4
1991	4.2
1992	3.0
1993	3.0
1994	2.6
1995	2.8
1996	3.0
1997	1.7

Source: U.S. Department of Labor.

_____

_____

_____

_____

_____

_____

_____

16.6 Productivity

Productivity is the amount of output per unit of input: for example, the quantity of a product produced per hour of labor. Suppose that five workers produce one car per day using certain equipment. Then managment decides to invest in better equipment that allows those same workers to produce two cars a day. Their productivity has doubled, or grown by 100%. Productivity growth is the real engine of more output and faster economic growth in any economy, and the basis for improvements in the standard of living.

Look at the productivity data below. Draw a line graph in the box provided. Then write a paragraph describing the trends revealed. During what periods of time did productivity grow the fastest?

Productivity Growth 1947-1997

Output per worker per hour, 1992=100			
1947 33.7	1960 51.4	1973 78.4	1986 94.0
1948 35.2	1961 53.2	1974 77.1	1987 94.0
1949 36.0	1962 55.7	1975 79.8	1988 94.6
1950 39.1	1963 57.9	1976 82.5	1989 95.4
1951 40.3	1964 60.5	1977 83.9	1990 96.1
1952 41.4	1965 62.7	1978 84.9	1991 96.7
1953 43.0	1966 65.2	1979 84.5	1992 100.0
1954 43.9	1967 66.6	1980 84.2	1993 100.2
1955 45.8	1968 68.9	1981 85.7	1994 100.6
1956 45.8	1969 69.2	1982 85.3	1995 100.5
1957 47.2	1970 70.5	1983 88.0	1996 102.0
1958 48.5	1971 73.6	1984 90.2	1997 104.0
1959 50.5	1972 76.0	1985 91.7	

Source: U.S. Department of Labor.

©1999 by The Center for Applied Research in Education

Name _____ Date _____ Class _____

16.7 The Service Economy

One of the most important changes in the U.S. economy since World War II has been the transition from a manufacturing economy, with factories as the primary source of income and jobs, to a service economy, dominated by service-producing industries such as business services, health care, government, and personal services. This change is illustrated in the graph below. Study the graph, then answer the questions.

1. What percentage of U.S. workers were employed in manufacturing in 1945? _____

2. What percentage were employed in manufacturing in 1996? _____

3. What percentage were employed in services in 1945? _____ In 1955? _____ In 1985? _____ In 1996? _____

4. In what year did services surpass manufacturing as the largest employer? _____

5. List four people you know who are employed (parents, neighbors, etc.) and whether they are employed in manufacturing or services. _____

_____

_____

_____

Share of employment in manufacturing and service industries 1945–1996

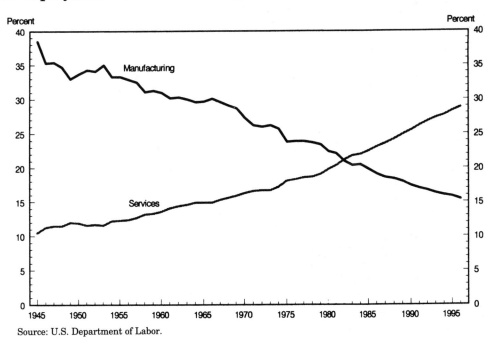

Source: U.S. Department of Labor.

16.8 Where Are the Jobs?

Economists analyze labor markets and project job growth in different industries and occupations. The graphs below were prepared by government economists. Look at the graphs and answer the questions.

1. What does the first graph measure?

_____

_____

2. What is the unit of measurement in the first graph? _____

3. What does the second graph measure?

_____

4. What is the unit of measurement in the second graph? _____

5. What period of time does the second graph cover? _____

6. What is the fastest growing occupation?

_____

_____

7. What was the most common occupation in 1996? _____

_____

8. What do the graphs indicate for someone interested in becoming a farmer?

_____

_____

9. List five jobs in the two occupations that are predicted to have the greatest growth between 1996 and 2006.

_____

_____

_____

_____

_____

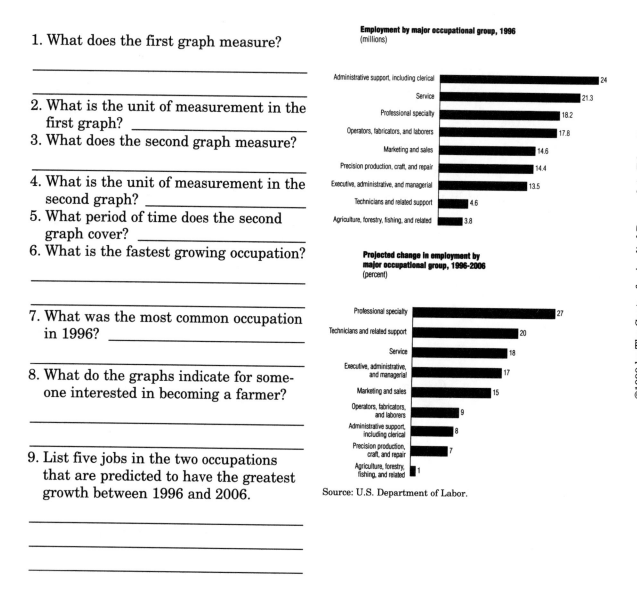

Employment by major occupational group, 1996
(millions)

Administrative support, including clerical	24
Service	21.3
Professional specialty	18.2
Operators, fabricators, and laborers	17.8
Marketing and sales	14.6
Precision production, craft, and repair	14.4
Executive, administrative, and managerial	13.5
Technicians and related support	4.6
Agriculture, forestry, fishing, and related	3.8

Projected change in employment by major occupational group, 1996-2006
(percent)

Professional specialty	27
Technicians and related support	20
Service	18
Executive, administrative, and managerial	17
Marketing and sales	15
Operators, fabricators, and laborers	9
Administrative support, including clerical	8
Precision production, craft, and repair	7
Agriculture, forestry, fishing, and related	1

Source: U.S. Department of Labor.

16.9 Jobs and Education

Read the table below and the explanations of the education and training requirements. On another sheet of paper write three paragraphs that describe the information in the table. Be sure to include information on the changes in job openings, the educational requirements for those jobs, and the earnings of workers in those jobs.

Table	Employment and total job openings, 1996-2006, and 1996 median weekly earnings by education and training category									

(Numbers in thousands of jobs)

Education and training category	Employment				Change		Total job openings due to growth and net replacements, 1996–2006[1]		1996 median weekly earnings, full-time workers
	Number		Percent distribution		Number	Percent	Number	Percent distribution	
	1996	2006	1996	2006					
Total, all occupations	132,353	150,927	100.0	100.0	18,574	14.0	50,563	100.0	$483
First professional degree	1,707	2,015	1.3	1.3	308	18.0	582	1.2	1,057
Doctoral degree	1,016	1,209	.8	.8	193	19.0	460	.9	847
Master's degree	1,371	1,577	1.0	1.0	206	15.0	430	.9	682
Work experience plus bachelor's or higher degree	8,971	10,568	6.8	7.0	1,597	17.8	3,481	6.9	786
Bachelor's degree	15,821	19,838	12.0	13.1	4,017	25.4	7,343	14.5	686
Associate's degree	4,122	5,036	3.1	3.3	915	22.2	1,614	3.2	639
Postsecondary vocational training ...	8,091	8,689	6.1	5.8	598	7.4	2,329	4.6	444
Work experience in a related occupation	9,966	11,177	7.5	7.4	1,211	12.2	3,285	6.5	534
Long-term on-the-job training	11,011	11,890	8.3	7.9	879	8.0	3,466	6.9	487
Moderate-term on-the-job training ...	16,792	18,260	12.7	12.1	1,468	8.7	5,628	11.1	434
Short-term on-the-job training	53,487	60,670	40.4	40.2	7,183	13.4	21,944	43.4	342

[1] Total job openings represent the sum of employment increases and net replacements. If employment change is negative, job openings due to growth are zero and total job openings equal net replacements.

Source: U.S. Department of Labor.

First professional degree. *Occupations that require a professional degree.* Completion of the academic program usually requires at least 6 years of full-time equivalent academic study, including college study prior to entering the professional degree program.

Doctoral degree. *Occupations that generally require a Ph.D. or other doctoral degree.* Completion of the degree program usually requires at least 3 years of full-time equivalent academic work beyond the bachelor's degree.

Master's degree. *Occupations that generally require a master's degree.* Completion of the degree program usually requires 1 or 2 years of full-time equivalent study beyond the bachelor's degree.

Work experience, plus a bachelor's or higher degree. *Occupations that generally require work experience in an occupation requiring a bachelor's or higher degree.* Most occupations in this category are managerial occupations that require experience in a related nonmanagerial position.

Bachelor's degree. *Occupations that generally require a bachelor's degree.* Completion of the degree program generally requires at least 4 years, but not more than 5 years, of full-time equivalent academic work.

Associate's degree. *Occupations that generally require an associate's degree.* Completion of the degree program generally requires at least 2 years of full-time equivalent academic work.

Post-secondary vocational training. *Occupations that generally require completion of vocational school training.* Some programs last only a few weeks while others may last more than a year. In some occupations, a license is needed that requires passing an examination after completion of the training.

Work experience in a related occupation. *Occupations that generally require skills obtained through work experience in a related occupation.* Some occupations requiring work experience are supervisory or managerial occupations.

Long-term on-the-job training. *Occupations that generally require more than 12 months of on-the-job training or combined work experience and formal classroom instruction for workers to develop the skills needed for average job performance.* This category includes formal and informal apprenticeships that may last up to 4 years and short-term intensive employer-sponsored training that workers must successfully complete. Individuals undergoing training are generally considered to be employed in the occupation. This category includes occupations in which workers may gain experience in nonwork activities, such as professional athletes who gain experience through participation in athletic programs in academic institutions.

Moderate-term on-the-job training. *Occupations in which workers can develop the skills needed for average job performance after 1 to 12 months of combined on-the-job experience and informal training.*

Short-term on-the-job training. *Occupations in which workers generally can develop the skills needed for average job performance after a short demonstration or up to 1 month of on-the-job experience and instruction.*

16.10 Calculating Change

The table below shows data for employment in different occupations over the twenty years from 1986-2006. Read the table and calculate the missing numbers for the two columns that are blank. After you've filled in the missing numbers, write a paragraph describing the trends in employment indicated by the data.

Table	Employment by major occupational group, 1986, 1996, and projected 2006									
(Numbers in thousands of jobs)										
Occupational group	Employment						Change			
	Number			Percent distribution			Number		Percent	
	1986	1996	2006	1986	1996	2006	1986–96	1996–2006	1986–96	1996–2006
Total, all occupations ...	111,375	132,353	150,927	100.0	100.0	100.0	20,978	18,574	18.8	14.0
Executive, administrative, and managerial	10,568	13,542	15,866	9.5	10.2		2,974	2,324	28.1	
Professional specialty	13,589	18,173	22,998	12.2	13.7		4,584	4,826	33.7	
Technicians and related support	3,724	4,618	5,558	3.3	3.5		894	940	24.0	
Marketing and sales	11,496	14,633	16,897	10.3	11.1		3,137	2,264	27.3	
Administrative support, including clerical	20,871	24,019	25,825	18.7	18.1		3,147	1,806	15.1	
Service	17,427	21,294	25,147	15.6	16.1		3,867	3,853	22.2	
Agriculture, forestry, fishing, and related occupations, .	3,661	3,785	3,823	3.3	2.9		124	37	3.4	
Precision production, craft, and repair	13,832	14,446	15,448	12.4	10.9		614	1,002	4.4	
Operators, fabricators, and laborers	16,206	17,843	19,365	14.6	13.5		1,637	1,522	10.1	

Source: U.S. Department of Labor.

(Use the back of this sheet if you need more space.)

16.11 How Much Do They Make?

The table here shows average compensation for full-time workers in different occupations in 1996. The table shows total compensation—wages plus benefits such as health insurance, paid time off, and pensions. Read the table, then create graphs in the spaces provided. Provide labels when needed.

Occupational groups	Total compensation	Wages and salaries	Benefit costs
All workers in private industry	$17.49	$12.58	$4.91
White-collar occupations	21.10	15.44	5.66
Executive, administrative, and managerial	33.12	24.07	9.05
Professional	30.80	22.49	8.31
Technical	24.84	17.90	6.94
Administrative support, including clerical	14.93	10.69	4.23
Sales occupations	14.34	11.09	3.25
Blue-collar occupations	17.04	11.61	5.44
Precision production, craft, and repair	22.12	15.10	7.02
Transportation and material moving	16.96	11.62	5.34
Machine operators, assemblers, and inspectors	15.48	10.22	5.27
Handlers, equipment cleaners, helpers, and laborers	12.07	8.48	3.59
Service occupations	8.61	6.53	2.07

Source: U.S. Department of Labor.

1. A pie chart showing wages and benefits as portions of total compensation for all workers.

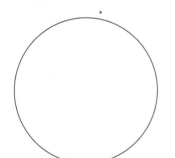

2. A bar chart comparing total compensation for nine occupations.

16.12 The Wage Gap

This table shows the median annual earnings in 1993 for men and women workers age 45-64 who worked in the same jobs with the same level of education. The gap between what men earn and what women earn is called the "wage gap." Although federal law prohibits employers from paying a woman a lower wage than a man working in the same job, the "wage gap" persists in most occupations. Study the table. Then, in the space provided, create a visual representation of all or some of the information in the table. You might draw a graph or a cartoon or an illustration that expresses the "wage gap."

Bachelor's degree	Median annual earnings		Women's earnings as percent of men's in same major
	Women	Men	
All major fields	$32,093	$49,392	65
Accounting	35,254	54,745	64
Agriculture	–	–	–
Architecture/environmental design	–	–	–
Biological/life sciences	32,715	43,260	76
Business, except accounting	33,613	50,897	66
Chemistry	36,671	52,149	70
Communications	37,418	49,985	75
Computer and information sciences	36,336	51,945	70
Criminal justice/protective service	–	–	–
Economics	42,743	52,264	82
Education, including physical education	30,010	38,313	78
Engineering	38,707	59,215	65
Engineering-related technologies	–	–	–
English language and literature	31,740	43,193	73
Foreign languages and linguistics	32,840	37,851	87
Health/medical technologies	36,038	37,448	96
History	30,283	42,321	72
Liberal arts/general studies	36,807	43,213	85
Mathematics	34,718	56,389	62
Nursing	40,908	–	–
Pharmacy	46,148	51,028	90
Political science and government	32,255	49,920	65
Psychology	32,076	45,514	70
Social work	28,953	30,205	96
Sociology	32,039	45,757	70
Theology, philosophy, and religion	33,592	30,516	110
Visual and performing arts	30,013	36,441	82

Source: U.S. Department of Labor.

Section 17

Corporate America

17.1 How Much Did the Company Make?

Here's an actual income statement from a company. The statement shows **revenues** (the money the company received from the sale of its goods and services), **expenses** (the cost of producing those goods and services, including labor and materials), and **net income** (the money left over after expenses, interest, income taxes, and other expenses have been paid). Read the statement, then answer the questions.

Statement of Consolidated Income

In thousands of dollars	1996	1995
Operating revenues	$ 328,493	$ 326,559
Operating expenses		
Operations and maintenance	170,928	156,713
Depreciation and amortization	30,573	30,142
General taxes	49,510	48,604
Total operating expenses	251,011	235,459
Operating income	77,482	91,100
Interest and other expenses	30,979	40,053
Income before income taxes	46,503	51,047
Provision for income taxes	20,579	20,075
Net income	25,924	30,972

1. What was the company's net income for 1996? _____

2. What percentage of 1996 revenues does its net income represent? _____

3. Did net income rise or fall from 1995 to 1996? _____ Why? _____

_____

Step Ahead!
On the back of this sheet, draw a graph representing the change in revenues, total expenses, and net income.

17.2 How Do You Spell "Money"?

When you earn money, spend it, or invest it, you'll encounter some new words and some tricky spelling problems. Study the words below. Then team up with a classmate and test each other on your spelling skills. Take turns calling out the words for a written quiz, then check each other's work.

1. revenues
2. investment
3. property
4. shareholders
5. management
6. corporation
7. business
8. partnership
9. dividends
10. equity

Step Ahead!

1. denomination
2. certificate
3. equilibrium
4. discounting
5. currency

17.3 Buying Companies

Newspaper headlines often announce mergers, acquisitions, and other situations where companies are bought and sold. Using all of the terms defined below, write your own newspaper story about these corporate transactions. Create some companies for your story.

Cartel: Agreement among firms that dominate a market. Price and output may be agreed to so that the members of the cartel maximize profits and exclude new competitors.

Conglomerate: A company that is made up of a holding firm and subsidiary companies. Usually the product of mergers or takeovers.

Monopoly: A situation whereby a commodity or service is supplied by only one agent.

Oligopoly: Situation where the majority of a market is controlled by a few large companies that may therefore exert considerable influence on that market.

Merger: A combination of two or more companies.

Acquisition: One company taking over controlling interest in another company.

Subsidiary: A company of which more than 50% of its voting shares are owned by another company, called the parent company.

_____

(Use the back of this sheet if you need more space.)

17.4 Saving for the Future

An important part of participating in the economy is saving and investing for the future—to buy a first home, send your children to college, or for retirement. An easy way to determine how long it will take you to double the amount of money that you save is the *Rule of 72*. This mathematical rule allows you to calculate the money you will accumulate by investing that money at a certain interest rate.

The higher the interest rate, the faster your money grows.

Suppose you can invest your savings with a 10% interest rate or return. Divide 72 by the interest rate, and the answer is the number of years it will take your money to double at that rate of interest.

Example: You save $1,000 and invest it at a 10% interest rate. 72 divided by 10 equals 7.2. Your initial savings of $1,000 will be worth $2,000 in 7.2 years.

Use the Rule of 72 to determine how much your savings will grow in the examples given below. Show your work.

1. You save $1,000 and put it in a savings account that pays 5% interest. How many years will it take you to double your money?

2. You save $20,000 and invest it at a 10% interest rate. How long will it take for your investment to grow to $40,000?

Step Ahead!
You are 20 years old. You plan to buy a home when you are 35 years old, and you will need a $20,000 down payment. With an interest rate of 10%, how much money do you need to invest *now* to reach your goal?

17.5 The Giants of Corporate America

The table below shows the five largest companies in America in 1997 ranked by revenues. Complete the table by calculating the missing numbers for the last two columns. Then create a graph that illustrates the differences in size and profitability for the five companies.

Company	Revenues $ millions	Profits $ millions	Profits as % of revenue	Rank by profitability
1. General Motors	$178,174.0	$6,698.0	3.8%	
2. Ford Motor Co.	153,627.0	6,920.0		
3. Exxon	122,379.0	8,460.0		
4. Wal-Mart	119,299.0	3,526.0		
5. General Electric	90,840.0	8,203.0		

Source: *Fortune*, April, 27 1998.

17.6 Money Talks

Study the terms below. Then write a story about a new company in which you plan to invest. Use all the terms listed and underline each term used in your story.

bond: a certificate issued by a corporation or a government that states the amount of a loan, the interest to be paid, and the time for repayment

book value: the difference between a company's assets and its liabilities

capital gains tax: a tax levied on the difference between the purchase price and the sale price of an asset—real estate, stocks, bonds

common stock: an ownership stake in a company

discount rate: the interest rate at which banks can borrow money from a central bank to loan to their customers

dividend: the amount paid per share to holders of common stock

loss: the amount by which expenses exceed revenues

net income/profits/earnings: the amount of money left after a company pays taxes and all other expenses

operating profit/loss: net income excluding income from sources other than the company's regular business

sales: the money a company received for goods and services sold

revenues: the amount of money a company takes in, including sales, interest earned, rents, and royalties

©1999 by The Center for Applied Research in Education

_____

_____

_____

_____

_____

_____

_____

_____

_____

_____

_____

_____

_____

Balance Sheet

(Use the back of this sheet if you need more space.)

17.7 Researching a Company

If you are looking for a job or thinking about buying stock, you may need to learn more about a company and its financial status. The best place to begin is the company's annual report and financial statements. Companies that are publicly owned and have more than 500 employees and assets in excess of $1 million are required to file annual reports and a Form 10-K with the Securities and Exchange Commission (SEC). These reports are publicly available by writing to the SEC. Many large libraries also have copies of the annual reports for major companies. Companies provide copies of their annual reports to shareholders.

The annual report includes a description of product lines and market information; debt history, including a summary of all loans, their term, and the interest rate; the amount of retired debt; a five-year financial operating summary; a list of operating facilities; and information on the officers and directors. Form 10-K usually includes the information in the annual report. It also includes information on pending court cases that may affect the company's profitability; principal stock owners and major stock transactions; records of shareholders' meetings; and changes in the company's stocks.

The company's income statement, also known as a profit-and-loss statement, shows how much money the company made or lost over the past few years and the company's expenses. If the company's revenues were greater than expenses, the company made a profit. If the revenues were less than expenses, the company experienced a loss. The income statement provides the most valuable information about a company's financial future because profits or losses indicate a firm's ability to hold sufficient cash to operate effectively and grow.

Privately held companies are likely to have financial statements and may even have annual reports, but they are not required to make that information publicly available. However, the company may be willing to provide information, or you may be able to find information about the company from business publications. You can also find information about both publicly held and privately held companies on the web. Many companies have web sites with detailed information about the company and contact information.

Although profit or loss is an important financial indicator, it does not tell the whole story about a company's financial position. Other indicators must also be considered, such as increases or decreases in profits over time. The source of profits should also be investigated. If the company is relying on profits from nonoperating sources, such as interest or dividends on investments, it may be in trouble because the investment income is basically covering up a losing operation.

Answer the following questions.

1. Name two documents that contain detailed information about companies. _____
_____

2. What information can be found in an annual report? _____
_____
_____

3. What information is found in an income statement? _____
_____

4. Why is profit-and-loss information important? _____
_____

17.8 McDonald's® Money

Actual financial information about McDonald's® is provided below. Using all of the information provided, write a news story about McDonald's® finances.

McDonald's
Headquarters: Oak Brook, Illinois
CEO: Michael R. Quinlin

1997 revenues ($ millions)	$11,408.8
% change from 1996	6.8
1997 profits ($ millions)	$1,642.5
% change from 1996	4.4
assets ($ millions)	$18,200.0
market value ($ millions)	$36,145.2
profits as % of revenue	14.4
number of employees	237,000

Source: *Fortune,* April 27, 1998.

_____
_____
_____
_____
_____
_____
_____
_____
_____
_____
_____
_____
_____
_____
_____
_____
_____

17.9 Calculate Coca-Cola®'s Profits

According to *Fortune* magazine, if all the Coca-Cola® ever produced were put into eight-ounce bottles, the stack would stretch to the moon and back again 1,057 times! Coke®'s stock returned 28% in 1997, on top of a gain of 43% in 1996 and 46% in 1995, making Coke® one of the most successful (profitable) companies in America.

   Use the information below to write a news story about Coca-Cola®'s financial status and stock performance in 1997. Calculate profits as a percent of revenues and include that information in your story. Earnings per share is the portion of a company's profit allocated to each outstanding share of common stock. For example, if a company earned $10 million last year and has $10 million shares outstanding, it would report earnings of $1 per share.

Coca-Cola®	
Headquarters: Atlanta, Georgia	
1997 revenues ($ millions)	$18,868.0
1997 profits ($ millions)	$4,129.0
1997 earnings per share	$1.64
% change from 1996	18.8
1997 total return to investors	27.9%
number of employees	29,500

Source: *Fortune,* April 27, 1998.

©1999 by The Center for Applied Research in Education

_____

_____

_____

_____

_____

_____

_____

_____

_____

_____

_____

_____

(Use the back of this sheet if you need more space.)

Section 18

Participating in Wall Street

©1999 by The Center for Applied Research in Education

Name _____ Date _____ Class _____

18.1 Wall Street Talk

Using at least 12 of the terms defined below, write a paragraph about a day in the life of a stock trader and his or her colleagues on Wall Street. Underline the terms you use from the list.

bear market: a long period of falling prices on the market
bearish: feeling pessimistic about the market
belly up: bankrupt
blue chip: a common stock of a large corporation with a long history of solid growth
bull market: a long period of rising prices in the market
bullish: feeling optimistic about the market
bottom fisher: an investor who looks for a stock whose price has sunk to its lowest level
closely held: describes a company whose stock is held by only a small number of shareholders
cash cow: a company that generates a lot of surplus cash
crash: a collapse of the stock market, with a sharp sudden drop in prices
dog: a poorly performing stock
floor: the trading floor of a stock exchange
hot issue: a new stock that is very popular with investors
junk bond: a high-risk, high-yield bond
parking: putting money in a safe, low-risk investment in times of market uncertainty
raider: someone who takes over a company by buying up a large portion of its stock
rally: a rise in stock prices after a low point or bear market
speculator: an investor who trades in high-risk securities
ticker: the electronic display board of stock trading activity
turkey: a poorly performing investment
Wall Street: the financial district in lower Manhattan where the stock exchanges and investment firms are located
war babies: the stocks and bonds of weapons manufacturers and defense contractors

_____
_____
_____
_____
_____
_____

(Use the back of this sheet if you need more space.)

18.2 Share Holding

Paul wants to invest some of his money in the stock market. He buys ten shares of stock in the Smith Corporation, which he plans to sell in four months. To keep track of his investment, Paul decides to keep a log. Fill it in for him, using the following information:

May 1   Paul buys ten shares of stock at 17 1/2 (which equals $17.50) per share.

June 1   The value of the stock goes up 5 3/8 ($5.375) per share.

July 1   The stock falls 3 7/8 ($3.875) per share.

Aug. 1   The stock falls 1 1/2 ($1.50) per share and then **splits** 2 to 1, doubling his shares (when a stock splits it becomes two stocks, each worth half the value of the original stock).

Sept. 1   The stock goes up 2 3/8 ($2.375) per share. Paul receives a dividend check of $1.89 per share. Paul sells all his shares.

©1999 by The Center for Applied Research in Education

Portfolio Log		
Shares in Portfolio	**$ Value per Share**	**$ Value of Portfolio**
Initial Value _____	_____	_____
June 1 _____	_____	_____
July 1 _____	_____	_____
August 1 _____	_____	_____
September 1 _____	_____	_____

Earnings from dividends _____
Paul's profit over his initial investment _____

Name ____________________ Date ____________ Class ________

18.3 Reading a Stock Report

An actual stock report from a newspaper appears below. Use the definitions to help you read the stock report. Then find the information for LA Gear™ and write a short summary of the company's stock performance.

Bold Type marks stocks that rose or fell at least 4 percent, but only if the change was at least 75 cents a share.

Underlining (on New York or American Stock Exchange) means stock traded more than 1 percent of its total shares outstanding.

Underlining (on Nasdaq) means stock traded more than 2 percent of its total shares outstanding.

52-Week High and Low shows highest and lowest prices reached by a stock over the last year, but not including yesterday.

Arrows

^ Yesterday's high was greater than 52-week high.

v Yesterday's low was less than 52-week low.

Both new high and new low were reached.

Yield is the ratio of the annual dividend to the closing price, expressed as a percentage.

Price/Earnings Ratio is the price of the stock, divided by earnings per share reported over the last four quarters.

High: Highest price at which the stock traded yesterday.

Low: Lowest price at which the stock traded yesterday.

Last: Final trade of the day.

Change: Difference between last trade and previous day's last price.

52-Week High	52-Week Low	Stock	Div	Yld %	P/E	Sales 100s	High	Low	Last	Chg
99 1/8	68 5/8	KimbClk	1.84	1.9	cc	4778	98 3/8	97 1/4	98 1/4	+ 3/4
30 1/4	25 1/4	Kimco s	1.56	5.4	19	490	28 3/4	28 1/2	28 5/8	+ 1/8
25	22	Kimc pfA	1.94	8.2	...	27	23 7/8	23 5/8	23 3/4	− 1/8
26 1/4	24	Kimc pfB	2.13	8.4	...	14	25 3/8	25 3/8	25 3/8	...
25 1/8	22 3/4	Kimc pfC	2.09	8.4	...	489	24 3/4	24 1/2	24 3/4	+ 1/8
8 5/8	3 1/4	Kimmin s	...	...	dd	60	3 3/4	3 5/8	3 3/4	− 1/8
45 1/8	34 1/8	KingWd	...	...	9	1208	37 3/4	37 3/8	37 3/8	− 3/8
10 5/8	6 3/4	Kinross g	...	...	...	75	7 1/2	7 3/8	7 1/2	...
20 1/2	15 1/4	Kirby	...	...	19	47	19 5/8	19 5/8	19 5/8	− 1/8
9 5/8	8 5/8	KBAust	.78 a	8.3	q	776	9 3/8	9 1/4	9 3/8	+ 1/8
40 5/8	29 7/8 ^	KnightR s	.80	2.0	30	9466	40 3/4	40 1/2	40 5/8	...
41 1/4	25 1/4	Kohls s	...	...	36	1440	39	38 1/8	38 1/4	− 1/2
15 5/8	9	Kolmor	.08	0.7	20	206	11 1/2	11 1/8	11 1/2	+ 1/2
21 1/2	15	Koor	.28 e	1.6	2	241	18	17 5/8	18	+ 1/8
28 1/4	16 7/8	KoreaElc	.32 e	1.7	...	3045	18 3/4	18 1/4	18 1/2	− 3/8
9 5/8	6 5/8	KoreaEqt	.02 e	0.3	q	78	7	6 7/8	6 7/8	− 1/8
24	15 7/8	Korea	.72 e	4.2	q	1173	17 1/8	17	17 1/8	...
18 3/8	12	KoreaM n	...	...	...	5970	14 3/8	13 3/4	14 3/8	+ 5/8
11 1/2	7 7/8	KoreaInv	.29 e	3.6	q	43	8 1/8	8	8	...
16 1/4	14 1/8	Kranzc	1.92	12.7	dd	360	15 1/4	15	15 1/8	− 1/8
47 1/2	32 7/8	Kroger	...	...	18	3561	47	46 1/4	46 5/8	+ 1/4
18 1/2	10 7/8	Kuhlm	.60	3.4	15	1348	17 7/8	17 1/2	17 5/8	...
162 1/2	126 1/2	Kyocer	1.18 e	0.9	...	83	131 3/4	130	130 1/2	− 5
29 7/8	21 1/2	Kysor	.66	2.2	10	72	29 5/8	29 1/4	29 5/8	+ 1/4
		L								
3 7/8	1 1/2	LA Gear	...	...	dd	471	2 1/2	2 3/8	2 3/8	− 1/8
37 1/4	16 3/8	LCI Intl	...	...	42	1795	33 3/4	33 1/4	33 3/8	− 3/8
24 1/2	20 3/8 ^	LG&E s	1.15 f	4.7	19	486	24 5/8	24	24 1/2	+ 1/2
5 1/8	3 1/8	LLE Ry	.78 e	16.4	10	251	4 3/4	4 5/8	4 3/4	+ 1/8
6 3/8	3 1/2	LSB Ind	.06	1.5	dd	136	4 1/4	4 1/8	4 1/8	− 1/8
39	30 7/32	LSB pfC	3.25	8.4	...	2	38 7/8	38 3/4	38 7/8	+ 1/2
48	**17**	**LSI Log**	...	...	**22**	**11397**	**31**	**29 1/8**	**31**	**+ 1 3/8**
17 5/8	14 1/2	LTC Prp	1.36	7.8	15	534	17 1/2	17 1/4	17 1/2	+ 1/8
15 7/8	10	LTV	.12	1.1	11	3566	10 3/4	10 1/2	10 5/8	− 1/8
3 1/8	5/8	LTV wt	...	...	...	85	3/4	11/16	3/4	...
24	15 5/8	LaQuinta s	.07	0.4	29	545	19 7/8	19 3/8	19 3/8	− 1/2
34	26 7/8	LaZ Boy	.76	2.5	13	99	30 1/2	30 1/4	30 1/4	− 3/8
17 1/2	11 1/4	LabChile	.51 e	3.0	...	70	17 1/8	16 7/8	17 1/8	+ 1/4
9 3/8	3	LabCp	...	...	dd	1313	3 1/8	3	3	...
13/16	5/64	LabCp wt	...	...	...	20	9/64	9/64	9/64	...
24 7/8	20	LaclGas	1.26	5.5	12	283	23	22 1/4	22 3/4	− 1/8
21 7/8	17 3/4	Lafarge	.40	2.1	11	608	19 5/8	19 1/4	19 1/2	+ 1/4
12 1/4	8 5/8	LaidlwB	.16	...	22	886	12	11 7/8	11 7/8	− 1/8
34	21 5/8	LakehdP	2.72 f	8.0	12	394	34	33 3/4	33 7/8	...
13 7/8	6 7/8	LamSes	...	...	7	516	7 7/8	7 3/8	7 7/8	+ 5/8
25 5/8	12 3/4	LandsE	...	...	22	1014	25 5/8	24 7/8	25 1/2	+ 1/2
10 7/8	7 1/4	Lasmo	.68 e	6.4	cc	207	10 5/8	10 5/8	10 5/8	...
26 1/8	23 7/8	Lasmo pf	2.50	9.7	...	15	26	25 7/8	25 7/8	...
14 7/8	11 5/8	LatADlr	1.50	10.6	q	125	14 1/4	14 1/8	14 1/8	...
16 1/4	11 7/8	LatAEqt	.06 e	0.4	q	349	14	13 3/4	13 3/4	...
11 3/4	9	LatinAGr	.20 p	...	q	86	10	10	10	...
14 1/4	8 5/8	LatADis	...	...	q	310	12 7/8	12 3/4	12 3/4	...
18 5/8	13 1/2	LatAInv	.20 e	1.3	q	232	15 7/8	15 5/8	15 5/8	− 1/8
12 1/2	10 3/8	Lawter	.40	3.4	20	421	12	11 7/8	11 7/8	...

18.4 Mutual Funds

An actual mutual funds report from a daily newspaper is shown below. Find information for the Evergreen family of funds. Then write a short news story comparing the performances of Evergreen's Blue Chip fund, International Growth fund, and Value fund.

Mutual fund groups are shown in bold type. Funds in each group are indented under the group name; funds not in groups are not indented.

NAV: Net asset value of the shares, as reported by the fund through Nasdaq. Shares are sold to the public at NAV, plus any sales charge, and are redeemed at NAV, less any redemption charges.

Daily % Ret: One-day total return, including reinvested dividends, if any.

YTD % Ret: Total return, year to date.

Expense ratio of fund, expressed as a percentage of assets, as shown in most recent filing with the Securities and Exchange Commission. Expenses include management fees, marketing fees, legal fees and the cost of shareholder communications, as well as other charges.

Calculations of total return assume reinvestment of all distributions.

Fund Family Fund Name	NAV	Dly % Ret.	YTD % Ret.	5-Yr. % Ret.
Found m	20.42	−0.2	+ 7.1	NA
GloLead m	16.06	+0.1	+16.0	NA
GloOpp m	24.34	−0.2	+11.8	+11.7
GrowInc m	29.76	−0.6	+ 5.3	NA
HiGrTxF m	11.34	...	+ 2.0	+ 5.9
HiYldBd m	4.47	...	NA	NA
IntTrmBd m	9.09	...	+ 2.8	+ 5.8
IntlGr m	8.71	−0.5	NA	NA
NJTaxF m	11.12	...	+ 2.3	+ 5.3
Omega m	24.33	...	+15.3	+18.0
PrecMet m	11.36	−0.6	NA	NA.
SmCapEq m	16.21	−0.9	− 3.6	NA
SmCoGr m	7.71	−0.4	NA	NA
StrGrow m	10.85	+0.3	NA	NA
StratInc m	7.15	...	+ 4.0	+ 6.3
TaxF m	7.75	...	NA	NA
TotRet m	21.94	...	+12.0	+18.1
TxStrat m	16.10	−0.3	+ 3.4	NA.
USGovt m	9.74	...	+ 3.8	+ 6.0
Util m	11.96	−0.4	+ 2.1	NA
Value m	22.54	−0.2	+ 6.7	+17.7
Evergreen B				
AggGrow m	22.68	−0.7	+ 9.0	NA
AmerRet m	15.94	−0.3	+ 1.7	NA
Bal m	12.90	+0.2	+ 8.0	+13.5
BlChip m	30.97	+0.1	+12.3	+18.0
DivrBd m	16.03	−0.1	+ 3.5	+ 6.3
Evergr m	24.00	−0.7	+ 6.1	NA
FLHiInc m	11.17	...	+ 2.8	NA
FLMuni m	10.01	...	+ 1.9	+ 5.1
Found m	20.31	−0.3	+ 6.6	NA
GloLead m	15.80	+0.1	+15.5	NA
GloOpp m	23.29	−0.3	+11.3	+10.8
GrowInc m	29.50	−0.6	+ 5.1	NA
HiGrTxF m	11.34	...	+ 1.6	+ 5.2
HiYldBd m	4.47	...	+ 4.7	+ 6.3
IncGrow m	23.57	−0.4	+ 0.9	NA
IntlGr m	8.68	−0.5	+25.8	+14.3
LatAm m	9.88	−0.4	−11.5	NA
NCMuni m	10.70	...	+ 2.1	+ 5.2
Omega m	23.02	...	+14.8	NA
PATaxF m	11.57	...	+ 1.8	+ 4.9
SmCapEq m	16.12	−0.9	− 4.0	NA
SmCoGr m	7.68	−0.4	− 4.2	+11.6
StrGrow m	10.81	+0.3	+16.2	+18.8
StratInc m	7.18	...	+ 3.5	+ 5.5
TaxF m	7.75	...	+ 1.3	+ 5.0
TxStrat m	16.06	−0.4	+ 3.0	NA
USGovt m	9.74	...	+ 3.4	+ 5.3
Util m	11.97	−0.4	+ 1.7	NA
Value m	22.52	−0.2	+ 6.5	+17.0

_____

_____

_____

_____

_____

_____

_____

_____

18.5 Mutual Funds Investing

A mutual fund is a company that brings together money from many people and invests it in stocks, bonds, or other securities. The combined holdings of stocks, bonds, or other securities and assets the fund owns are known as its portfolio. Each investor owns shares, which represent a part of these holdings.

Mutual funds can be a good way for people to invest in stocks, bonds, and other securities. Why? Mutual funds are managed by professional money managers.

By owning shares in a mutual fund instead of buying individual stocks or bonds directly, your investment risk is spread out. Because your mutual fund buys and sells large amounts of securities at a time, its costs are often lower than what you would pay on your own.

Mutual funds are not guaranteed or insured by any bank or government agency. You can lose money. Mutual funds always carry investment risks. Some types carry more risk than others. A higher rate of return typically involves a higher risk of loss. All mutual funds have costs that lower your investment returns.

There are sources of information that you should consult before you invest in mutual funds. The most important of these is the prospectus of any fund you are considering. The prospectus is the fund's selling document and contains information about costs, risks, past performance, and the fund's investment goals.

You can buy some mutual funds by contacting them directly. Others are sold mainly through brokers, banks, financial planners, or insurance agents. All mutual funds will redeem (buy back) your shares on any business day and must send you the payment within seven days.

You can find out the value of your shares in the financial pages of major newspapers. After the fund's name, look for the column marked NAV. Net Asset Value per share (NAV) is the value of one share in a fund. A fund's NAV goes up or down daily as its holdings change in value.

Example: You invest $1,000 in a mutual fund with an NAV of $10.00. You will therefore own 100 shares of the fund. If the NAV drops to $9.00 (because the value of the fund's portfolio has dropped), you will still own 100 shares, but your investment is now worth $900. If the NAV goes up to $11.00, your investment is worth $1,100. (This example assumes no sales charge.)

Answer the following questions.

1. What is a mutual fund? _____

_____

2. What is a NAV? _____

3. How do you invest in a mutual fund? _____

_____

4. What is a prospectus? _____

5. Can you lose money in a mutual fund? _____

6. If you invest $5,000 in a fund with a NAV of $20, and the value drops to $19, how much will

your investment be worth? _____ What if the value rises to $22? _____

18.6 Types of Mutual Funds

The three main categories of mutual funds are money market funds, bond funds, and stock funds. There are a variety of types within each category.

1. **Money market funds** have relatively low risks compared with other mutual funds. They are limited by law to certain high-quality, short-term investments. Money market funds try to keep their value (NAV) at a stable $1.00 per share, but NAV may fall below $1.00 if their investments perform poorly. Investor losses have been rare, but they are possible.

2. **Bond funds** (also called fixed income funds) have higher risks than money market funds, but seek to pay higher yields. Unlike money market funds, bond funds are not restricted to high-quality or short-term investments. Because there are many different types of bonds, bond funds can vary dramatically in their risks and rewards.

Most bond funds have credit risk, which is the risk that companies or other issuers whose bonds are owned by the fund may fail to pay their debts (including the debt owed to holders of their bonds). Some funds have a little credit risk, such as those that invest in insured bonds or U.S. Treasury bonds. But nearly all bond funds have interest-rate risk, which means that the market value of the bonds they hold will go down when interest rates go up. Because of this, you can lose money in any bond fund, including those that invest only in insured bonds or Treasury bonds.

Long-term bond funds invest in bonds with longer maturities (length of time until the final payout). The values (NAVs) of long-term bond funds can go up or down more rapidly than those of shorter-term bond funds.

3. **Stock funds** (also called equity funds) generally involve more risk than money market or bond funds, but they also can offer the highest returns. A stock fund's value (NAV) can rise and fall quickly over the short term, but historically stocks have performed better over the long term than other types of investments.

Not all stock funds are the same. For example, growth funds focus on stocks that may not pay a regular dividend but have the potential for large capital gains. Others specialize in a particular industry segment such as technology stocks.

Write a summary of the three types of funds and their relative risks.

_____

_____

_____

_____

_____

_____

_____

18.7 Write for Information

Below is a list of all the Securities and Exchange Commission (SEC) offices in the U.S. Find the office closest to you, and write a letter to the public information officer requesting information on a specific company. The SEC distributes Form 10-K for all large publicly owned companies. A 10-K includes detailed financial information about the company. Also ask the SEC for information about investing in the stock market.

SEC Offices

U.S. Securities and Exchange Commission Headquarters
Office of Investor Education and Assistance
450 Fifth Street, N.W.
Washington, D.C. 20549

Northeast Regional Office
7 World Trade Center, Suite 1300
New York, NY 10048

Boston District Office
73 Tremont Street, Suite 600
Boston, MA 02108-3912

Philadelphia District office
601 Walnut Street, Suite 1005 E
Philadelphia, PA 19106-3322

Southeast Regional Office
1401 Brickell Avenue, Suite 200
Miami, FL 33131

Atlanta District Office
3475 Lenox Road, N.E. , Suite 1000
Atlanta, GA 30326-1232

Midwest Regional Office
500 West Madison Street, Suite 1400
Chicago, IL 60661-2511

Central Regional Office
1801 California Street, Suite 4800
Denver, CO 80202-2648

Fort Worth District Office
801 Cherry Street, 19th Floor
Fort Worth, TX 76102

Pacific Regional office
5670 Wilshire Boulevard, 11th Floor
Los Angeles, CA 90036-3648

San Francisco District Office
44 Montgomery Street, Suite 1100
San Francisco, CA 94104

18.8 Stock Talk

Write the number of each definition on the line next to the correct term.

_____ across the board   1. an investor's diversified holdings

_____ bellweather   2. stocks, bonds, notes

_____ bond   3. a new stock or bond offering

_____ buyout   4. initial public offering—a company's first sale of stock to the public

_____ closely held   5. a right granted to buy or sell a security at a set price

_____ dividend   6. any means of protecting one's investments against losses

_____ futures   7. a corporation's controlling stock held by a small number of shareholders

_____ hedge   8. earnings distributed to shareholders

_____ IPO   9. commodities such as metals, grains, foods

_____ new issue   10. a security whose price activity indicates which way the rest of the market will go

_____ option   11. stock market activity in which prices move in the same direction

_____ portfolio   12. an interest-bearing certificate of debt—a formal IOU

_____ securities   13. the purchase of a controlling interest in a company

The Market

IV. STATE AND LOCAL GOVERNMENTS

- State Government
- Local Government

Section 19

State Government

19.1 Federal/State Relations

Each of the fifty states in the Union has its own constitution and has a legislature to make laws for the people of that state. The United States Constitution has placed certain prohibitions on the states, mainly to prevent them from passing laws that are the business of the national government:

1. No state can declare war. Only Congress can declare war. A state may, however, defend itself if invaded.
2. No state can coin money.
3. No state can make treaties with other states or with foreign countries.
4. No state can tax exported or imported goods.
5. No state can grant titles of nobility.

For each of these five prohibited acts, summarize the reasons why the authors of the Constitution believed the acts should be prohibited for the states and reserved only for the federal government.

1. _____

_____

_____

_____

2. _____

_____

_____

_____

3. _____

_____

_____

_____

4. _____

_____

_____

_____

5. _____

_____

_____

_____

19.2 State and Federal Courts

Throughout the United States there are two judicial systems. One system consists of state and local courts established under the authority of the state governments. The other is the U.S. Supreme Court and the federal court system, created by Congress under the authority of the Constitution of the United States.

The state courts have general, unlimited power to decide nearly every type of case, subject only to the limitations of the U.S. Constitution, their own state constitutions, and state law. The state and local courts are located in virtually every town and county and are the courts with which citizens most often have contact. These courts handle most criminal matters and the great bulk of legal business concerning probate of estates, marital disputes, dealings in land, commercial contracts, and other day-to-day matters.

The federal courts, in contrast, have power to decide only those cases over which the Constitution gives them authority. These courts are located principally in the larger cities. Only carefully selected types of cases may be heard in the federal courts. The controversies that may be decided in the federal courts are identified in Article III, Section 2 of the Constitution. They include cases in which the United States government or one of its officers is either suing someone or being sued.

The federal courts also may decide cases for which state courts are inappropriate or might be suspected of partiality. Thus, federal courts may decide, in the language of the Constitution, "...Controversies between two or more states—between a State and Citizens of another State—between Citizens of different States—between Citizens of the same State claiming Lands under Grants of different States..." For example, one state might be sued by another state for the pollution of its air. Since the impartiality of the courts in either state could be questioned, such a suit might be decided in a federal court.

Answer the following questions.

1. Describe the two judicial systems that exist in the U.S.

   _____

   _____

2. What are the powers of the state courts?

   _____

   _____

3. What types of cases are tried in federal courts?

   _____

   _____

   _____

   _____

19.3 State Legislatures

Read the information below. Then draw a diagram representing the structure of state government in your state, and another diagram representing the process by which a bill becomes a law.

    Each of the fifty states has a constitution of its own which is the supreme law of that particular state. The only restriction on the state constitutions is that they must not conflict with the United States Constitution. The legislative branch of the state government is usually called a state legislature or state assembly, divided into two groups or houses. The upper house is usually called the Senate and the members of that house, called state senators, are usually elected for four-year terms. The members of the lower house, which may be known as the State House of Representatives, or State Assembly, usually serve for two-year terms.

    Any legislator who desires to make a new law presents a bill to the particular house to which he or she belongs. This document is known as a bill. If the bill is passed by the house in which it is introduced, it goes to the other house for approval. After it passes both houses, it goes to the governor of the state for his or her signature. If the governor vetoes it or refuses to sign it, the bill will not become a state law unless the legislators vote on the bill again and decide to pass it without the governor's approval. Most state laws require a two-thirds vote of the members of each house of the legislature in order to pass a law after the governor has vetoed the bill.

19.4 Steps in a Court Case

Most state court cases follow ten basic steps. Study the steps, then write your own story about a crime committed. Include all ten steps in your story.

1. **Investigation:** The police investigate a reported crime.

2. **Arrest:** The suspect (someone believed to be the offender) is arrested.

3. **Booking:** The suspect is detained at a jail, fingerprinted, photographed, and told of the charges against him or her.

4. **Initial appearance:** The defendant (accused person) makes his or her first court appearance. The defendant is told of his or her rights, the charges are read aloud, and bail is decided.

5. **Indictment:** Documents issued by a prosecutor (information) or grand jury (indictment) that list all of the charges against a suspect. Some states use a grand jury trial to determine whether or not the government should prosecute an accused person. Some states use a preliminary hearing, where a judge reviews the evidence to see if there is enough to continue toward a trial.

6. **Arraignment:** Defendant pleads "guilty" or "not guilty" to the charges. Charges may be dismissed at this point.

7. **Trial or guilty plea:** Someone who tries to get the crime reduced or changed in exchange for a guilty plea is plea bargaining. Almost 90 percent of all criminal cases are resolved in this way. Very few persons accused of a felony ever seek a trial to determine guilt or innocence.

8. **Sentencing:** The judge determines the punishment.

9. **Corrections:** For civil cases, a typical penalty is a fine. Failure to pay a fine may result in a jail sentence or probation. For criminal cases, a convicted person may be imprisoned, fined, or given an alternative sentence.

10. **Appeal:** A convicted person may appeal his or her conviction to a court of appeal. Most verdicts are upheld by appellate courts.

19.5 Criminal or Civil?

Look at the following examples and decide if a crime or a civil wrong has occurred. Write either "criminal," "civil," or "both" in the blank.

1. A bank employee pockets your cash deposit. _____

2. A driver refuses to take a breathalyzer test. _____

3. A neighbor accidentally backs his car over your bike. _____

4. There are loud parties at the apartment next door. _____

5. You write a check knowing that there is not enough money in the bank account.

   _____

6. You accidentally leave a store with a book you didn't pay for. _____

7. Someone refuses to help a police officer when ordered to do so. _____

8. You make a $20.00 bet in a card game. _____

9. There are rats in the kitchen of a restaurant. _____

10. A drug company uses false advertising. _____

11. You are caught hunting without a license. _____

12. A person takes a friend's car without permission. _____

13. A factory dumps toxic waste into the water supply. _____

14. A bus driver drives a bus while he is intoxicated. _____

15. A pickpocket steals a wallet. _____

16. A car manufacturer knowingly makes defective autos. _____

17. You forget to put on your seatbelt while sitting in the front seat of a car.

    _____

18. A hospital overcharges for its services. _____

19. A surgeon removes the wrong organ from a patient. _____

19.6 Court Talk

Use the words in the box to fill in this puzzle.

Across

3. A court decision in an earlier case with facts and law similar to a dispute currently before a court.
6. When an appellate court sends a case back to a lower court for further proceedings.
10. A civil wrong to another person.
11. The geographical location in which a case is tried.
12. To place a paper in the official custody of the clerk of court to enter into the records of a case.
13. Another name for the court; where the judges sit.

Down

1. A judge's written explanations of a decision of the court or of a majority of judges.
2. A request asking another to decide whether a trial was conducted properly.
6. When an appellate court sets aside the decision of a lower court because of an error.
7. A log containing brief entries of court proceedings.
8. Laws passed by a legislature.
9. Information presented to a judge or jury.

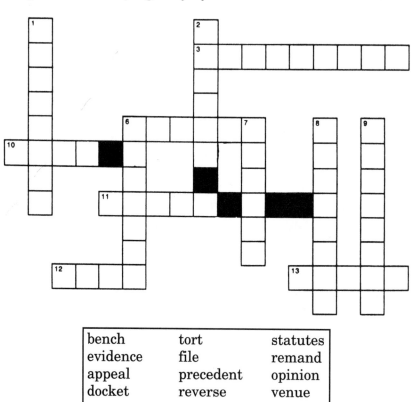

bench	tort	statutes
evidence	file	remand
appeal	precedent	opinion
docket	reverse	venue

©1999 by The Center for Applied Research in Education

19.7 The Richest and the Poorest

The U.S. Department of Commerce collects a number of statistics on the states. The tables below show the 10 states with the highest per capita (per person) income in 1997, and the 10 states with the lowest. Study the tables, then answer the questions.

The 10 states with the highest per capita income in 1997 were:	Dollars		Rank	
	1996	1997	1996	1997
Connecticut	34,174	36,263	1	1
New Jersey	31,265	32,654	2	2
Massachusetts	29,808	31,524	3	3
New York	29,221	30,752	4	4
Delaware	27,782	29,022	5	5
Maryland	27,676	28,969	6	6
Illinois	26,855	28,202	7	7
New Hampshire	26,772	28,047	8	8
Colorado	25,740	27,051	10	9
Minnesota	25,699	26,797	11	10

The 10 states with the lowest per capita income in 1997 were:	Dollars		Rank	
	1996	1997	1996	1997
Kentucky	19,773	20,657	42	41
Oklahoma	19,574	20,556	44	42
Idaho	19,865	20,478	41	43
Utah	19,384	20,432	45	44
North Dakota	20,479	20,271	38	45
Montana	19,278	20,046	46	46
New Mexico	18,814	19,587	48	47
Arkansas	18,967	19,585	47	48
West Virginia	18,225	18,957	49	49
Mississippi	17,561	18,272	50	50

1. What was the richest state in the nation in 1997? _____ The poorest? _____

2. How great is the gap between the richest and the poorest in dollar terms? _____ As a percentage? _____

3. What was the percent change between 1996 and 1997 for per capita income in Connecticut? _____ New York? _____ West Virginia? _____ Mississippi? _____

19.8 State Growth

The table below shows the population of each state and the percent change in population for 1993-1997. Select three states and write a summary of the population trends in those states.

| | [Thousands of persons] | | | | | Percent change | | | |
	1993	1994	1995	1996	1997	1993-94	1994-95	1995-96	1996-97
United States	257,753	260,292	262,761	265,179	267,636	1.0	0.9	0.9	0.9
New England									
Connecticut	3,273	3,270	3,267	3,267	3,270	-.1	-.1	0	.1
Maine	1,237	1,236	1,234	1,239	1,242	-.1	-.1	.4	.3
Massachusetts	6,008	6,029	6,061	6,085	6,118	.4	.5	.4	.5
New Hampshire	1,122	1,134	1,146	1,160	1,173	1.1	1.1	1.2	1.1
Rhode Island	998	994	990	988	987	-.4	-.4	-.2	-.1
Vermont	574	579	583	586	589	.9	.7	.6	.4
Mideast									
Delaware	698	706	716	723	732	1.2	1.3	1.1	1.1
District of Columbia	577	566	552	539	529	-1.9	-2.4	-2.4	-1.9
Maryland	4,945	4,989	5,027	5,060	5,094	.9	.8	.7	.7
New Jersey	7,869	7,911	7,956	8,002	8,053	.5	.6	.6	.6
New York	18,139	18,154	18,146	18,134	18,137	.1	0	-.1	0
Pennsylvania	12,022	12,043	12,046	12,040	12,020	.2	0	0	-.2
Great Lakes									
Illinois	11,675	11,737	11,795	11,845	11,896	.5	.5	.4	.4
Indiana	5,700	5,742	5,788	5,828	5,864	.7	.8	.7	.6
Michigan	9,524	9,580	9,655	9,731	9,774	.6	.8	.8	.4
Ohio	11,058	11,095	11,133	11,163	11,186	.3	.3	.3	.2
Wisconsin	5,038	5,075	5,113	5,146	5,170	.7	.8	.6	.5
Plains									
Iowa	2,820	2,829	2,841	2,848	2,852	.3	.4	.3	.2
Kansas	2,535	2,554	2,570	2,579	2,595	.8	.6	.4	.6
Minnesota	4,524	4,567	4,607	4,649	4,686	1.0	.9	.9	.8
Missouri	5,238	5,281	5,325	5,364	5,402	.8	.8	.7	.7
Nebraska	1,613	1,623	1,636	1,649	1,657	.6	.8	.8	.5
North Dakota	637	640	641	643	641	.4	.3	.2	-.3
South Dakota	723	730	735	738	738	1.0	.7	.4	.1
Southeast									
Alabama	4,193	4,232	4,262	4,287	4,319	.9	.7	.6	.7
Arkansas	2,424	2,451	2,481	2,506	2,523	1.1	1.2	1.0	.7
Florida	13,712	13,956	14,181	14,419	14,654	1.8	1.6	1.7	1.6
Georgia	6,896	7,049	7,192	7,334	7,486	2.2	2.0	2.0	2.1
Kentucky	3,793	3,824	3,856	3,882	3,908	.8	.8	.7	.7
Louisiana	4,285	4,307	4,329	4,341	4,352	.5	.5	.3	.3
Mississippi	2,635	2,663	2,691	2,711	2,731	1.1	1.0	.8	.7
North Carolina	6,948	7,062	7,187	7,309	7,425	1.6	1.8	1.7	1.6
South Carolina	3,625	3,654	3,683	3,717	3,760	.8	.8	.9	1.2
Tennessee	5,083	5,158	5,235	5,307	5,368	1.5	1.5	1.4	1.1
Virginia	6,465	6,538	6,601	6,666	6,734	1.1	1.0	1.0	1.0
West Virginia	1,816	1,819	1,822	1,820	1,816	.1	.2	-.1	-.3
Southwest									
Arizona	3,994	4,149	4,308	4,434	4,555	3.9	3.8	2.9	2.7
New Mexico	1,617	1,656	1,686	1,711	1,730	2.4	1.8	1.5	1.1
Oklahoma	3,229	3,248	3,271	3,295	3,317	.6	.7	.7	.7
Texas	18,035	18,385	18,738	19,091	19,439	1.9	1.9	1.9	1.8
Rocky Mountain									
Colorado	3,563	3,657	3,742	3,816	3,893	2.6	2.3	2.0	2.0
Idaho	1,101	1,135	1,165	1,188	1,210	3.1	2.6	1.9	1.9
Montana	840	855	869	877	879	1.8	1.6	.9	.2
Utah	1,875	1,929	1,974	2,018	2,059	2.9	2.4	2.2	2.1
Wyoming	469	475	479	480	480	1.3	.7	.3	-.1
Far West									
Alaska	597	601	602	605	609	.7	.1	.6	.7
California	31,183	31,369	31,558	31,858	32,268	.6	.6	.9	1.3
Hawaii	1,160	1,173	1,179	1,183	1,187	1.1	.5	.3	.3
Nevada	1,382	1,459	1,530	1,601	1,677	5.5	4.8	4.7	4.7
Oregon	3,036	3,089	3,143	3,196	3,243	1.7	1.8	1.7	1.5
Washington	5,250	5,339	5,436	5,520	5,610	1.7	1.8	1.5	1.6

Source: Bureau of the Census, U.S. Department of Commerce.

©1999 by The Center for Applied Research in Education

19.9 In Civil Court

You are a lawyer trying a civil case. Decide what your case is about and who you represent. Then write a summary of your case and the court proceedings using all of the terms defined below.

affirmed: In the practice of the appellate courts, the decree or order is declared valid and will stand as rendered in the lower court.

answer: The formal written statement by a defendant responding to a civil complaint and setting forth the grounds for defense.

brief: A written statement submitted by the lawyer for each side in a case that explains to the judges why they should decide the case or a particular part of a case in favor of that lawyer's client.

case law: The law as laid down in cases that have been decided in the decisions of the courts.

chambers: A judge's office.

complaint: A written statement by the plaintiff stating the wrongs allegedly committed by the defendant.

defendant: In a civil suit, the person complained against; in a criminal case, the person accused of the crime.

docket: A log containing brief entries of court proceedings.

file: To place a paper in the official custody of the clerk of court to enter into the files or records of a case.

case law: The law as laid down in cases that have been decided in the decisions of the courts.

hearsay: Statements by a witness who did not see or hear the incident in question, but heard about it from someone else. Hearsay is usually not admissible as evidence in court.

injunction: An order of the court prohibiting (or compelling) the performance of a specific act to prevent irreparable damage or injury.

jurisdiction: The legal authority of a court to hear and decide a case; the geographic area over which the court has authority to decide cases.

parties: Plaintiffs and defendants (petitioners and respondents) to lawsuits; also known as appellants and appellees in appeals, and their lawyers.

plaintiff: The person who files the complaint in a civil lawsuit.

precedent: A court decision in an earlier case with facts and law similar to a dispute currently before a court. Precedent will ordinarily govern the decision of a later similar case, unless a party can show that it was wrongly decided or that it differed in some significant way.

settlement: Parties to a lawsuit resolve their difference without having a trial. Settlements often involve the payment of compensation by one party in satisfaction of the other party's claims.

_____

_____

_____

_____

_____

_____

_____

_____

_____

_____

(Use the back of this sheet if you need more space.)

19.10 Decide the Case

You are a judge in the state court. Create a case with real parties and issues, and write your decision. Use all of the terms defined below, and underline the terms in your story.

appeal: A request made after a trial, asking another court (usually the court of appeals) to decide whether the trial was conducted properly. To make such a request is "to appeal" or "to take an appeal." One who appeals is called the appellant.

chief judge: The judge who has primary responsibility for the administration of a court but also decides cases; chief judges are determined by seniority.

clerk of court: An officer appointed by the court to work with the chief judge in overseeing the court's administration, especially to assist in managing the flow of cases through the court and to maintain court records.

contract: An agreement between two or more persons that creates an obligation to do or not to do a particular thing.

counsel: Legal advice; a term used to refer to lawyers in a case.

counterclaim: A claim that a defendant makes against a plaintiff.

court reporter: A person who makes a word-for-word record of what is said in court and produces a transcript of the proceedings upon request.

damages: Money paid by defendants to successful plaintiffs in civil cases to compensate the plaintiffs for their injuries.

instructions: Judge's explanation to the jury before it begins deliberations of the questions it must answer and the law governing the case.

issue: The disputed point in a disagreement between parties in a lawsuit.

judgment: The official decision of a court finally determining the respective rights and claims of the parties to a suit.

statute: A law passed by a legislature.

statute of limitations: A law that sets the time within which parties must take action to enforce their rights.

subpoena: A command to a witness to appear and give testimony.

tort: A civil wrong or breach of a duty to another person, as outlined by law. A very common tort is negligent operation of a motor vehicle that results in property damage and personal injury in an automobile accident.

transcript: A written, word-for-word record of what was said, either in a proceeding such as a trial or during some other conversation, as in a transcript of a hearing or oral deposition.

©1999 by The Center for Applied Research in Education

_____
_____
_____
_____
_____
_____
_____
_____
_____

(Use the back of this sheet if you need more space.)

19.11 Your City and State

How much do you know about the state and city governments that affect so much of your life? See how many of these blanks you can fill in.

1. Your state's governor: _____

2. Your state's lieutenant governor: _____

3. Does your state legislature have an assembly or a house of representatives? _____

4. Your state senate leader: _____

5. The dominant party in your state senate: _____

6. The dominant party in your state assembly: _____

7. Your governor's political party _____

8. Your mayor: _____

9. Does your city or town have a council? _____ How many members? _____

10. Does your county have a board? _____ How many members? _____

11. Your mayor's political party: _____

12. Average property taxes in your town: _____

13. State sales tax: _____%

14. Superintendent of your school district: _____

15. Chairperson of your school board: _____

16. State capital: _____

17. State motto: _____

18. Describe the state flag: _____

19. State flower: _____

20. State bird: _____

21. Origins of the state's name: _____

22. Year your state joined the Union: _____

23. All states that share borders with your state: _____

24. Most important industry in your state: _____

25. Total state population: _____

Section 20

Local Government

20.1 Structure of Local Government

Local governments do not have constitutions; rather, they receive a charter (plan of government) from the state government. There are different types of local governments: town, village, borough, city and county. In the space provided, describe your local government. Refer to the divisions of local government outlined below.

CITY GOVERNMENT
MAYOR: Usually elected by the citizens.
CITY COUNCIL: Usually elected by the citizens. The council makes the laws and directs the city manager.
CITY MANAGER: Some cities use a city manager, who is hired by the city council to carry out the city's business.
COMMISSION: Usually elected by the citizens and acts as both executive and legislature.

COUNTY GOVERNMENT
COUNTY BOARD or BOARD OF COMMISSIONERS or BOARD OF SUPERVISORS: The county board is usually elected by the citizens of the county. It makes plans for the county, controls the county budget, and enforces state laws.

LOCAL COURTS
Local governments have a court system that handles local issues. A judge in a local court is usually called judge, magistrate, or justice of the peace.

_____
_____
_____
_____
_____
_____
_____

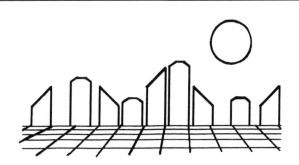

©1999 by The Center for Applied Research in Education

20.2. City Government

Cities may choose from several different forms of government. The constitution of a city is usually called a *charter*. The city—like the nation, the state, and the county—often has three departments of government. The Chief Executive of a city is called the *Mayor*. The legislative branch of a city is usually the *City Council* or the Board of Supervisors. The judicial branch of a city consists of the *Police Courts* and *Justice Courts*.

Among the usual city officers are the *Treasurer, Tax Collector, Assessor, Auditor, Health Officer, Clerk, Engineer, Police Chief, Fire Chief* and several minor officers. Some of these officers are elected by the voters and others are appointed by the Mayor.

City laws are called *ordinances*. Among the well-known ordinances in cities are the automobile regulation ordinances, bicycle-riding ordinances, milk-delivery ordinances, ordinances regulating domestic animals, building ordinances, and health ordinances. These ordinances differ in various communities, in accordance with the wishes of the citizens.

Create your own city. In the space provided, describe your city, its charter, its officials, and its most important ordinances, using the terms underlined above. Don't forget to give your city a name and a location!

_____

_____

_____

_____

_____

_____

_____

_____

_____

_____

_____

_____

_____

_____

_____

_____

(Use the back of this sheet if you need more space.)

20.3 Who Do You Call?

Using the chart below as your guide, fill in each blank with the name of the department you could call to solve the following problems.

1. You see an automobile accident on your way home.

   _____

2. The water coming from your tap is brown. _____

3. Your neighbor's dog barks all night. _____

4. There's broken glass at the city park playground. _____

5. Your school's textbooks are out-of-date. _____

6. You see smoke coming from your neighbor's apartment. _____

7. You see a drunken man leave a bar and get into his car.

   _____

8. You want to fence your yard but you've heard there are local restrictions.

   _____

Water Department	Makes sure drinking water is safe
Highway Department	Repairs local roads, signs, bridges
Board of Education	Hires teaches: decides salaries and curriculum
Sanitation Department	Collects trash: keeps public areas clean
Police Department	Enforces laws: protects people
Fire Department	Puts out fires: saves people in emergencies
Court	Hears cases about local laws and family problems
Tax Department	Collects money to pay for services
Clerk's Office	Keeps records and certificates

20.4 Spell "Criminal Court"

Study the spellings and definitions of the terms below. Then team up with a classmate and test each other.

acquittal: Judgment that a criminal defendant has not been proved guilty beyond a reasonable doubt.

arraignment: A proceeding in which an individual who is accused of committing a crime is brought into court, told of the charges, and asked to plead guilty or not guilty.

circumstantial evidence: All evidence except eyewitness testimony.

conviction: A judgment of guilt against a criminal defendant.

defendant: The person accused of the crime.

habeas corpus: A writ that is usually used to bring a prisoner before the court to determine the legality of his or her imprisonment. It may also be used to bring a person in custody before the court to give testimony, or to be prosecuted.

hearsay: Statements by a witness who did not see or hear the incident in question but heard about it from someone else. Hearsay is usually not admissible as evidence in court.

indictment: The formal charge issued by a grand jury stating that there is enough evidence that the defendant committed the crime to justify having a trial; it is used primarily for felonies.

misdemeanor: Usually a petty offense, a less serious crime than a felony, punishable by less than a year of confinement.

probation: A sentencing alternative to imprisonment in which the court releases convicted defendants under supervision as long as certain conditions are observed.

prosecute: To charge someone with a crime. A prosecutor tries a criminal case on behalf of the government.

sequester: To separate. Sometimes juries are sequestered from outside influences during their deliberations.

sidebar: A conference between the judge and lawyers held out of earshot of the jury and spectators.

testimony: Evidence presented orally by witnesses during trials or before grand juries.

warrant: A written order directing the arrest of a party. A search warrant orders that a specific location be searched for items, that, if found, can be used in court as evidence.

20.5 Whose Jurisdiction?

For each of the crimes listed below, indicate which jurisdiction is responsible for enforcing the law. Use **F** for federal jurisdiction, **S** for state jurisdiction, and **L** for local jurisdiction. Some crimes may fall under more than one jurisdiction.

1. Shoplifting _____

2. Murdering your neighbor _____

3. Speeding on Main Street _____

4. Stealing a car _____

5. Robbing a bank _____

6. Printing counterfeit money _____

7. Stealing someone's mail _____

8. Child abuse _____

9. Hijacking a plane _____

10. Cheating on your income taxes _____

11. Loitering _____

12. Collecting money for a faked workplace injury _____

13. Stalking the President. _____

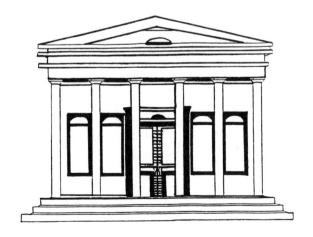

20.6 In Criminal Court

If you are charged with a crime or asked to serve on a jury in criminal court, you must be familiar with the words found in the box. Search the puzzle for the words listed and circle them. They may be printed horizontally, vertically, diagonally, forward, or backward.

CRIMINAL	SENTENCING	FRAUD
DUE PROCESS	ARRAIGNMENT	COURTS
MISDEMEANOR	JURY	WITNESSES
ARRESTED	TRIAL	CONVICTION
FELONY	LARCENY	PAROLE
PARDON	HEARING	

```
K L O U Y T R E F G H B N I G N I R A E H G F T R E D F G T
F D U E P R O C E S S F E L O N Y X X A R R E S T E D M N U
C O N V I C T I O N E P O P L I U L B F E P A R D O N N O I
R X O L N V C D E R K L M J H T R A D E D E E R T E N M T O
I P L O I U G R F E D I O P O T G R D S W F R A U D I M T H
M C V D F E E I O L M I M R N B G C R T F N B V C X S D W E
I S I J H G F E Q W S A C P A L K E I T F E D T G I H I U B
N S S S E S S E N T I W B I H P G N E I O L U T R I A L E N
A O L K U T R E W Q S A I L M N B Y F D D I L K O P O I U I
L M E E E T N E M N G I A R R A W U Y T E F G F E D E S I L
L L K O U A N L L Y U I O P P W W U I J E R I O E K H T E I
X D S F B I M V B N K J U R Y H I P L U P L O M L P P R L M
N F M S M W O A M I S D E M E A N O R P K H F D O I U U F W
M M D K S M L R R N M H U O P D E Y M N J F D N O L T O G N
W S E N T E N C I N G O O L A R C E N Y O D E R R Y Y C I A
```

Step Ahead!
What is *due process?* _____

_____

Name _____   Date _____   Class _____

20.7 Reading Crime Rates

Using the charts shown below, answer the following questions:

1. What is the most common violent crime? _____

2. What is the most common property crime? _____

3. Of all the crimes depicted in the two charts, which has increased the most?

_____

4. Of all the crimes depicted in the two charts, which has decreased the most?

_____

5. Pick one crime and describe the trend shown in the chart. Has the number increased or decreased over time? Discuss the possible causes for the increase/decrease. _____

_____

_____

_____

_____

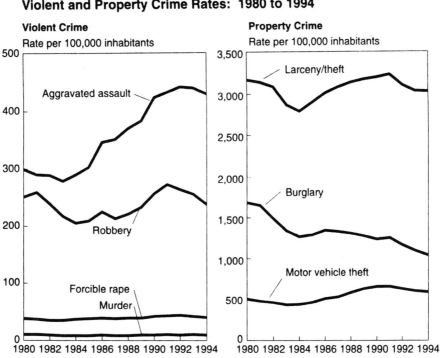

Violent and Property Crime Rates: 1980 to 1994

Source: Chart prepared by U.S. Bureau of the Census.

20.8 Progression of Civil Actions

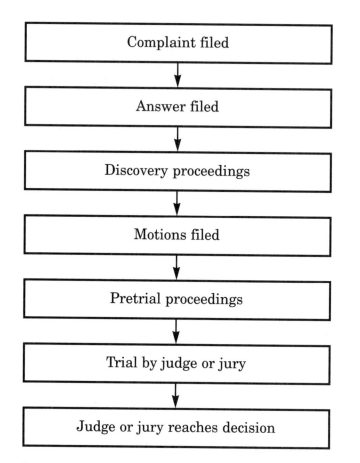

The diagram above shows the steps in a civil lawsuit from the time a complaint is filed with the court to the time a decision is reached by the court. Using the diagram to name each of the steps, write a paragraph describing the progression of a civil action. Fill in as many details as possible as you trace the progression of the case.

_____

_____

_____

_____

_____

_____

_____

(Use the back of this sheet if you need more space.)

©1999 by The Center for Applied Research in Education

20.9 Trials in Criminal Actions

Defendant arrested ——▶ Preliminary hearing ——▶ Grand Jury returns indictment

Discovery proceedings ——▶ Motions filed ——▶ Trial ——▶ Opening statements

Prosecutor presents case ——▶ Presentation of evidence

Defendant's lawyer presents case ——▶ Prosecutor presents rebuttal

Closing arguments ——▶ Judge instructs jury ——▶ Deliberations ——▶ **VERDICT**

This diagram shows the steps in a criminal trial from the time a defendant is arrested to the time a jury reaches a verdict. In the space below, write your own story of a defendant's criminal trial. Include all the steps shown above and use the correct terms for each step. Describe the defendant, the crime, the trial, the jury's deliberations, and the verdict. Use the back of this sheet if necessary.

_____
_____
_____
_____
_____
_____
_____
_____
_____
_____
_____
_____
_____
_____
_____
_____

20.10 Law and Order

Imagine that you are a reporter covering the trial of a murder case. Write a paragraph about it using at least eight of the defined words below.

Alibi: An accounting of a person's whereabouts during the time a crime was committed

Conspiracy: a crime committed by two or more people

cross-examination: The questioning of a witness by the lawyer who did not call him or her to the stand having to do with information previously given by the witness

jump bail: to not appear in court after bail is posted

manslaughter: the murder of another human being without the intention or desire to do so

mistrial: a trial that is called off or terminated before a verdict is reached due to court errors: the death of a juror, judge, or attorney: or a jury that can't agree on a verdict

plea bargaining: the decision between the prosecutor and the accused on whether or not to plead guilty in turn for a lesser sentence

polygraph: a device that detects lies through the measuring of stress levels

premeditation: thinking over or planning a crime beforehand, usually what distinguishes manslaughter from murder

search warrant: an order issued for a police officer by a judge allowing the officer to search a place for persons or objects and bring them before the court

taking the Fifth: pleading the Fifth Amendment right to decide not to give evidence that will incriminate oneself

©1999 by The Center for Applied Research in Education

_____
_____
_____
_____
_____
_____
_____
_____
_____

(Use the back of this sheet if you need more space.)

20.11 Police Talk

Write the number of the definition next to the appropriate abbreviation.

_____ A.D.A

_____ I.A.D

_____ M.O.

_____ R.K.C.

_____ S.W.A.T.

_____ C.S.U.

_____ C of D

_____ C of O

_____ A.C.U.

_____ A.P.B.

_____ division

_____ D.A.

_____ fugitive section

_____ homicide division

_____ commissioner

_____ the book

_____ narcotics division

1. modus operandi; the method by which a criminal operates

2. special weapons and tactics: a paramilitary trained police force

3. Assistant District Attorney

4. District Attorney

5. Internal Affairs Division; a division that investigates complaints about the police or other department personnel

6. chief of detectives

7. chief of operations

8. crime scene unit

9. all points bulletin; issued for other police units to help locate a suspect who is fleeing

10. a city official who supervises the police

11. a precinct

12. recently known criminal

13. a division that deals with narcotics

14. a division in a department that investigates murders and brings the cases to court

15. anti-crime unit

16. the rules and regulations of law

17. a division in a department that finds and captures fugitives of the law

APPENDIX

Virginia's Declaration of Rights

Virginia's Declaration of Rights was drawn upon by Thomas Jefferson for the opening paragraphs of the Declaration of Independence. It was widely copied by the other colonies and became the basis of the Bill of Rights. Written by George Mason, it was adopted by the Virginia Constitutional Convention on June 12, 1776.

A DECLARATION OF RIGHTS made by the representatives of the good people of Virginia, assembled in full and free convention which rights do pertain to them and their posterity, as the basis and foundation of government.

Section 1. That all men are by nature equally free and independent and have certain inherent rights, of which, when they enter into a state of society, they cannot, by any compact, deprive or divest their posterity; namely, the enjoyment of life and liberty, with the means of acquiring and possessing property, and pursuing and obtaining happiness and safety.

Section 2. That all power is vested in, and consequently derived from, the people; that magistrates are their trustees and servants and at all times amenable to them.

Section 3. That government is, or ought to be, instituted for the common benefit, protection, and security of the people, nation, or community; of all the various modes and forms of government, that is best which is capable of producing the greatest degree of happiness and safety and is most effectually secured against the danger of maladministration. And that, when any government shall be found inadequate or contrary to these purposes, a majority of the community has an indubitable, inalienable, and indefeasible right to reform, alter, or abolish it, in such manner as shall be judged most conducive to the public weal.

Section 4. That no man, or set of men, is entitled to exclusive or separate emoluments or privileges from the community, but in consideration of public services; which, nor being descendible, neither ought the offices of magistrate, legislator, or judge to be hereditary.

Section 5. That the legislative and executive powers of the state should be separate and distinct from the judiciary; and that the members of the two first may be restrained from oppression, by feeling and participating the burdens of the people, they should, at fixed periods, be reduced to a private station, return into that body from which they were originally taken, and the vacancies be supplied by frequent, certain, and regular elections, in which all, or any part, of the former members, to be again eligible, or ineligible, as the laws shall direct.

Section 6. That elections of members to serve as representatives of the people, in assembly ought to be free; and that all men, having sufficient evidence of permanent common interest with, and attachment to, the community, have the right of suffrage and cannot be taxed or deprived of their property for public uses without their own consent or that of their representatives so elected, nor bound by any law to which they have not, in like manner, assembled for the public good.

Section 7. That all power of suspending laws, or the execution of laws, by any authority, without consent of the representatives of the people, is injurious to their rights and ought not to be exercised.

Section 8. That in all capital or criminal prosecutions a man has a right to demand the cause and nature of his accusation, to be confronted with the accusers and witnesses, to call for evidence in his favor, and to a speedy trial by an impartial jury of twelve men of his vicinage, without whose unanimous consent he cannot be found guilty; nor can he be compelled to give evidence against himself; that no man be deprived of his liberty except by the law of the land or the judgment of his peers.

Section 9. That excessive bail ought not to be required, nor excessive fines imposed, nor cruel and unusual punishments inflicted.

Section 10. That general warrants, whereby an officer or messenger may be commanded to search suspected places without evidence of a fact committed, or to seize any person or persons not named, or whose offense is not particularly described and supported by evidence, are grievous and oppressive and ought not to be granted.

Section 11. That in controversies respecting property, and in suits between man and man, the ancient trial by jury is preferable to any other and ought to be held sacred.

Section 12. That the freedom of the press is one of the great bulwarks of liberty, and can never be restrained but by despotic governments.

Section 13. That a well-regulated militia, composed of the body of the people, trained to arms, is the proper, natural, and safe defense of a free state; that standing armies, in time of peace, should be avoided as dangerous to liberty; and that in all cases the military should be under strict subordination to, and governed by, the civil power.

Section 14. That the people have a right to uniform government; and, therefore, that no government separate from or independent of the government of Virginia ought to be erected or established within the limits thereof.

Section 15. That no free government, or the blessings of liberty, can be preserved to any people but by a firm adherence to justice, moderation, temperance, frugality, and virtue and by frequent recurrence to fundamental principles.

Section 16. That religion, or the duty which we owe to our Creator, and the manner of discharging it, can be directed only by reason and conviction, not by force or violence; and therefore all men are equally entitled to the free exercise of religion, according to the dictates of conscience; and that it is the mutual duty of all to practice Christian forbearance, love, and charity toward each other.

The Declaration of Independence

IN CONGRESS, July 4, 1776.

A DECLARATION By the REPRESENTATIVES of the UNITED STATES OF AMERICA,

When in the Course of human events, it becomes necessary for one people to dissolve the political bands which have connected them with another, and to assume among the powers of the earth, the separate and equal station to which the Laws of Nature and of Nature's God entitle them, a decent respect to the opinions of mankind requires that they should declare the causes which impel them to the separation.

We hold these truths to be self-evident, that all men are created equal, that they are endowed by their Creator with certain unalienable Rights, that among these are Life, Liberty, and the pursuit of Happiness—That to secure these rights, Governments are instituted among Men, deriving their just powers from the consent of the governed, that whenever any Form of Government becomes destructive of these ends, it is the Right of the People to alter or to abolish it, and to institute new Government, laying its foundation on such principles, and organizing its powers in such form, as to them shall seem most likely to effect their Safety and Happiness. Prudence, indeed, will dictate that Governments long established should not be changed for light and transient causes; and accordingly all experience hath shewn, that mankind are more disposed to suffer, while evils are sufferable, than to right themselves by abolishing the forms to which they are accustomed. But when a long train of abuses and usurpations, pursuing invariably the same Object evinces a design to reduce them under absolute Despotism, it is their right, it is their duty, to throw off such Government, and to provide new Guards for their future security. Such has been the patient sufferance of these Colonies; and such is now the necessity which constrains them to alter their former Systems of Government. The history of the present King of Great Britain is a history of repeated injuries and usurpations, all having in direct object the establishment of an absolute Tyranny over these States. To prove this, let Facts be submitted to a candid world.

He has refused his Assent to Laws, the most wholesome and necessary for the public good.

He has forbidden his Governors to pass Laws of immediate and pressing importance, unless suspended in their operation till his Assent should be obtained; and when so suspended, he has utterly neglected to attend to them.

He has refused to pass other Laws for the accommodation of large districts of people, unless those people would relinquish the right of Representation in the Legislature, a right inestimable to them and formidable to tyrants only.

He has called together legislative bodies at places unusual, uncomfortable, and distant from the depository of their public Records, for the sole purpose of fatiguing them into compliance with his measures.

He has dissolved Representative Houses repeatedly, for opposing with manly firmness his invasions on the rights of the people.

He has refused for a long time, after such dissolutions, to cause others to be elected; whereby the Legislative powers, incapable of Annihilation, have returned to the People at large for their exercise; the State remaining in the mean time exposed to all the dangers of invasion from without, and convulsions within.

He has endeavoured to prevent the population of these States; for that purpose obstructing the Laws for Naturalization of Foreigners; refusing to pass others to encourage their migrations hither, and raising the conditions of new Appropriations of Lands.

He has obstructed the Administration of Justice, by refusing his Assent to Laws for establishing Judiciary powers.

He has made Judges dependent on his Will alone, for the tenure of their offices, and the amount and payment of their salaries.

He has erected a multitude of New Offices, and sent hither swarms of Officers to harrass our people, and eat out their substance.

He has kept among us, in times of peace, Standing Armies, without the Consent of our legislatures.

He has affected to render the Military independent, of and superior to the Civil power.

He has combined with others to subject us to a jurisdiction foreign to our constitution, and unacknowledged by our laws; giving his Assent to their Acts of pretended Legislation:

For Quartering large bodies of armed troops among us:

For protecting them, by a mock Trial, from punishment for any Murders which they should commit on the Inhabitants of these States:

For cutting off our Trade with all parts of the world:

For imposing Taxes on us without our Consent:

For depriving us, in many cases, of the benefits of Trial by Jury:

For transporting us beyond Seas to be tried for pretended offen[c]es:

For abolishing the free System of English Laws in a neighbo[u]ring Province, establishing therein an Arbitrary government, and enlarging its Boundaries, so as to render it at once an example and fit instrument for introducing the same absolute rule into these Colonies:

For taking away our Charters, abolishing our most valuable Laws, and altering fundamentally the Forms of our Governments:

For suspending our own Legislatures, and declaring themselves invested with power to legislate for us in all cases whatsoever.

He has abdicated Government here, by declaring us out of his Protection and waging War against us.

He has plundered our seas, ravaged our Coasts, burnt our towns, and destroyed the lives of our people.

He is, at this time, transporting large Armies of foreign Mercenaries to complete the works of death, desolation, and tyranny, already begun with circumstances of Cruelty and perfidy, scarcely paralleled in the most barbarous ages, and totally unworthy the Head of a civilized nation.

He has constrained our fellow Citizens taken Captive on the high Seas to bear Arms against their Country, to become the executioners of their friends and Brethren, or to fall themselves by their Hands.

He has excited domestic insurrections amongst us, and has endeavoured to bring on the inhabitants of our frontiers, the merciless Indian Savages, whose known rule of warfare, is an undistinguished destruction, of all ages, sexes and conditions.

In every stage of these Oppressions We have Petitioned for Redress in the most humble terms: Our repeated Petitions have been answered only by repeated injury. A Prince, whose character is thus marked by every act which may define a Tyrant, is unfit to be the ruler of a free people.

Nor have We been wanting in attentions to our British brethren. We have warned them from time to time of attempts by their legislature to extend an unwarrantable jurisdiction over us. We have reminded them of the circumstances of our emigration and settlement here. We have appealed to their native justice and magnanimity, and we have conjured them by the ties of our common kindred to disavow these usurpations, which, would inevitably interrupt our connections and correspondence. They too have been deaf to the voice of justice and of consanguinity. We must, therefore, acquiesce in the necessity, which denounces our Separation, and hold them, as we hold the rest of mankind, Enemies in War, in Peace, Friends.

We, therefore, the Representatives of the united States of America, in General Congress, Assembled, appealing to the Supreme Judge of the world for the rectitude of our intentions, do, in the Name, and by Authority of the good People of these Colonies, solemnly publish and declare, That these United Colonies are, and of Right ought to be, Free and Independent States; that they are Absolved from all Allegiance to the British Crown, and that all political connection between them and the State of Great Britain, is and ought to be totally dissolved; and that as Free and Independent States, they have full Power to levy War, conclude Peace, contract Alliances, establish Commerce, and to do all other Acts and Things which Independent States may of right do. And for the support of this Declaration, with a firm reliance on the protection of divine Providence, we mutually pledge to each other our Lives, our Fortunes, and our sacred Honor.

John Hancock

The 56 signatures on the Declaration:

Connecticut
Roger Sherman
Samuel Huntington
William Williams
Oliver Wolcott

Delaware
Caesar Rodney
George Read
Thomas McKean

Georgia
Button Gwinnett
Lyman Hall
George Walton

Maryland
Samuel Chase
William Paca
Thomas Stone
Charles Carroll of Carrollton

Massachusetts
Samuel Adams

John Adams
Robert Treat Paine
Elbridge Gerry

New Hampshire
Josiah Bartlett
William Whipple
Matthew Thornton

New Jersey
Richard Stockton
John Witherspoon
Francis Hopkinson
John Hart
Abraham Clark

New York
William Floyd
Philip Livingston
Francis Lewis
Lewis Morris

North Carolina
William Hooper

Joseph Hewes
John Penn

Pennsylvania
Robert Morris
Benjamin Rush
Benjamin Franklin
John Morton
George Clymer
James Smith
George Taylor
James Wilson
George Ross

Rhode Island
Stephen Hopkins

William Ellery

South Carolina
Edward Rutledge
Thomas Heyward, Jr.
Thomas Lynch, Jr.
Arthur Middleton

Virginia
George Wythe
Richard Henry Lee
Thomas Jefferson
Benjamin Harrison
Thomas Nelson, Jr.
Francis Lightfoot Lee
Carter Braxton

Constitution of the United States of America

We the People of the United States, in Order to form a more perfect Union, establish Justice, insure domestic Tranquility, provide for the common defence, promote the general Welfare, and secure the Blessings of Liberty to ourselves and our Posterity, do ordain and establish this Constitution for the United States of America.

ARTICLE I.

Section 1.

All legislative Powers herein granted shall be vested in a Congress of the United States, which shall consist of a Senate and House of Representatives.

Section 2.

The House of Representatives shall be composed of Members chosen every second Year by the People of the several States, and the Electors in each State shall have the Qualifications requisite for Electors of the most numerous Branch of the State Legislature.

No Person shall be a Representative who shall not have attained to the Age of twenty-five Years, and been seven Years a Citizen of the United States, and who shall not, when elected, be an Inhabitant of that State in which he shall be chosen.

Representatives and direct Taxes shall be apportioned among the several States which may be included within this Union, according to their respective Numbers, which shall be determined by adding to the whole Number of free Persons, including those bound to Service for a Term of Years, and excluding Indians not taxed, three-fifths of all other Persons. The actual Enumeration shall be made within three Years after the first Meeting of the Congress of the United States, and within every subsequent Term of ten Years, in such Manner as they shall by Law direct. The Number of Representatives shall not exceed one for every thirty Thousand, but each State shall have at Least one Representative; and until such enumeration shall be made, the State of New Hampshire shall be entitled to [chuse] three, Massachusetts eight, Rhode[-]Island and Providence Plantations one, Connecticut five, New[-]York six, New Jersey four, Pennsylvania eight, Delaware one, Maryland six, Virginia ten, North Carolina five, South Carolina five, and Georgia three.

When vacancies happen in the Representation from any State, the Executive Authority thereof shall issue Writs of Election to fill such Vacancies.

The House of Representatives shall [chuse] their Speaker and other Officers; and shall have the sole Power of Impeachment.

Section 3.

The Senate of the United States shall be composed of two Senators from each State, chosen by the Legislature thereof for six Years; and each Senator shall have one Vote.

Immediately after they shall be assembled in Consequence of the first Election, they shall be divided as equally as may be into three Classes. The Seats of the Senators of the first Class shall be vacated at the Expiration of the second Year, of the second Class at the Expiration of the fourth Year, and of the third Class at the Expiration of the sixth Year, so that one third may be chosen every second Year; and if Vacancies happen by Resignation, or otherwise, during the Recess of the Legislature of any State, the Executive thereof may make temporary Appointments until the next Meeting of the Legislature, which shall then fill such Vacancies.

No Person shall be a Senator who shall not have attained to the Age of thirty Years, and been nine Years a Citizen of the United States, and who shall not, when elected, be an Inhabitant of that State for which he shall be chosen.

The Vice President of the United States shall be President of the Senate, but shall have no Vote, unless they be equally divided.

The Senate shall [chuse] their other Officers, and also a President pro tempore, in the Absence of the Vice President, or when he shall exercise the Office of President of the United States.

The Senate shall have the sole Power to try all Impeachments. When sitting for that Purpose, they shall be on Oath or Affirmation. When the President of the United States is tried, the Chief Justice shall preside: And no Person shall be convicted without the Concurrence of two thirds of the Members present.

Judgment in Cases of Impeachment shall not extend further than to removal from Office, and disqualification to hold and enjoy any Office of honor, Trust or Profit under the United States: but the Party convicted shall nevertheless be liable and subject to Indictment, Trial, Judgment and Punishment, according to Law.

Section 4

The Times, Places and Manner of holding Elections for Senators and Representatives, shall be prescribed in each State by the Legislature thereof; but the Congress may at any time by Law make or alter such Regulations, except as to the Place of [chusing] Senators.

The Congress shall assemble at least once in every Year, and such Meeting shall be on the first Monday in December, unless they shall by Law appoint a different Day.

Section 5.

Each House shall be the Judge of the Elections, Returns and Qualifications of its own Members, and a Majority of each shall constitute a Quorum to do Business; but a smaller Number may adjourn from day to day, and may be authorized to compel the Attendance of absent Members, in such Manner, and under such Penalties as each House may provide.

Each House may determine the Rules of its Proceedings, punish its Members for disorderly Behavior, and, with the Concurrence of two thirds, expel a Member.

Each House shall keep a Journal of its Proceedings, and from time to time publish the same, excepting such Parts as may in their Judgment require Secrecy; and the Yeas and Nays of the Members of either House on any question shall, at the Desire of one fifth of those Present, be entered on the Journal.

Neither House, during the Session of Congress, shall, without the Consent of the other, adjourn for more than three days, nor to any other Place than that in which the two Houses shall be sitting.

Section 6.

The Senators and Representatives shall receive a Compensation for their Services, to be ascertained by Law, and paid out of the Treasury of the United States. They shall in all Cases, except Treason, Felony and Breach of the Peace, be privileged from Arrest during their Attendance at the Session of their respective Houses, and in going to and returning from the same; and for any Speech or Debate in either House, they shall not be questioned in any other Place.

No Senator or Representative shall, during the Time for which he was elected, be appointed to any civil Office under the Authority of the United States, which shall have been created, or the Emoluments whereof shall have been encreased during such time; and no Person holding any Office under the United States, shall be a Member of either House during his Continuance in Office.

Section 7.

All Bills for raising Revenue shall originate in the House of Representatives; but the Senate may propose or concur with Amendments as on other Bills.

Every Bill which shall have passed the House of Representatives and the Senate, shall, before it become a Law, be presented to the President of the United States: If he approve he shall sign it, but if not he shall return it, with his Objections to that House in which it shall have originated, who shall enter the Objections at large on their Journal, and proceed to reconsider it. If after such Reconsideration two thirds of that House shall agree to pass the Bill, it shall be sent, together with the Objections, to the other House, by which it shall likewise be reconsidered, and if approved by two thirds of that House, it shall become a Law. But in all such Cases the Votes of both Houses shall be determined by Yeas and Nays, and the Names of the Persons voting for and against the Bill shall be entered on the Journal of each House respectively. If any Bill shall not be returned by the President within ten Days (Sundays excepted) after it shall have been presented to him, the Same shall be a Law, in like Manner as if he had signed it, unless the Congress by their Adjournment prevent its Return, in which Case it shall not be a Law.

Every Order, Resolution, or Vote to which the Concurrence of the Senate and House of Representatives may be necessary (except on a question of Adjournment) shall be presented to the President of the United States; and before the Same shall take Effect, shall be approved by him, or being disapproved by him, shall be repassed by two thirds of the Senate and House of Representatives, according to the Rules and Limitations prescribed in the Case of a Bill.

Section 8.

The Congress shall have Power To lay and collect Taxes, Duties, Imposts and Excises, to pay the Debts and provide for the common Defen[c]e and general Welfare of the United States; but all Duties, Imposts and Excises shall be uniform throughout the United States;

To borrow Money on the credit of the United States;

To regulate Commerce with foreign Nations, and among the several States, and with the Indian Tribes;

To establish a[n] uniform Rule of Naturalization, and uniform Laws on the subject of Bankruptcies throughout the United States;

To coin Money, regulate the Value thereof, and of foreign Coin, and fix the Standard of Weights and Measures;

To provide for the Punishment of counterfeiting the Securities and current Coin of the United States;

To establish Post Offices and post Roads;

To promote the Progress of Science and useful Arts, by securing for limited Times to Authors and Inventors the exclusive Right to their respective Writings and Discoveries;

To constitute Tribunals inferior to the supreme Court;

To define and punish Piracies and Felonies committed on the high Seas, and Offen[c]es against the Law of Nations;

To declare War, grant Letters of Marque and Reprisal, and make Rules concerning Captures on Land and Water;

To raise and support Armies, but no Appropriation of Money to that Use shall be for a longer Term than two Years;

To provide and maintain a Navy;

To make Rules for the Government and Regulation of the land and naval Forces;

To provide for calling forth the Militia to execute the Laws of the Union, suppress Insurrections and repel Invasions;

To provide for organizing, arming, and disciplining, the Militia, and for governing such Part of them as may be employed in the Service of the United States, reserving to the States respectively, the Appointment of the Officers, and the Authority of training the Militia according to the discipline prescribed by Congress;

To exercise exclusive Legislation in all Cases whatsoever, over such District (not exceeding ten Miles square) as may, by Cession of particular States, and the Acceptance of Congress, become the Seat of the Government of the United States, and to exercise like Authority over all Places purchased by the Consent of the Legislature of the State in which the Same shall be, for the Erection of Forts, Magazines, Arsenals, dock-Yards, and other needful Buildings;—And

To make all Laws which shall be necessary and proper for carrying into Execution the foregoing Powers, and all other Powers vested by this Constitution in the Government of the United States, or in any Department or Officer thereof.

Section 9.

The Migration or Importation of such Persons as any of the States now existing shall think proper to admit, shall not be prohibited by the Congress prior to the Year one thousand eight hundred and eight, but a tax or duty may be imposed on such Importation, not exceeding ten dollars for each Person.

The Privilege of the Writ of Habeas Corpus shall not be suspended, unless when in Cases of Rebellion or Invasion the public Safety may require it.

No Bill of Attainder or ex post facto Law shall be passed.

No Capitation, or other direct, Tax shall be laid, unless in Proportion to the Census or enumeration herein before directed to be taken.

No Tax or Duty shall be laid on Articles exported from any State.

No Preference shall be given by any Regulation of Commerce or Revenue to the Ports of one State over those of another; nor shall Vessels bound to, or from, one State, be obliged to enter, clear, or pay Duties in another.

No Money shall be drawn from the Treasury, but in Consequence of Appropriations made by Law; and a regular Statement and Account of the Receipts and Expenditures of all public Money shall be published from time to time.

No Title of Nobility shall be granted by the United States: and no Person holding any Office of Profit or Trust under them, shall, without the Consent of the Congress, accept of any present, Emolument, Office, or Title, of any kind whatever, from any King, Prince, or foreign State.

Section 10.

No State shall enter into any Treaty, Alliance, or Confederation; grant Letters of Marque and Reprisal; coin Money; emit Bills of Credit; make any Thing but gold and silver Coin a Tender in Payment of Debts; pass any Bill of Attainder, ex post facto Law, or Law impairing the Obligation of Contracts, or grant any Title of Nobility.

No State shall, without the Consent of the Congress, lay any Imposts or Duties on Imports or Exports, except what may be absolutely necessary for executing its inspection Laws: and the net Produce of all Duties and Imposts, laid by any State on Imports or Exports, shall be for the Use of the Treasury of the United States; and all such Laws shall be subject to the Revision and Controul of the Congress.

No State shall, without the Consent of Congress, lay any Duty of Tonnage, keep Troops, or Ships of War in time of Peace, enter into any Agreement or Compact with another State, or with a foreign Power, or engage in War, unless actually invaded, or in such imminent Danger as will not admit of delay.

ARTICLE II.

Section 1.
The executive Power shall be vested in a President of the United States of America. He shall hold his Office during the Term of four Years, and, together with the Vice President, chosen for the same Term, be elected, as follows:

Each State shall appoint, in such Manner as the Legislature thereof may direct, a Number of Electors, equal to the whole Number of Senators and Representatives to which the State may be entitled in the Congress: but no Senator or Representative, or Person holding an Office of Trust or Profit under the United States, shall be appointed an Elector.

The Electors shall meet in their respective States, and vote by Ballot for two Persons, of whom one at least shall not be an Inhabitant of the same State with themselves. And they shall make a List of all the Persons voted for, and of the Number of Votes for each; which List they shall sign and certify, and transmit sealed to the Seat of the Government of the United States, directed to the President of the Senate. The President of the Senate shall, in the Presence of the Senate and House of Representatives, open all the Certificates, and the Votes shall then be counted. The Person having the greatest Number of Votes shall be the President, if such Number be a Majority of the whole Number of Electors appointed; and if there be more than one who have such Majority, and have an equal Number of Votes, then the House of Representatives shall immediately [chuse] by Ballot one of them for President; and if no Person have a Majority, then from the five highest on the List the said House shall in like Manner [chuse] the President. But in [chusing] the President, the Votes shall be taken by States, the Representation from each State having one Vote; a quorum for this purpose shall consist of a Member or Members from two thirds of the States, and a Majority of all the States shall be necessary to a Choice. In every Case, after the Choice of the President, the Person having the greatest Number of Votes of the Electors shall be the Vice President. But if there should remain two or more who have equal Votes, the Senate shall [chuse] from them by Ballot the Vice President.

The Congress may determine the Time of [chusing] the Electors, and the Day on which they shall give their Votes; which Day shall be the same throughout the United States.

No Person except a natural born Citizen, or a Citizen of the United States, at the time of the Adoption of this Constitution, shall be eligible to the Office of President; neither shall any Person be eligible to that Office who shall not have attained to the Age of thirty-five Years, and been fourteen Years a Resident within the United States.

In Case of the Removal of the President from Office, or of his Death, Resignation, or Inability to discharge the Powers and Duties of the said Office, the Same shall devolve on the Vice President, and the Congress may by Law provide for the Case of Removal, Death, Resignation or Inability, both of the President and Vice President, declaring what Officer shall then act as President, and such Officer shall act accordingly, until the Disability be removed, or a President shall be elected.

The President shall, at stated Times, receive for his Services, a Compensation, which shall neither be increased nor diminished during the Period for which he shall have been elected, and he shall not receive within that Period any other Emolument from the United States, or any of them.

Before he enter on the Execution of his Office, he shall take the following Oath or Affirmation:—"I do solemnly swear (or affirm) that I will faithfully execute the Office of President of the United States, and will to the best of my Ability, preserve, protect and defend the Constitution of the United States."

Section 2.

The President shall be Commander in Chief of the Army and Navy of the United States, and of the Militia of the several States, when called into the actual Service of the United States; he may require the Opinion, in writing, of the principal Officer in each of the executive Departments, upon any Subject relating to the Duties of their respective Offices, and he shall have Power to grant Reprieves and Pardons for Offen[c]es against the United States, except in Cases of Impeachment.

He shall have Power, by and with the Advice and Consent of the Senate, to make Treaties, provided two thirds of the Senators present concur; and he shall nominate, and by and with the Advice and Consent of the Senate, shall appoint Ambassadors, other public Ministers and Consuls, Judges of the supreme Court, and all other Officers of the United States, whose Appointments are not herein otherwise provided for, and which shall be established by Law: but the Congress may by Law vest the Appointment of such inferior Officers, as they think proper, in the President alone, in the Courts of Law, or in the Heads of Departments.

The President shall have Power to fill up all Vacancies that may happen during the Recess of the Senate, by granting Commissions which shall expire at the End of their next Session.

Section 3.

He shall from time to time give to the Congress Information of the State of the Union, and recommend to their Consideration such Measures as he shall judge necessary and expedient; he may, on extraordinary Occasions, convene both Houses, or either of them, and in Case of Disagreement between them, with Respect to the Time of Adjournment, he may adjourn them to such Time as he shall think proper; he shall receive Ambassadors and other public Ministers; he shall take Care that the Laws be faithfully executed, and shall Commission all the Officers of the United States.

Section 4.

The President, Vice President and all civil Officers of the United States, shall be removed from Office on Impeachment for, and Conviction of, Treason, Bribery, or other high Crimes and Misdemeanors.

ARTICLE III.

Section 1.

The judicial Power of the United States shall be vested in one supreme Court, and in such inferior Courts as the Congress may from time to time ordain and establish. The Judges, both of the supreme and inferior Courts, shall hold their Offices during good

Behavio[u]r, and shall, at stated Times, receive for their Services a Compensation, which shall not be diminished during their Continuance in Office.

Section 2.

The judicial Power shall extend to all Cases, in Law and Equity, arising under this Constitution, the Laws of the United States, and Treaties made, or which shall be made, under their Authority;—to all Cases affecting Ambassadors, other public Ministers and Consuls;—to all Cases of admiralty and maritime Jurisdiction;—to Controversies to which the United States shall be a Party;—to Controversies between two or more States;—between a State and Citizens of another State;—between Citizens of different States;—between Citizens of the same State claiming Lands under Grants of different States, and between a State, or the Citizens thereof, and foreign States, Citizens or Subjects.

In all Cases affecting Ambassadors, other public Ministers and Consuls, and those in which a State shall be Party, the supreme Court shall have original Jurisdiction. In all the other Cases before mentioned, the supreme Court shall have appellate Jurisdiction, both as to Law and Fact, with such Exceptions, and under such Regulations as the Congress shall make.

The Trial of all Crimes, except in Cases of Impeachment, shall be by Jury; and such Trial shall be held in the State where the said Crimes shall have been committed; but when not committed within any State, the Trial shall be at such Place or Places as the Congress may by Law have directed.

Section 3.

Treason against the United States, shall consist only in levying War against them, or in adhering to their Enemies, giving them Aid and Comfort. No Person shall be convicted of Treason unless on the Testimony of two Witnesses to the same overt Act, or on Confession in open Court.

The Congress shall have Power to declare the Punishment of Treason, but no Attainder of Treason shall work Corruption of Blood, or Forfeiture except during the Life of the Person attainted.

ARTICLE IV.

Section 1.

Full Faith and Credit shall be given in each State to the public Acts, Records, and judicial Proceedings of every other State. And the Congress may by general Laws prescribe the Manner in which such Acts, Records and Proceedings shall be proved, and the Effect thereof.

Section 2.

The Citizens of each State shall be entitled to all Privileges and Immunities of Citizens in the several States.

A Person charged in any State with Treason, Felony, or other Crime, who shall flee from Justice, and be found in another State, shall on Demand of the executive Authority of the State from which he fled, be delivered up, to be removed to the State having Jurisdiction of the Crime.

No Person held to Service or Labo[u]r in one State, under the Laws thereof, escaping into another, shall, in Consequence of any Law or Regulation therein, be discharged from such Service or Labo[u]r, but shall be delivered up on Claim of the Party to whom such Service or Labo[u]r may be due.

Section 3.

New States may be admitted by the Congress into this Union; but no new State shall be formed or erected within the Jurisdiction of any other State; nor any State be formed by the Junction of two or more States, or Parts of States, without the Consent of the Legislatures of the States concerned as well as of the Congress.

The Congress shall have Power to dispose of and make all needful Rules and Regulations respecting the Territory or other Property belonging to the United States; and nothing in this Constitution shall be so construed as to Prejudice any Claims of the United States, or of any particular State.

Section 4.

The United States shall guarantee to every State in this Union a Republican Form of Government, and shall protect each of them against Invasion; and on Application of the Legislature, or of the Executive (when the Legislature cannot be convened), against domestic Violence.

ARTICLE V.

The Congress, whenever two thirds of both Houses shall deem it necessary, shall propose Amendments to this Constitution, or, on the Application of the Legislatures of two thirds of the several States, shall call a Convention for proposing Amendments, which, in either Case, shall be valid to all Intents and Purposes, as Part of this Constitution, when ratified by the Legislatures of three-fourths of the several States, or by Conventions in three-fourths thereof, as the one or the other Mode of Ratification may be proposed by the Congress; Provided that no Amendment which may be made prior to the Year One thousand eight hundred and eight shall in any Manner affect the first and fourth Clauses in the Ninth Section of the first Article; and that no State, without its Consent, shall be deprived of its equal Suffrage in the Senate.

ARTICLE VI.

All Debts contracted and Engagements entered into, before the Adoption of this Constitution, shall be as valid against the United States under this Constitution, as under the Confederation.

This Constitution, and the Laws of the United States which shall be made in Pursuance thereof; and all Treaties made, or which shall be made, under the Authority of the United States, shall be the supreme Law of the Land; and the Judges in every State shall be bound thereby, any Thing in the Constitution or Laws of any State to the Contrary notwithstanding.

The Senators and Representatives before mentioned, and the Members of the several State Legislatures, and all executive and judicial Officers, both of the United States and of the several States, shall be bound by Oath or Affirmation, to support this Constitution; but no religious Test shall ever be required as a Qualification to any Office or public Trust under the United States.

ARTICLE VII.

The Ratification of the Conventions of nine States, shall be sufficient for the Establishment of this Constitution between the States so ratifying the Same.

(The Word, "the," being interlined between the seventh and eighth Lines of the first Page, the Word "Thirty" being partly written on an Erazure in the fifteenth Line of the first Page, The Words "is tried" being interlined between the thirty second and thirty third Lines of the first Page and the Word "the" being interlined between the forty third and forty fourth Lines of the second Page.)

Attest: William Jackson Secretary

Done in Convention by the Unanimous Consent of the States present the Seventeenth Day of September in the Year of our Lord one thousand seven hundred and Eighty seven and of the Independence of the United States of America the Twelfth.

In witness whereof We have hereunto subscribed our Names.

G. Washington,
Presidt and deputy from Virginia

Delaware
    Geo: Read
    Gunning Bedford jun
    John Dickinson
    Richard Bassett
    Jaco: Broom

Maryland
    James McHenry
    Dan: of St Thos Jenifer
    Danl Carroll

Virginia
    John Blair
    James Madison Jr.

North Carolina
    Wm Blount
    Richd. Dobbs Spaight
    Hu Williamson

South Carolina
    J. Rutledge
    Charles Cotesworth Pinckney
    Charles Pinckney
    Pierce Butler

Georgia
    William Few
    Abr Baldwin

New Hampshire
    John Langdon
    Nicholas Gilman

Massachusetts
    Nathaniel Gorham
    Rufus King

Connecticut
    Wm Saml Johnson
    Roger Sherman

New York
    Alexander Hamilton

New Jersey
    Wil: Livingston
    David Brearley
    Wm Paterson
    Jona: Dayton

Pennsylvania
    B Franklin
    Thomas Mifflin
    Robt. Morris
    Geo. Clymer
    Thos. FitzSimons
    Jared Ingersoll
    James Wilson
    Gouv Morris

Ten Original Amendments: The Bill of Rights

The following text is a transcription of the first 10 amendments to the Constitution in their original form. These amendments were ratified December 15, 1791, and form what is known as the "Bill of Rights."

AMENDMENT I.

Congress shall make no law respecting an establishment of religion, or prohibiting the free exercise thereof; or abridging the freedom of speech, or of the press; or the right of the people peaceably to assemble, and to petition the Government for a redress of grievances.

AMENDMENT II.

A well regulated Militia, being necessary to the security of a free State, the right of the people to keep and bear Arms, shall not be infringed.

AMENDMENT III.

No Soldier shall, in time of peace be quartered in any house, without the consent of the Owner, nor in time of war, but in a manner to be prescribed by law.

AMENDMENT IV.

The right of the people to be secure in their persons, houses, papers, and effects, against unreasonable searches and seizures, shall not be violated, and no Warrants shall issue, but upon probable cause, supported by Oath or affirmation, and particularly describing the place to be searched, and the persons or things to be seized.

AMENDMENT V.

No person shall be held to answer for a capital, or otherwise infamous crime, unless on a presentment or indictment of a Grand Jury, except in cases arising in the land or naval forces, or in the Militia, when in actual service in time of War or public danger; nor shall any person be subject for the same offen[c]e to be twice put in jeopardy of life or limb; nor shall be compelled in any criminal case to be a witness against himself, nor be deprived of life, liberty, or property, without due process of law; nor shall private property be taken for public use, without just compensation.

AMENDMENT VI.

In all criminal prosecutions, the accused shall enjoy the right to a speedy and public trial, by an impartial jury of the State and district wherein the crime shall have been committed, which district shall have been previously ascertained by law, and to be informed of the nature and cause of the accusation; to be confronted with the witnesses against him; to have compulsory process for obtaining witnesses in his favor, and to have the Assistance of Counsel for his defen[c]e.

AMENDMENT VII.

In suits at common law, where the value in controversy shall exceed twenty dollars, the right of trial by jury shall be preserved, and no fact tried by a jury, shall be otherwise reexamined in any Court of the United States, than according to the rules of the common law.

AMENDMENT VIII.

Excessive bail shall not be required, nor excessive fines imposed, nor cruel and unusual punishments inflicted.

AMENDMENT IX.

The enumeration in the Constitution, of certain rights, shall not be construed to deny or disparage others retained by the people.

AMENDMENT X.

The powers not delegated to the United States by the Constitution, nor prohibited by it to the States, are reserved to the States respectively, or to the people.

Amendments 11-27 to the Constitution of the United States

AMENDMENT XI.

Passed by Congress March 4, 1794. Ratified February 7, 1795.
Note: *Article III, Section 2 of the Constitution was modified by Amendment XI.*

The Judicial power of the United States shall not be construed to extend to any suit in law or equity, commenced or prosecuted against one of the United States by Citizens of another State, or by Citizens or Subjects of any Foreign State.

AMENDMENT XII.

Passed by Congress December 9, 1803. Ratified June 15, 1804.
Note: *A portion of Article II, section 1 of the Constitution was superseded by Amendment XII.*

The Electors shall meet in their respective states and vote by ballot for President and Vice[-]President, one of whom, at least, shall not be an inhabitant of the same state with themselves; they shall name in their ballots the person voted for as President, and in distinct ballots the person voted for as Vice[-]President, and they shall make distinct lists of all persons voted for as President, and of all persons voted for as Vice[-]President, and of the number of votes for each, which lists they shall sign and certify, and transmit sealed to the seat of the government of the United States, directed to the President of the Senate;—the President of the Senate shall, in the presence of the Senate and House of Representatives, open all the certificates and the votes shall then be counted;—The person having the greatest number of votes for President, shall be the President, if such number be a majority of the whole number of Electors appointed; and if no person have such majority, then from the persons having the highest numbers not exceeding three on the list of those voted for as President, the House of Representatives shall choose immediately, by ballot, the President. But in choosing the President, the votes shall be taken by states, the representation from each state having one vote; a quorum for this purpose shall consist of a member or members from two-thirds of the states, and a majority of all the states shall be necessary to a choice. (And if the House of Representatives shall not choose a President whenever the right of choice shall devolve upon them, before the fourth day of March next following, then the Vice[-]President shall act as President, as in case of the death or other constitutional disability of the President.—)* The person having the greatest number of votes as Vice[-]President, shall be the Vice[-]President, if such number be a majority of the whole number of Electors appointed, and if no person have a majority, then from the two highest numbers on the list, the Senate shall choose the Vice[-]President; a quorum for the purpose shall consist of two-thirds of the whole number of Senators, and a majority of the whole number shall be necessary to a choice. But no person constitutionally ineligible to the office of President shall be eligible to that of Vice[-]President of the United States.

*Superseded by Section 3 of Amendment XX.

AMENDMENT XIII.

Passed by Congress January 31, 1865. Ratified December 6, 1865.

Note: *A portion of Article IV, Section 2 of the Constitution was superseded by Amendment XIII.*

Section 1.

Neither slavery nor involuntary servitude, except as a punishment for crime whereof the party shall have been duly convicted, shall exist within the United States, or any place subject to their jurisdiction.

Section 2.

Congress shall have power to enforce this article by appropriate legislation.

AMENDMENT XIV.

Passed by Congress June 13, 1866. Ratified July 9, 1868.

Note: *Article I, Section 2 of the Constitution was modified by Section 2 of Amendment XIV.*

Section 1.

All persons born or naturalized in the United States, and subject to the jurisdiction thereof, are citizens of the United States and of the State wherein they reside. No State shall make or enforce any law which shall abridge the privileges or immunities of citizens of the United States; nor shall any State deprive any person of life, liberty, or property, without due process of law; nor deny to any person within its jurisdiction the equal protection of the laws.

Section 2.

Representatives shall be apportioned among the several States according to their respective numbers, counting the whole number of persons in each State, excluding Indians not taxed. But when the right to vote at any election for the choice of electors for President and Vice[-]President of the United States, Representatives in Congress, the Executive and Judicial officers of a State, or the members of the Legislature thereof, is denied to any of the male inhabitants of such State, being twenty-one years of age,* and citizens of the United States, or in any way abridged, except for participation in rebellion, or other crime, the basis of representation therein shall be reduced in the proportion which the number of such male citizens shall bear to the whole number of male citizens twenty-one years of age in such State.

Section 3.

No person shall be a Senator or Representative in Congress, or elector of President and Vice[-]President, or hold any office, civil or military, under the United States, or under any State, who, having previously taken an oath, as a member of Congress, or as an officer of the United States, or as a member of any State legislature, or as an executive or judicial officer of any State, to support the Constitution of the United States, shall have engaged in insurrection or rebellion against the same, or given aid or comfort to the enemies thereof. But Congress may by a vote of two-thirds of each House, remove such disability.

Section 4.

The validity of the public debt of the United States, authorized by law, including debts incurred for payment of pensions and bounties for services in suppressing insurrection or rebellion, shall not be questioned. But neither the United States nor any State shall assume or pay any debt or obligation incurred in aid of insurrection or rebellion against the United States, or any claim for the loss or emancipation of any slave; but all such debts, obligations and claims shall be held illegal and void.

Section 5.

The Congress shall have the power to enforce, by appropriate legislation, the provisions of this article.

*Changed by Section 1 of Amendment XXVI.

AMENDMENT XV.

Passed by Congress February 26, 1869. Ratified February 3, 1870.

Section 1.

The right of citizens of the United States to vote shall not be denied or abridged by the United States or by any State on account of race, color, or previous condition of servitude—

Section 2.

The Congress shall have the power to enforce this article by appropriate legislation.

AMENDMENT XVI.

Passed by Congress July 2, 1909. Ratified February 3, 1913.
Note: *Article I, Section 9 of the Constitution was modified by Amendment XVI.*

The Congress shall have power to lay and collect taxes on incomes, from whatever source derived, without apportionment among the several States, and without regard to any census or enumeration.

AMENDMENT XVII.

Passed by Congress May 13, 1912. Ratified April 8, 1913.
Note: *Article I, Section 3 of the Constitution was modified by Amendment XVII.*

The Senate of the United States shall be composed of two Senators from each State, elected by the people thereof, for six years; and each Senator shall have one vote. The electors in each State shall have the qualifications requisite for electors of the most numerous branch of the State legislatures.

When vacancies happen in the representation of any State in the Senate, the executive authority of such State shall issue writs of election to fill such vacancies: *Provided,* That the legislature of any State may empower the executive thereof to make temporary appointments until the people fill the vacancies by election as the legislature may direct.

This amendment shall not be so construed as to affect the election or term of any Senator chosen before it becomes valid as part of the Constitution.

AMENDMENT XVIII.

Passed by Congress December 18, 1917. Ratified January 16, 1919. Repealed by Amendment XXI.

Section 1.

After one year from the ratification of this article the manufacture, sale, or transportation of intoxicating liquors within, the importation thereof into, or the exportation thereof from the United States and all territory subject to the jurisdiction thereof for beverage purposes is hereby prohibited.

Section 2.

The Congress and the several States shall have concurrent power to enforce this article by appropriate legislation.

Section 3.

This article shall be inoperative unless it shall have been ratified as an amendment to the Constitution by the legislatures of the several States, as provided in the Constitution, within seven years from the date of the submission hereof to the States by the Congress.

AMENDMENT XIX.

Passed by Congress June 4, 1919. Ratified August 18, 1920.

The right of citizens of the United States to vote shall not be denied or abridged by the United States or by any State on account of sex.

Congress shall have power to enforce this article by appropriate legislation.

AMENDMENT XX.

Passed by Congress March 2, 1932. Ratified January 23, 1933.

Note: *Article I, Section 4 of the Constitution was modified by Section 2 of this amendment. In addition, a portion of Amendment XII was superseded by Section 3.*

Section 1.

The terms of the President and the Vice President shall end at noon on the 20th day of January, and the terms of Senators and Representatives at noon on the 3d day of January, of the years in which such terms would have ended if this article had not been ratified; and the terms of their successors shall then begin.

Section 2.

The Congress shall assemble at least once in every year, and such meeting shall begin at noon on the 3d day of January, unless they shall by law appoint a different day.

Section 3.

If, at the time fixed for the beginning of the term of the President, the President elect shall have died, the Vice President elect shall become President. If a President shall not have been chosen before the time fixed for the beginning of his term, or if the President elect shall have failed to qualify, then the Vice President elect shall act as President until a President shall have qualified; and the Congress may by law provide for the case wherein neither a President elect nor a Vice President shall have qualified, declaring who shall then act as President, or the manner in which one who is to act shall be selected, and such person shall act accordingly until a President or Vice President shall have qualified.

Section 4.

The Congress may by law provide for the case of the death of any of the persons from whom the House of Representatives may choose a President whenever the right of choice shall have devolved upon them, and for the case of the death of any of the persons from whom the Senate may choose a Vice President whenever the right of choice shall have devolved upon them.

Section 5.

Sections 1 and 2 shall take effect on the 15th day of October following the ratification of this article.

Section 6.

This article shall be inoperative unless it shall have been ratified as an amendment to the Constitution by the legislatures of three-fourths of the several States within seven years from the date of its submission.

AMENDMENT XXI.

Passed by Congress February 20, 1933. Ratified December 5, 1933.

Section 1.

The eighteenth article of amendment to the Constitution of the United States is hereby repealed.

Section 2.

The transportation or importation into any State, Territory, or Possession of the United States for delivery or use therein of intoxicating liquors, in violation of the laws thereof, is hereby prohibited.

Section 3.

This article shall be inoperative unless it shall have been ratified as an amendment to the Constitution by conventions in the several States, as provided in the Constitution, within seven years from the date of the submission hereof to the States by the Congress.

AMENDMENT XXII,

Passed by Congress March 21, 1947. Ratified February 27, 1951.

Section 1.

No person shall be elected to the office of the President more than twice, and no person who has held the office of President, or acted as President, for more than two years of a term to which some other person was elected President shall be elected to the office of President more than once. But this Article shall not apply to any person holding the office of President when this Article was proposed by Congress, and shall not prevent any person who may be holding the office of President, or acting as President, during the term within which this Article becomes operative from holding the office of President or acting as President during the remainder of such term.

Section 2.

This article shall be inoperative unless it shall have been ratified as an amendment to the Constitution by the legislatures of three-fourths of the several States within seven years from the date of its submission to the States by the Congress.

AMENDMENT XXIII.

Passed by Congress June 16, 1960. Ratified March 29, 1961.

Section 1.

The District constituting the seat of Government of the United States shall appoint in such manner as Congress may direct:

A number of electors of President and Vice President equal to the whole number of Senators and Representatives in Congress to which the District would be entitled if it were a State, but in no event more than the least populous State; they shall be in addition to those appointed by the States, but they shall be considered, for the purposes of the election of President and Vice President, to be electors appointed by a State; and they shall meet in the District and perform such duties as provided by the twelfth article of amendment.

Section 2.

The Congress shall have power to enforce this article by appropriate legislation.

AMENDMENT XXIV.

Passed by Congress August 27, 1962. Ratified January 23, 1964.

Section 1.

The right of citizens of the United States to vote in any primary or other election for President or Vice President, for electors for President or Vice President, or for Senator or Representative in Congress, shall not be denied or abridged by the United States or any State by reason of failure to pay poll tax or other tax.

Section 2.

The Congress shall have power to enforce this article by appropriate legislation.

AMENDMENT XXV.

Passed by Congress July 6, 1965. Ratified February 10, 1967.
Note: *Article II, Section 1 of the Constitution was affected by this amendment.*

Section 1.

In case of the removal of the President from office or of his death or resignation, the Vice President shall become President.

Section 2.

Whenever there is a vacancy in the office of the Vice President, the President shall nominate a Vice President who shall take office upon confirmation by a majority vote of both Houses of Congress.

Section 3.

Whenever the President transmits to the President pro tempore of the Senate and the Speaker of the House of Representatives his written declaration that he is unable to discharge the powers and duties of his office, and until he transmits to them a written declaration to the contrary, such powers and duties shall be discharged by the Vice President as Acting President.

Section 4.

Whenever the Vice President and a majority of either the principal officers of the executive departments or of such other body as Congress may by law provide, transmit to the President pro tempore of the Senate and the Speaker of the House of Representatives their written declaration that the President is unable to discharge the powers and duties of his office, the Vice President shall immediately assume the powers and duties of the office as Acting President.

Thereafter, when the President transmits to the President pro tempore of the Senate and the Speaker of the House of Representatives his written declaration that no inability exists, he shall resume the powers and duties of his office unless the Vice President and a majority of either the principal officers of the executive department or of such other body as Congress may by law provide, transmit within four days to the President pro tempore of the Senate and the Speaker of the House of Representatives their written declaration that the President is unable to discharge the powers and duties of his office. Thereupon Congress shall decide the issue, assembling within forty-eight hours for that purpose if not in session. If the Congress, within twenty-one days after receipt of the latter written declaration, or, if Congress is not in session, within twenty-one days after Congress is required to assemble, determines by two-thirds vote of both Houses that the President is unable to discharge the powers and duties of his office, the Vice President shall continue to discharge the same as Acting President; otherwise, the President shall resume the powers and duties of his office.

AMENDMENT XXVI.

Passed by Congress March 23, 1971. Ratified July 1, 1971.

Note: *Amendment 14, Section 2 of the Constitution was modified by Section 1 of this amendment.*

Section 1.

The right of citizens of the United States, who are eighteen years of age or older, to vote shall not be denied or abridged by the United States or by any State on account of age.

Section 2.

The Congress shall have power to enforce this article by appropriate legislation.

AMENDMENT XXVII.

Originally proposed September 25, 1789. Ratified May 7, 1992.

No law, varying the compensation for the services of the Senators and Representatives, shall take effect, until an election of representatives shall have intervened.

The Founding Fathers: Delegates to the Constitutional Convention

On February 21, 1787 the Continental Congress resolved that:

> "... it is expedient that on the second Monday in May next a Convention of delegates who shall have been appointed by the several States be held at Philadelphia for the sole and express purpose of revising the Articles of Confederation ..."

The original states, except Rhode Island, collectively appointed 70 individuals to the Constitutional Convention, but a number did not accept or could not attend. Those who did not attend included Richard Henry Lee, Patrick Henry, Thomas Jefferson, John Adams, Samuel Adams, and John Hancock.

In all, 55 delegates attended the Constitutional Convention sessions, but only 39 actually signed the Constitution. The delegates ranged in age from Jonathan Dayton, aged 26, to Benjamin Franklin, aged 81, who was so infirm that he had to be carried to sessions in a sedan chair.

(*Indicates delegates who did not sign the Constitution)

Connecticut
Oliver Ellsworth (Elsworth)*
William S. Johnson
Roger Sherman

Delaware
Richard Bassett (Basset)
Gunning Bedford, Jr.
Jacob Broom
John Dickinson
George Read

Georgia
Abraham Baldwin
William Few
William Houstoun*
William L. Pierce*

Maryland
Daniel Carroll
Daniel Jenifer of St. Thomas
Luther Martin*
James McHenry

John F. Mercer*

Massachusetts
Elbridge Gerry*
Nathaniel Gorham
Rufus King
Caleb Strong*

New Hampshire
Nicholas Gilman
John Langdon

New Jersey
David Brearly (Brearley)
Jonathan Dayton
William C. Houston*
William Livingston
William Paterson (Patterson)

New York
Alexander Hamilton
John, Jr. Lansing*
Robert Yates *

North Carolina
William Blount
William R. Davie*
Alexander Martin*
Richard D. Spaight
Hugh Williamson

Pennsylvania
George Clymer
Thomas Fitzsimons (FitzSimons; Fitzsimmons)
Benjamin Franklin
Jared Ingersoll
Thomas Mifflin
Gouverneur Morris
Robert Morris
James Wilson

South Carolina
Pierce Butler
CharlesPinckney
Charles Cotesworth Pinckney
John Rutledge

Rhode Island
Rhode Island did not send any delegates to the Constitutional Convention.

Virginia
John Blair
James Madison
George Mason*
James McClurg*
Edmund J. Randolph*
George Washington
George Wythe*

U.S. Presidents and Vice Presidents

©1999 by The Center for Applied Research in Education

Year	President/VP	Party
1789	George Washington (VA) John Adams (MA)	No party designations
1792	George Washington (VA) John Adams (MA)	No party designations
1796	John Adams (MA) Thomas Jefferson (VA)	Federalist Democratic-Republican
1800	Thomas Jefferson (VA) Aaron Burr (NY)	Democratic-Republican
1804	Thomas Jefferson (VA) George Clinton (NY)	Democratic-Republican
1808	James Madison (VA) George Clinton (NY)	Democratic-Republican
1812	James Madison (VA) Elbridge Gerry (MA)	Democratic-Republican
1816	James Monroe (VA) Daniel Tompkins (NY)	Democratic-Republican
1820	James Monroe (VA) Daniel Tompkins (NY)	Democratic-Republican
1824	John Quincy Adams (MA) John C. Calhoun (SC)	Democratic-Republican Democratic-Republican
1828	Andrew Jackson (TN) John C. Calhoun (SC)	Democratic
1832	Andrew Jackson (TN) Martin Van Buren (NY)	Democratic
1836	Martin Van Buren (NY) Richard M. Johnson (KY)	Democratic
1840	William H. Harrison (OH) John Tyler (VA)	Whig
1841	John Tyler (VA) (no Vice President)	Whig
1844	James K. Polk (TN) George M. Dallas (PA)	Democratic

Year	President/VP	Party
1848	Zachary Taylor (LA) Millard Fillmore (NY)	Whig
1850	Millard Fillmore (NY) (no Vice President)	Whig
1852	Franklin Pierce (N.H.) William King (AL)	Democratic
1856	James Buchanan (PA) John C. Breckinridge (KY)	Democratic
1860	Abraham Lincoln (IL) Hannibal Hamlin (ME)	Republican
1864	Abraham Lincoln (IL) Andrew Johnson (TN)	Republican
1864	Andrew Johnson (TN) (no Vice President)	Republican
1868	Ulysses S. Grant (OH) Schuyler Colfax (IN)	Republican
1872	Ulysses S. Grant (OH) Henry Wilson (MA)	Republican
1876	Rutherford B. Hayes (OH) William A. Wheeler (NY)	Republican
1880	James A. Garfield (OH) Chester A. Arthur (NY)	Republican
1881	Chester A. Arthur (NY) (no Vice President)	Republican
1884	Grover Cleveland (NY) Thomas A. Hendricks (IN)	Democratic
1888	Benjamin Harrison (IN) Levi. P. Morton (NY)	Republican
1892	Grover Cleveland (NY) Adlai E. Stevenson (IL)	Democratic
1896	William McKinley (OH) Garret Hobart (VA)	Republican
1900	William McKinley (OH) Theodore Roosevelt (NY)	Republican
1901	Theodore Roosevelt (NY) (no Vice President)	Republican
1904	Theodore Roosevelt (NY) Charles Fairbanks (IN)	Republican

Year	President/VP	Party
1908	William H. Taft (OH) James Sherman (NY)	Republican
1912	Woodrow Wilson (NJ) Thomas Marshall (IN)	Democratic
1916	Woodrow Wilson (NJ) Thomas Marshall (IN)	Democratic
1920	Warren G. Harding (OH) Calvin Coolidge (MA)	Republican
1923	Calvin Coolidge (MA) (no Vice President)	Republican
1924	Calvin Coolidge (MA) Charles Dawes (OH)	Republican
1928	Herbert C. Hoover (IA) Charles Curtis (KS)	Republican
1932	Franklin D. Roosevelt (NY) John Nance Garner (TX)	Democratic
1936	Franklin D. Roosevelt (NY) John Nance Garner (TX)	Democratic
1940	Franklin D. Roosevelt (NY) Henry A. Wallace (IA)	Democratic
1944	Franklin D. Roosevelt (NY) Harry S. Truman (MO)	Democratic
1945	Harry S. Truman (MO) (no Vice President)	Democratic
1948	Harry S. Truman (MO) Alben Barkley (KY)	Democratic
1952	Dwight D. Eisenhower (KS) Richard M. Nixon (CA)	Republican
1956	Dwight D. Eisenhower (KS) Richard M. Nixon (CA)	Republican
1960	John F. Kennedy (MA) Lyndon Johnson (TX)	Democratic
1963	Lyndon Johnson (TX) (no Vice President)	Democratic
1964	Lyndon Johnson (TX) Hubert H. Humphrey (MN)	Democratic
1968	Richard M. Nixon (CA) Spiro T. Agnew (MD)	Republican

Year	President/VP	Party
1972	Richard M. Nixon (CA) Spiro T. Agnew (MD)	Republican
1974	Gerald Ford (NE) Nelson Rockefeller (ME)	Republican
1976	Jimmy Carter (GA) Walter Mondale (MN)	Democratic
1980	Ronald Reagan (CA) George Bush (TX)	Republican
1984	Ronald Reagan (CA) George Bush (TX)	Republican
1988	George Bush (TX) Dan Quayle (IN)	Republican
1992	Bill Clinton (AR) Al Gore, Jr. (TN)	Democratic
1996	Bill Clinton (AR) Al Gore, Jr. (TN)	Democratic

Justices of the U.S. Supreme Court

Justice	Dates*	Appointed By
John Jay	1789-95	George Washington
John Rutledge	1789-91	George Washington
William Cushing	1789-1810	George Washington
James Wilson	1789-98	George Washington
John Blair	1789-96	George Washington
James Iredell	1790-99	George Washington
Thomas Johnson	1791-93	George Washington
William Paterson	1793-1806	George Washington
John Rutledge#	1795	George Washington
Samuel Chase	1796-1811	George Washington
Oliver Ellsworth+	1796-99	George Washington
Bushrod Washington	1798-1829	John Adams
Alfred Moore	1799-1804	John Adams
John Marshall+	1801-35	John Adams
William Johnson	1804-34	Thomas Jefferson
Henry B. Livingston	1806-23	Thomas Jefferson
Thomas Todd	1807-26	Thomas Jefferson
Joseph Story	1811-45	James Madison
Gabriel Duval	1811-35	James Madison
Smith Thompson	1823-43	James Monroe
Robert Trimble	1826-28	John Quincy Adams
John McLean	1829-61	Andrew Jackson
Henry Baldwin	1830-44	Andrew Jackson
James M. Wayne	1835-67	Andrew Jackson
Roger B. Taney+	1836-64	Andrew Jackson
Philip P. Barbour	1836-41	Andrew Jackson
John Catron	1837-65	Andrew Jackson
John McKinley	1837-52	Martin Van Buren
Peter V. Daniel	1841-60	Martin Van Buren
Samuel Nelson	1845-72	John Tyler
Levi Woodbury	1845-51	James K. Polk
Robert C. Grier	1846-70	James K. Polk
Benjamin R. Curtis	1851-57	Millard Fillmore
John A. Campbell	1853-61	Franklin Pierce
Nathan Clifford	1858-81	James Buchanan
Noah H. Swayne	1862-81	Abraham Lincoln
Samuel F. Miller	1862-90	Abraham Lincoln
David Davis	1862-77	Abraham Lincoln
Stephen J. Field	1863-97	Abraham Lincoln
Salmon P. Chase+	1864-73	Abraham Lincoln

Justice	Dates*	Appointed By
William Strong	1870-80	Ulysses S. Grant
Joseph P. Bradley	1870-92	Ulysses S. Grant
Ward Hunt	1872-82	Ulysses S. Grant
Morrison R. Waite+	1874-88	Ulysses C. Grant
John Marshall Harlan	1877-1911	Rutherford B. Hayes
William B. Woods	1880-87	Rutherford B. Hayes
Stanley Matthews	1881-89	James A. Garfield
Horace Gray	1881-1902	Chester A. Arthur
Samuel Blatchford	1882-93	Chester A. Arthur
Lucius Q. C. Lamar	1888-93	Grover Cleveland
Melville W. Fuller+	1888-1910	Grover Cleveland
David J. Brewer	1889-1910	Benjamin Harrison
Henry B. Brown	1890-1906	Benjamin Harrison
George Shiras	1892-1903	Benjamin Harrison
Howell E. Jackson	1893-95	Benjamin Harrison
Edward D. White	1894-1910	Grover Cleveland
Rufus W. Peckham	1895-1909	Grover Cleveland
Joseph McKenna	1898-1925	William McKinley
Oliver W. Holmes	1902-32	Theodore Roosevelt
William R. Day	1903-22	Theodore Roosevelt
William H. Moody	1906-10	Theodore Roosevelt
Horace H. Lurton	1910-14	William H. Taft
Charles Evans Hughes	1910-16	William H. Taft
Edward D. White+	1910-21	William H. Taft
W. Van Devanter	1910-37	William H. Taft
Joseph R. Lamar	1911-16	William H. Taft
Mahlon Pitney	1912-22	William H. Taft
James C. McReynolds	1914-41	Woodrow Wilson
Louis D. Brandeis	1916-39	Woodrow Wilson
John H. Clarke	1916-22	Woodrow Wilson
William Howard Taft	1921-30	Warren G. Harding
George Sutherland	1922-38	Warren G. Harding
Pierce Butler	1922-39	Warren G. Harding
Edward T. Sanford	1923-30	Warren G. Harding
Harlan F. Stone	1925-41	Calvin Coolidge
Charles Evans Hughes+	1930-41	Herbert Hoover
Owen J. Roberts	1930-45	Herbert Hoover
Benjamin N. Cardozo	1932-38	Herbert Hoover
Hugo L. Black	1937-71	Franklin D. Roosevelt
Stanley Reed	1938-57	Franklin D. Roosevelt
Felix Frankfurter	1939-62	Franklin D. Roosevelt
William O. Douglas	1939-75	Franklin D. Roosevelt
Frank Murphy	1940-49	Franklin D. Roosevelt
James F. Byrnes	1941-42	Franklin D. Roosevelt
Harlan F. Stone+	1941-46	Franklin D. Roosevelt
Robert H. Jackson	1941-54	Franklin D. Roosevelt
Wiley Rutledge	1943-49	Franklin D. Roosevelt

Justice	Dates*	Appointed By
Harold H. Burton	1945-58	Harry S. Truman
Frederick M. Vinson+	1946-53	Harry S. Truman
Tom C. Clark	1949-67	Harry S. Truman
Sherman Minton	1949-56	Harry S. Truman
Earl Warren+	1953-69	Dwight D. Eisenhower
John Marshall Harlan	1955-71	Dwight D. Eisenhower
William J. Brennan, Jr.	1956-90	Dwight D. Eisenhower
Charles E. Whittaker	1957-62	Dwight D. Eisenhower
Potter Stewart	1958-81	Dwight D. Eisenhower
Byron R. White	1962-93	John Kennedy
Arthur J. Goldberg	1962-65	John Kennedy
Abe Fortas#	1965-69	Lyndon Johnson
Thurgood Marshall	1967-91	Lyndon Johnson
Warren E. Burger+	1969-86	Richard Nixon
Harry A. Blackmun	1970-94	Richard Nixon
Lewis F. Powell Jr.	1972-87	Richard Nixon
William H. Rehnquist	1972-86	Richard Nixon
John Paul Stevens	1976-	Gerald Ford
Sandra Day O'Connor	1981-	Ronald Reagan
William H. Rehnquist+	1986-	Ronald Reagan
Antonin Scalia	1986-	Ronald Reagan
Anthony M. Kennedy	1987-	Ronald Reagan
David H. Souter	1990-	George Bush
Clarence Thomas	1991-	George Bush
Ruth Bader Ginsburg	1993-	Bill Clinton
Stephen G. Breyer	1994-	Bill Clinton

* Dates begin with year of nomination.
+Chief justices.
#Never confirmed by the Senate as chief justice.

U.S. Secretaries of State

Year
appointed

1789	Thomas Jefferson
1794	Edmund Randolph
1795	Timothy Pickering
1800	John Marshall
1801	James Madison
1809	Robert Smith
1811	James Monroe
1817	John Quincy Adams
1825	Henry Clay
1829	Martin Van Buren
1831	Edward Livingston
1833	Louis McLane
1834	John Forsyth
1841	Daniel Webster
1843	Abel P. Upshur
1844	John C. Calhoun
1845	James Buchanan
1849	John M. Clayton
1850	Daniel Webster
1852	Edward Everett
1853	William L. Marcy
1857	Lewis Cass
1860	Jeremiah S. Black
1861	William H. Seward
1869	Elihu B. Washburne
1869	Hamilton Fish
1877	William M. Evarts
1881	James G. Blaine
1881	F.T. Frelinghuysen
1885	Thomas F. Bayard
1889	James G. Blaine
1892	John W. Foster
1893	Walter Q. Gresham
1895	Richard Olney
1897	John Sherman
1898	William R. Day
1898	John Hay
1905	Elihu Root
1909	Robert Bacon
1909	Philander C. Knox
1913	William J. Bryan
1915	Robert Lansing

1920	Bainbridge Colby
1921	Charles E. Hughes
1925	Frank B. Kellogg
1929	Henry L. Stimson
1933	Cordell Hull
1944	E.R. Stettinius, Jr.
1945	James F. Byrnes
1947	George C. Marshall
1949	Dean G. Acheson
1953	John Foster Dulles
1959	Christian A. Herter
1961	Dean Rusk
1969	William P. Rogers
1973	Henry A. Kissinger
1977	Cyrus R. Vance
1980	Edmund S. Muskie
1981	Alexander M. Haig, Jr.
1982	George P. Shultz
1989	James Baker, 3d
1992	Lawrence S. Eagleburger
1993	Warren M. Christopher
1997	Madeleine K. Albright

Senators of the 105th Congress

Alabama
Sessions, Jeff (R)
Shelby, Richard C. (R)

Alaska
Murkowski, Frank H. (R)
Stevens, Ted (R)

Arizona
Kyl, Jon (R)
McCain, John (R)

Arkansas
Bumpers, Dale (D)
Hutchinson, Tim (R)

California
Boxer, Barbara (D)
Feinstein, Dianne (D)

Colorado
Allard, Wayne A. (R)
Campbell, Ben Nighthorse (R)

Connecticut
Dodd, Christopher J. (D)
Lieberman, Joseph I. (D)

Delaware
Biden, Joseph R., Jr. (D)
Roth, William V., Jr. (R)

Florida
Graham, Bob (D)
Mack, Connie (R)

Georgia
Cleland, Max (D)
Coverdell, Paul (R)

Hawaii
Akaka, Daniel K. (D)
Inouye, Daniel K. (D)

Idaho
Craig, Larry E. (R)
Kempthorne, Dirk (R)

Illinois
Durbin, Richard J. (D)
Moseley-Braun, Carol (D)

Indiana
Coats, Dan (R)
Lugar, Richard G. (R)

Iowa
Grassley, Chuck (R)
Harkin, Tom (D)

Kansas
Brownback, Sam (R)
Roberts, Pat (R)

Kentucky
Ford, Wendell H. (D)
McConnell, Mitch (R)

Louisiana
Breaux, John B. (D)
Landrieu, Mary (D)

Maine
Collins, Susan (R)
Snowe, Olympia J. (R)

Maryland
Mikulski, Barbara A. (D)
Sarbanes, Paul S. (D)

Massachusetts
Kennedy, Edward M. (D)
Kerry, John F. (D)

Michigan
Abraham, Spencer (R)
Levin, Carl (D)

Minnesota
    Grams, Rod (R)
    Wellstone, Paul D. (D)

Mississippi
    Cochran, Thad (R)
    Lott, Trent (R)

Missouri
    Ashcroft, John (R)
    Bond, Christopher S. (R)

Montana
    Baucus, Max (D)
    Burns, Conrad R. (R)

Nebraska
    Hagel, Chuck (R)
    Kerrey, J. Robert (D)

Nevada
    Bryan, Richard H. (D)
    Reid, Harry (D)

New Hampshire
    Gregg, Judd (R)
    Smith, Bob (R)

New Jersey
    Lautenberg, Frank R. (D)
    Torricelli, Robert (D)

New Mexico
    Bingaman, Jeff (D)
    Domenici, Pete V. (R)

New York
    D'Amato, Alfonse M. (R)
    Moynihan, Daniel Patrick (D)

North Carolina
    Faircloth, Lauch (R)
    Helms, Jesse (R)

North Dakota
    Conrad, Kent (D)
    Dorgan, Byron L. (D)

Ohio
    DeWine, Mike (R)
    Glenn, John (D)

Oklahoma
    Inhofe, James M. (R)
    Nickles, Don (R)

Oregon
    Smith, Gordon(R)
    Wyden, Ron (D)

Pennsylvania
    Santorum, Rick (R)
    Specter, Arlen (R)

Rhode Island
    Chafee, John H. (R)
    Reed, Jack (D)

South Carolina
    Hollings, Ernest F. (D)
    Thurmond, Strom (R)

South Dakota
    Daschle, Thomas A. (D)
    Johnson, Tim (D)

Tennessee
    Frist, William H. (R)
    Thompson, Fred (R)

Texas
    Gramm, Phil (R)
    Hutchison, Kay Bailey (R)

Utah
    Bennett, Robert F. (R)
    Hatch, Orrin G. (R)

Vermont
    Jeffords, James M. (R)
    Leahy, Patrick J. (D)

Virginia
    Robb, Charles S. (D)
    Warner, John W. (R)

Washington
    Gorton, Slade (R)
    Murray, Patty (D)

West Virginia
    Byrd, Robert C. (D)
    Rockefeller, John D., IV (D)

Wisconsin
    Feingold, Russell D. (D)
    Kohl, Herb (D)

Wyoming
    Enzi, Mike (R)
    Thomas, Craig (R)

55 Republicans, 45 Democrats as of February 4, 1998

Membership of the United Nations 1996

Member	Date of Admission
Afghanistan	Nov. 19, 1946
Albania	Dec. 14, 1955
Algeria	Oct. 8, 1962
Andorra	July 28, 1993
Angola	Dec. 1, 1976
Antigua and Barbuda	Nov. 11, 1981
Argentina*	Oct. 24, 1945
Armenia	Mar. 2, 1992
Australia*	Nov. 1, 1945
Austria	Dec. 14, 1955
Azerbaijan	Mar. 2, 1992
Bahamas	Sept. 18, 1973
Bahrain	Sept. 21, 1971
Bangladesh	Sept. 17, 1974
Barbados	Dec. 9, 1966
Belarus*	Oct. 24, 1945
Belgium*	Dec. 27, 1945
Belize	Sept. 25, 1981
Benin (formerly Dahomey)	Sept. 20, 1960
Bhutan	Sept. 21, 1971
Bolivia*	Nov. 14, 1945
Bosnia and Herzegovina	May 22, 1992
Botswana	Oct. 17, 1966
Brazil*	Oct. 24, 1945
Brunei	Sept. 21, 1984
Bulgaria	Dec. 14, 1955
Burkina Faso (formerly Upper Volta)	Sept. 20, 1960
Burundi	Sept. 18, 1962
Cambodia	Dec. 14, 1955
Cameroon	Sept. 20, 1960
Canada*	Nov. 9, 1945
Cape Verde	Sept. 16, 1975
Central African Republic	Sept. 20, 1960
Chad	Sept. 20, 1960
Chile*	Oct. 24, 1945
China*+	Oct. 24, 1945
Colombia*	Nov. 5, 1945
Comoros	Nov. 12, 1975
Congo	Sept. 20, 1960
Costa Rica*	Nov. 2, 1945

Member	Date of Admission
Croatia	May 22, 1992
Cuba*	Oct. 24, 1945
Cyprus	Sept. 20, 1960
Czech Republic**	Jan. 19, 1993
Denmark*	Oct. 24, 1945
Djibouti	Sept. 20, 1977
Dominica	Sept. 18, 1978
Dominican Republic*	Oct. 24, 1945
Ecuador*	Dec. 21, 1945
Egypt*	Oct. 24, 1945
El Salvador*	Oct. 24, 1945
Equatorial Guinea	Nov. 12, 1968
Eritrea	May 28, 1993
Estonia	Sept. 17, 1991
Ethiopia*	Nov. 13, 1945
Fiji	Oct. 13, 1970
Finland	Dec. 14, 1955
France*	Oct. 24, 1945
Gabon	Sept. 20, 1960
Gambia	Sept. 21, 1965
Georgia	Mar. 2, 1992
Germany++	Sept. 18, 1973
Ghana	Mar. 8, 1957
Greece*	Oct. 25, 1945
Grenada	Sept. 17, 1974
Guatemala*	Nov. 21, 1945
Guinea	Dec. 12, 1958
Guinea-Bissau	Sept. 17, 1974
Guyana	Sept. 20, 1966
Haiti*	Oct. 24, 1945
Honduras*	Dec. 17, 1945
Hungary	Dec. 14, 1955
Iceland	Nov. 19, 1946
India*	Oct. 30, 1945
Indonesia	Sept. 28, 1950
Iran*	Oct. 24, 1945
Iraq*	Dec. 21, 1945
Ireland	Dec. 14, 1955
Israel	May 11, 1949
Italy	Dec. 14, 1955
Ivory Coast	Sept. 20, 1960
Jamaica	Sept. 18, 1962
Japan	Dec. 18, 1956
Jordan	Dec. 14, 1955
Kazakhstan	Mar. 2, 1992
Kenya	Dec. 16, 1963
Korea, North	Sept. 17, 1991

Member	Date of Admission
Korea, South	Sept. 17, 1991
Kuwait	May 14, 1963
Kyrgyzstan	Mar. 2, 1992
Laos	Dec. 14, 1955
Latvia	Sept. 17, 1991
Lebanon*	Oct. 24, 1945
Lesotho	Oct. 17, 1966
Liberia*	Nov. 2, 1945
Libya	Dec. 14, 1955
Liechtenstein	Sept. 18, 1990
Lithuania	Sept. 17, 1991
Luxembourg*	Oct. 24, 1945
Macedonia	Apr. 8, 1993
Madagascar (Malagasy Republic)	Sept. 20, 1960
Malawi	Dec. 1, 1964
Malaysia	Sept. 17, 1957
Maldives	Sept. 21, 1965
Mali	Sept. 28, 1960
Malta	Dec. 1, 1964
Marshall Islands	Sept. 17, 1991
Mauritania	Oct. 27, 1961
Mauritius	Apr. 24, 1968
Mexico*	Nov. 7, 1945
Micronesia	Sept. 17, 1991
Moldova	Mar. 2, 1992
Monaco	May 28, 1993
Mongolia	Oct. 27, 1961
Morocco	Nov. 12, 1956
Mozambique	Sept. 16, 1975
Namibia	Apr. 23, 1990
Nepal	Dec. 14, 1955
Netherlands*	Dec. 10, 1945
New Zealand*	Oct. 24, 1945
Nicaragua*	Oct. 24, 1945
Niger	Sept. 20, 1960
Nigeria	Oct. 7, 1960
Norway*	Nov. 27, 1945
Oman	Oct. 7, 1971
Pakistan	Sept. 30, 1947
Palau	Dec. 15, 1994
Panama*	Nov. 13, 1945
Papua New Guinea	Oct. 10, 1975
Paraguay*	Oct. 24, 1945
Peru*	Oct. 31, 1945
Philippines*	Oct. 24, 1945
Poland*	Oct. 24, 1945
Portugal	Dec. 14, 1955

Member	Date of Admission
Qatar	Sept. 21, 1971
Romania	Dec. 14, 1955
Russia*	Oct. 24, 1945
Rwanda	Sept. 18, 1962
Saint Kitts and Nevis	Sept. 23, 1983
Saint Lucia	Sept. 18, 1979
Saint Vincent and the Grenadines	Sept. 16, 1980
Samoa	Dec. 15, 1976
San Marino	Mar. 2, 1992
Sao Tome and Principe	Sept. 16, 1975
Saudi Arabia*	Oct. 24, 1945
Senegal	Sept. 28, 1960
Seychelles	Sept. 21, 1976
Sierra Leone	Sept. 27, 1961
Singapore	Sept. 21, 1965
Slovakia**	Jan. 19, 1993
Slovenia	May 22, 1992
Solomon Islands	Sept. 19, 1978
Somalia	Sept. 20, 1960
South Africa*	Nov. 7, 1945
Spain	Dec. 14, 1955
Sri Lanka	Dec. 14, 1955
Sudan	Nov. 12, 1956
Suriname	Dec. 4, 1975
Swaziland	Sept. 24, 1968
Sweden	Nov. 19, 1946
Syrian Arab Republic*	Oct. 24, 1945
Tajikistan	Mar. 2, 1992
Tanzania	Dec. 14, 1961
Thailand	Dec. 16, 1946
Togo	Sept. 20, 1960
Trinidad and Tobago	Sept. 18, 1962
Tunisia	Nov. 12, 1956
Turkey*	Oct. 24, 1945
Turkmenistan	Mar. 2, 1992
Uganda	Oct. 25, 1962
Ukraine*	Oct. 24, 1945
United Arab Emirates	Dec. 9, 1971
United Kingdom of Great Britain and Northern Ireland*	Oct. 24, 1945
United States of America*	Oct. 24, 1945
Uruguay*	Dec. 18, 1945
Uzbekistan	Mar. 2, 1992
Vanuatu	Sept. 15, 1981
Venezuela*	Nov. 15, 1945
Vietnam	Sept. 20, 1977
Western Samoa	Dec. 15, 1976

Yemen	Sept. 30, 1947
Yugoslavia*+++	Oct. 24, 1945
Zaire	Sept. 20, 1960
Zambia	Dec. 1, 1964
Zimbabwe	Aug. 25, 1980

*Original member

+The Republic of China (Taiwan) represented China until 1971, when the UN voted to have China represented by the People's Republic of China.

(Russia now has the seat formerly occupied by the Union of Soviet Socialist Republics.)

**Czech Republic and Slovakia admitted on Jan. 19, 1993; Czechoslovakia was a founding member.

++Date of admission of East Germany and West Germany.

+++Yugoslavia's membership is under suspension.

Population of the United States by Census Year

Census Year	Population
1790	3,929,214
1800	5,308,483
1810	7,239,881
1820	9,638,453
1830	12,866,020
1840	17,069,453
1850	23,191,876
1860	31,443,321
1870	39,818,449
1880	50,155,783
1890	62,947,714
1900	75,994,575
1910	91,972,266
1920	105,710,620
1930	122,775,046
1940	131,669,275
1950	151,325,798
1960	179,323,175
1970	203,211,926
1980	226,504,825
1990	248,709,873

ANSWER KEY

SECTION 1

1.1 Answers will vary.

1.2

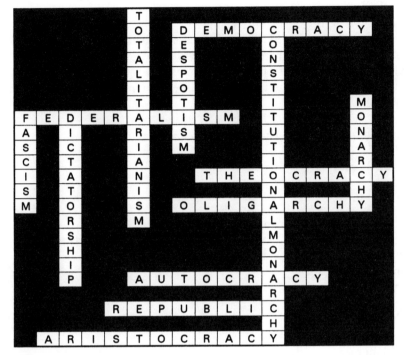

1.3 Answers will vary.

1.4 Answers will vary.

1.5 Answers will vary.

1.6 Answers will vary.

1.7 Classmates make sure words are spelled correctly.

1.8 early, twilight's, ramparts, bombs, home, sweet, died, pride, mountain-side, Author, land, holy, Great: amber, grain, majesties, fruited, crown, patriot, alabaster, tears

1.9 Answers will vary.

SECTION 2

2.1 Answers will vary.

2.2   1. California
      2. Michigan
      3. California
      4. Maryland
      5. 96,456,345
      6. 49.08%

2.3 Answers will vary.

2.4 Answers will vary.

2.5 Answers will vary.

2.6 Answers will vary.

2.7 Answers will vary.

2.8 Answers will vary.

2.9 Answers will vary.

SECTION 3

3.1 Answers will vary.

3.2 b, b, c, a, a, c, a, a, b

3.3 We, the People of the United States, in Order to form a more perfect Union, establish Justice, insure domestic Tranquility, provide for the common defen[c]e, promote the general Welfare, and secure the Blessings of Liberty to ourselves and our Posterity, do ordain and establish this Constitution for the United States of America.

3.4 Answers will vary.

3.5 As listed in section 2 of Article III.

3.6 Students make sure each other's answers are correct.

3.7 A, I, E, B, F, G, C, D, H

3.8 Answers will vary.

SECTION 4

4.1   1. blacks, women, immigrants, Native Americans
      2. mental incompetents, felons, those under age 18, non-citizens
      3. Answers will vary.

4.2 Answers will vary.

4.3 Answers will vary.

4.4 Answers will vary.

4.5   1. Billings
      2. Andrews
      3. Carruthers
      4. Answers will vary.

4.6 Answers will vary.

4.7 Pie charts.

4.8   1. 30%
      2. A
      3. A
      4. 70%

SECTION 5

5.1 Answers will vary.

5.2 Answers will vary.

5.3 Answers will vary.

5.4 Answers will vary.

5.5 Answers will vary.

5.6 Answers will vary.

5.7   Federal: 1, 4, 6, 8, 10, 15
      State: 2, 4, 5, 12
      Local: 3, 7, 9, 11, 12, 13, 14, 16, 17

5.8   President: 1, 2, 3, 4, 7, 8, 9, 11, 12, 13, 14
      Vice President: 4, 5, 6, 10, 14

SECTION 6

6.1 1. amendment
     2. whip
     3. Senate
     4. civil liberties
     5. mandate
6.2 All items should be checked.
6.3 Answers will vary.
6.4 Answers will vary.
6.5 H, I, G, E, F, C, D, B, A
6.6 Answers will vary.
6.7 Answers will vary.
6.8 Answers will vary.
6.9 Answers will vary.
6.10 Answers will vary.
6.11 Qualifications for Federal Office
     1. Senator, Representative
     2. Any office.
     3. Any office.
     4. Vice President, Senator, Representative.
     5. Representative.
     6. None.
6.12 Answers will vary.

SECTION 7

7.1 Answers will vary.
7.2 Answers will vary
7.3 8, 6, 10, 7, 1, 4, 9, 5, 2, 3
7.4 Answers will vary.
7.5 1800—D; 1804—H; 1812—F; 1862—E; 1879—A; 1903—G; 1908—G; 1917—B;
    1920—B; 1924—I; 1941—L; 1964—K; 1971—C; 1982—J
7.6 3, 2, 8, 9, 1, 6, 5, 4, 7, 12, 11, 10, 13, 15, 14
7.7 Answers will vary.
7.8 As indicated.

7.9

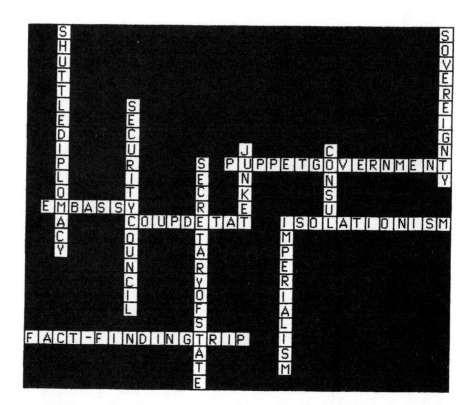

7.10

7.11

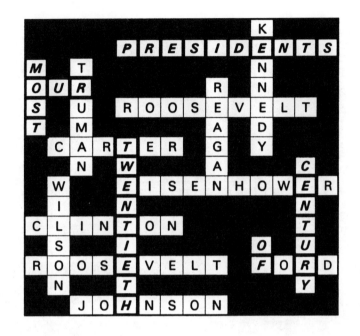

SECTION 8

8.1 Answers will vary.

8.2. Answers will vary.

8.3. 1. 535
     2. 6 years, 2 years
     3. by population of the state
     4. from January until end of business
     5. Vice President
     6. Speaker
     7. Speaker of the House

8.4 As indicated.

8.5 As indicated.

8.6 As indicated.

8.7

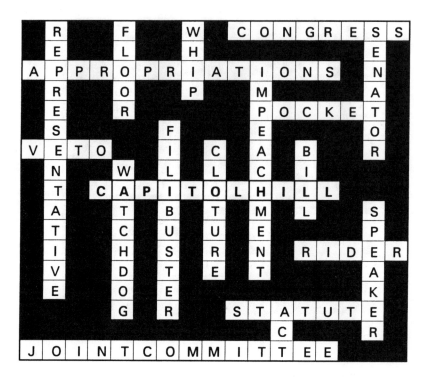

8.8 As indicated.

8.9 Answers will vary.

8.10

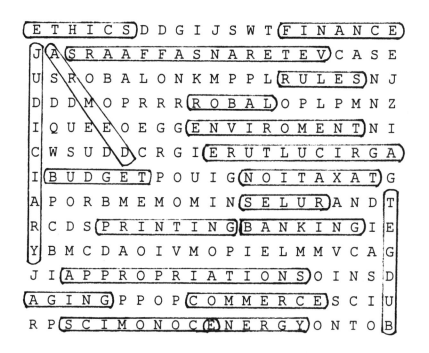

8.11

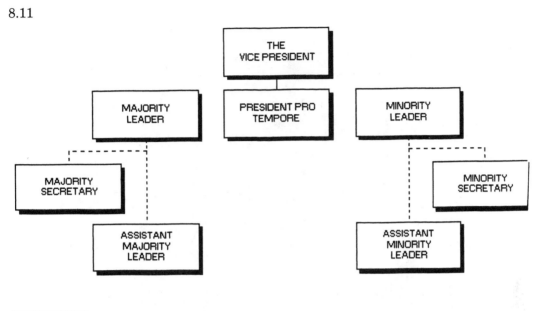

SECTION 9

9.1 As indicated.
9.2

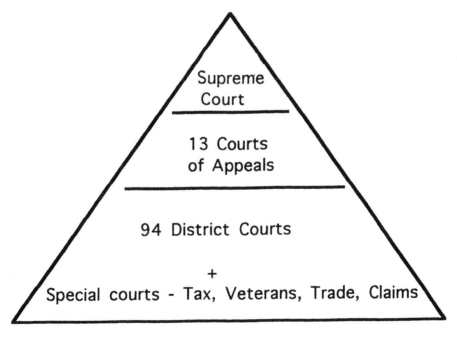

9.3 1. John Marshall
     2. 12.5 years
     3. 31%
     4. 0 (to date)

9.4

9.5 1. 64

2. 22%

3. all over age 48; all law school graduates; all prior court experience

9.6 Answers will vary.

9.7 As indicated.

9.8

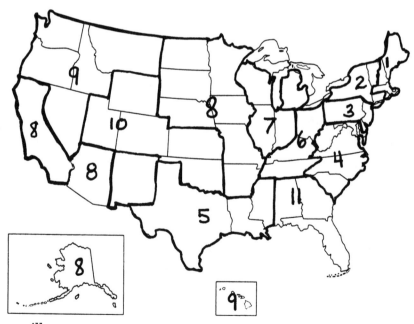

9.9 Answers will vary.

9.10 Classmates will test each other.

SECTION 10

10.1 Answers will vary.
10.2 Answers will vary.
10.3 Answers will vary.
10.4 Answers will vary.
10.5 Answers will vary.
10.6 Answers will vary.
10.7 Classmates will test each other.
10.8 Answers will vary.
10.9 Answers will vary.
10.10 Answers will vary.
10.11 Answers will vary.

SECTION 11

11.1 Answers will vary.
11.2 Answers will vary.
11.3 Variations on: candidate supported by minority of voters could win; race could result in three-way tie
11.4 A, C, D, G, I; 418,000; 53%; 25; 30; HeHe. Answers will vary for *Step Ahead*.
11.5 1. Belgium, Cyprus, and Australia
    2. Bulgaria, Japan, and Zimbabwe
    3. Answers will vary
11.6 Answers will vary.
11.7 *left column:* H, G, C, M, K, F, E, F; *right column:* D, J, O, I, N, B, A
11.8 2, 5, 4, 1, 2, 4, 3, 5, 1 (but allow for variations)
11.9 Answers will vary.
11.10 1. 6; 35%
    2. 6
    3. 13; 76%
    4. 4; 24%
    5. 20
    6. NY
    7. AL, AK, AZ, CO, CT, DE, FL, HI, ID, IL, LA, ME, MI, MS, MT, NE, NV, NH, NM, NC, ND, OK, OR, PA, RI, SC, SD, UT, VT, VA, WA, WV, WI, WY
11.11 Refer to chart.

SECTION 12

12.1. Answers will vary.
12.2. Answers will vary.
12.3. smear campaign; mudslinging; red herrings; deep sixed; bandwagon; rhetoric

12.4.

Q	W	E	R	T	Y	U	I	O	P	A	S	D	F	G	H	J	K	L	Z
X	P	U	N	D	I	T	C	V	B	N	M	Q	W	T	E	R	T	Y	U
I	O	O	P	A	S	N	D	F	G	H	J	K	L	N	Z	X	C	V	B
N	M	Q	L	W	E	A	R	T	Y	U	I	O	A	U	P	A	S	D	F
G	H	J	K	I	L	C	Z	X	C	V	B	M	N	H	M	Q	W	E	R
T	Y	F	U	I	T	O	P	A	S	D	E	G	H	H	J	K	L	Z	X
C	V	E	B	N	M	I	Q	W	E	C	R	T	Y	C	U	I	O	P	A
S	D	N	F	G	H	J	C	K	N	L	Z	X	C	T	V	B	N	M	Q
W	E	C	R	T	Y	U	I	A	O	P	A	S	D	I	F	G	H	J	K
Z	X	E	C	V	B	N	V	M	L	Q	W	E	R	W	T	Y	U	I	O
P	A	M	A	D	F	D	S	G	H	F	J	L	K	Z	X	V	C	B	N
M	Q	E	H	W	A	E	T	R	Y	U	O	I	K	I	O	O	P	A	S
D	F	N	A	G	H	J	K	L	Z	E	X	O	C	V	B	N	M	Z	X
Q	W	D	H	E	E	R	O	T	M	Y	U	I	T	H	E	H	I	L	L
A	D	I	U	F	H	O	O	E	A	J	H	K	L	B	Z	X	C	V	B
N	M	N	O	Q	W	E	C	R	T	Y	U	I	P	O	A	S	D	F	
G	H	G	R	O	U	N	D	S	W	E	L	L	H	K	L	L	Z	X	C
V	B	N	B	N	E	M	Q	E	R	T	Y	U	I	O	P	A	L	S	D
F	G	H	J	F	K	L	Z	X	C	V	B	N	M	Q	E	W	R	T	Y
U	I	S	D	H	L	I	O	A	R	E	K	A	R	D	U	M	C	V	B

12.5. Answers will vary.

12.6.

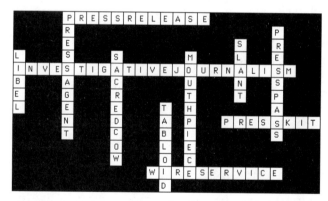

12.7. rag; fluff; muckrakers; correspondents; hacks; editorializing; editorials; killed; banner; bury a story; bylines; datelines

12.8. Answers will vary.

SECTION 13

13.1 Answers will vary.

13.2 Who Pays?

     1. $748,600,000,000

     2. $192,600,000,000

     3. 45.9%

     4. 11.8%

Step Ahead; Answers will vary.

13.3 Tax Time!
> Answers will vary.

13.4 Where Does It All Go?
> 1. Social security; National defense; Net interest; Income security; Medicare
>
> 2. 79.4%
>
> 3. National defense, energy, agriculture, commerce and housing credit
>
> Step Ahead! Answers will vary.

13.5 1. $4,804
> 2. $5,989
>
> 3. $6,659
>
> 4. $7,185
>
> 5. $7,961

13.6 Answers will vary.

13.7 1. New York
> 2. Alabama
>
> 3. Answers will vary.

13.8 Charts will depict percentages.

SECTION 14

14.1 Answers will vary.

14.2 Answers will vary.

14.3 Answers will vary.

14.4 Answers will vary.

14.5 Answers will vary.

14.6 Answers will vary.

14.7 Answers will vary.

14.8 Answers will vary.

14.9 Answers will vary.

14.10 Answers will vary.

SECTION 15

15.1 4, 3, 5, 6, 1, 8, 7, 2, 9

15.2 Answers will vary.

15.3 Answers will vary.

15.4

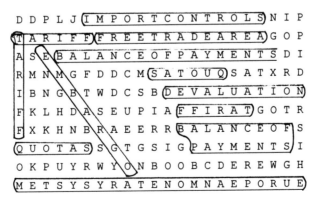

15.5 Answers will vary.
15.6 Answers will vary.
15.7 Answers will vary.
15.8.

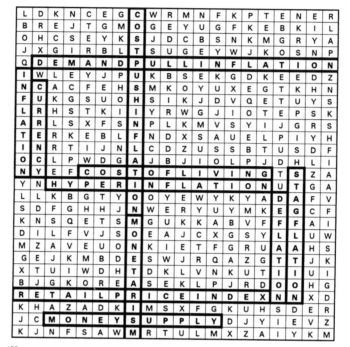

15.9 Answers will vary.
15.10 Answers will vary.
15.11 Answers will vary.
15.12 Answers will vary.

SECTION 16

16.1 Answers will vary.
16.2 7, 5, 9, 8, 11, 4, 1, 10, 3, 6, 2
16.3 9.9%; Urology; $14,000; Otolaryngology; 10
16.4 Answers will vary.
16.5 Answers will vary.
16.6 Answers will vary.
16.7 1. 38.5%
    2. 15%
    3. 10.5%; 12%; 20%; 29%
    4. 1982
    5. Answers will vary.
16.8 1. Employment by major occupation
    2. Millions of people
    3. Projected change in employment
    4. Percent increase
    5. 1996-2006

      6. Professional specialty

      7. Administrative support, including clerical

      8. There are few farmers, and little growth expected in farming jobs.

      9. Answers will vary.

16.9 Answers will vary.

16.10

Percent distribution			Number		Percent	
1986	**1996**	**2006**	**1986–96**	**1996–2006**	**1986–96**	**1996–2006**
100.0	100.0	100.0	20,978	18,574	18.8	14.0
9.5	10.2	10.5	2,974	2,324	28.1	17.2
12.2	13.7	15.2	4,584	4,826	33.7	26.6
3.3	3.5	3.7	894	940	24.0	20.4
10.3	11.1	11.2	3,137	2,264	27.3	15.5
18.7	18.1	17.1	3,147	1,806	15.1	7.5
15.6	16.1	16.7	3,867	3,853	22.2	18.1
3.3	2.9	2.5	124	37	3.4	1.0
12.4	10.9	10.2	614	1,002	4.4	6.9
14.6	13.5	12.8	1,637	1,522	10.1	8.5

16.11 Graphs will vary.

16.12 Answers will vary.

SECTION 17

17.1 1. $25, 924,000

      2. 7.89%

      3. fell; expenses rose

      Step Ahead: Answers will vary.

17.2 Answers will vary.

17.3 Students will check each other.

17.4 1. 14.4

      2. 7.2

      Step Ahead: $5,000

17.5 1. 3.8% 4th

      2. 4.5% 3rd

      3. 6.9% 2nd

      4. 3.0% 5th

      5. 9.0% 1st

17.6 Answers will vary.

17.7 Answers will vary.

17.8 Answers will vary.

17.9 Answers will vary.

SECTION 18

18.1 Answers will vary.
18.2

"Share Holding"

Portfolio Log:	Share in Portfolio	$ Value per Share	$ Value of Portfolio
Initial Value	10	17.50	175.00
June 1	10	22.875	228.75
July 1	10	19.00	190.00
August 1	20	8.75	175.00
September 1	20	11.125	222.50

Earnings from dividends: 37.80

Paul's profit over his initial investment: 85.30

18.3 Answers will vary.
18.4 Answers will vary.
18.5 Answers will vary.
18.6 Answers will vary.
18.7 Answers will vary.
18.8 11, 10, 12, 13, 7, 8, 9, 6, 4, 3, 5, 1, 2

SECTION 19

19.1 Answers will vary.
19.2 Answers will vary.
19.3 Answers will vary.
19.4 Answers will vary.
19.5 Both: 1, 9, 10, 13, 14, 19
     Civil: 3, 4, 17, 18
     Criminal: 2, 5, 6, 7, 8, 11, 12, 15, 16
19.6

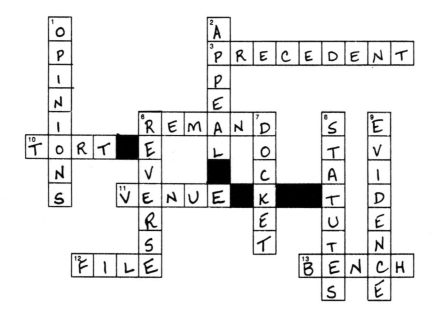

19.7 1. Connecticut; Mississippi
     2. $17,991; 98%
     3. 6%; 5%; 4%; 4%
19.8 Answers will vary.
19.9 Answers will vary.
19.10 Answers will vary.
19.11 Answers will vary.

SECTION 20

20.1 Answers will vary.
20.2 Answers will vary.
20.3 Who Do You Call?
     1. Police
     2. Water
     3. Police
     4. Sanitation
     5. Board of Education
     6. Fire
     7. Police
     8. Clerk's Office
20.4 Students check each other's answers
20.5 Whose Jurisdiction?
     1. S   6. F   10. F
     2. S   7. F   11. L
     3. L   8. S   12. S
     4. S, F   9. F   13. F
     5. S, F
20.6

```
K L O U Y T R E F G H B N I(G N I R A E H)G F T R E D F G T
F(D U E P R O C E S S(F E L O N Y)X X(A R R E S T E D)M N U
C O N V I C T I O N E P O P L I U L B F E(P A R D O N)N O I
R X O L N V C D E R K L M J H T R A D E D E E R T E N M T O
I P L O I U G R F E D I O P O T G R D S W(F R A U D)I M T H
M C V D F E E I O L M I M R N B G C R T F N B V C X S D W E
I S I J H G F E Q W S A C P A L K E I T F E D T G I H I U B
N S S(S E S S E N T I W)B I H P G N E I O L U(T R I A L)E N
A O L K U T R E W Q S A I L M N B Y F D D I L K O P O I U I
L M E E E(T N E M N G I A R R A)W U Y T E F G F E D E S I L
L L K O U A N L L Y U I O P P W W U I J E R I O E K H T E I
X D S F B I M V B N K(J U R Y)H I P L U P L O M L P P R L M
N F M S M W O A(M I S D E M E A N O R)P K H F D O I U U F W
M M D K S M L R R N M H U O P D E Y M N J F D N O L T O G N
W(S E N T E N C I N G)O O(L A R C E N Y)O D E R R Y Y C I A
```

20.7 Reading Crime Rates
    1. Aggravated assault
    2. Larceny/theft
    3. Aggravated assault
    4. Burglary
    5. Answers will vary.
20.8 Answers will vary.
20.9 Answers will vary.
20.10 Answers will vary.
20.11 3, 5, 1, 12, 2, 8, 6, 7, 15, 9, 11, 4, 17, 14, 10, 16, 13